T0189338

Robotic Tactile Perception and Understanding

Huaping Liu · Fuchun Sun

Robotic Tactile Perception and Understanding

A Sparse Coding Method

 Springer

Huaping Liu ⓘ
Department of Computer Science
 and Technology
Tsinghua University
Beijing
China

Fuchun Sun
Department of Computer Science
 and Technology
Tsinghua University
Beijing
China

ISBN 978-981-13-3873-1   ISBN 978-981-10-6171-4   (eBook)
https://doi.org/10.1007/978-981-10-6171-4

Printed on acid-free paper

This Springer imprint is published by Springer Nature
The registered company is Springer Nature Singapore Pte Ltd.
The registered company address is: 152 Beach Road, #21-01/04 Gateway East, Singapore 189721, Singapore

Foreword

Robotic manipulation and grasping is one of the most challenging problems in the field of robotics. It requires the robot to have the ability to perceive and understand its environment via multimodal sensing and strategies.

Compared with visual sensing modality, human's understanding of the tactile sensing modality remains limited. It is mainly because of the complexity of the tactile signals, the restriction of the tactile perception techniques, and the lack of the available tactile data. Moreover, since tactile sensing is highly coupled with other sensory modalities, investigating its mechanism can largely improve the development of cognitive science.

Recently, with the rapid development of artificial intelligence, and especially machine learning techniques, the area of robotics has revealed great advances and potential. I am pleased to see this book by Huaping and Fuchun. To the best of my knowledge, this is the first book for a comprehensive approach to tactile perception using machine learning. For the problem of tactile sensing in robotic manipulation, they have established a novel technical framework, sparse coding, and dictionary learning. With this framework, the complex tactile signals can be reconstructed as new coding vectors. The sparsity is utilized to characterize many features such as the correlations between multiple fingers and different tactile attributes. Moreover, under the proposed framework, the authors also successfully solve the heterogeneous visual–tactile sensing fusion problem.

Therefore, I believe there are mainly three contributions in this book. Firstly, it provides a comprehensive survey of tactile object recognition and of visual–tactile fusion recognition technology, together with an analysis of the different representations for tactile and visual modalities. Secondly, it systematically unravels the object attribute recognition problem in the field of robotic tactile perception and understanding. Finally, it establishes a complete machine learning approach for the multimodal sensing fusion task. This work provides a good way of solving robotic manipulation and grasping in unstructured and complex environments.

This book provides readers with an intuitive understanding and exciting applications in robotic tactile sensing. The tactile sensing promises to play a critical role in robotic manipulation. I believe this book will reveal enormous practical impact as well as scientific insights into tactile sensing research and education.

Prof. Angelo Cangelosi
University of Manchester

Preface

Intelligent service robots have great potential in various application scenarios such as home services, public health, and warehouse logistics. Robotic manipulator and dexterous finger system are two key components of service robots to perform tasks which require manipulation and grasp capability, for example, caring for the elderly, surgical operations, and space or underwater exploration.

The technical challenges of manipulation and grasp involve a number of aspects including mechanical structure, hand material, object property, environment perception, and grasp planning. Among them, environment perception of service robots brings obvious challenges to existing technologies for industrial robots used for structured environments, due to the fact that service robots usually work in more complex, dynamic, and uncertain environments. This requires the robots to perceive and understand its environment in an accurate and timely manner. Referring to humans' approaches for sensing the environment through looking, listening, tasting, smelling, touching, and then unintentionally integrate the information from all channels, it is tempting to equip service robots with various sensors.

For both humans and robots, tactile sensing is the core approach used for exploration and manipulation of objects. Unlike visual sensors, tactile sensors are capable of perceiving some physical properties (e.g., softness/hardness, texture, temperature) of an object. Incorporating tactile perception to the robots can not only simulate human perception and cognitive mechanisms but also enable robots to perform more satisfyingly at practical applications.

Furthermore, visual and tactile modalities are quite different from each other. First of all, the format, frequency, and range of perceived object information are different. Tactile sensing obtains information through constant physical contact with target object, while the visual modality can simultaneously obtain multiple different features of an object at a distance. Furthermore, some features can only be obtained by one single perceptual mode. For example, the color of an object can only be obtained visually, while the texture, hardness, and temperature of a surface are obtained through tactile sensing.

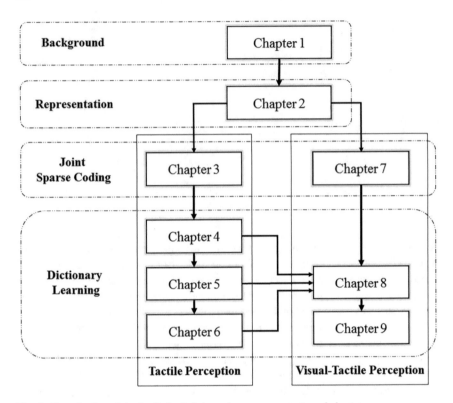

Fig. 1 Organization of the book: logical dependency among parts and chapters

To tackle those intrinsically difficult problems in tactile perception and visual–tactile fusion problems, we establish a unified sparse coding and dictionary learning framework, which forms the main contents of this book. Furthermore, a set of structured sparse coding models is developed to address the issues of dynamic tactile sensing. The book then proves that the proposed framework is effective in solving some challenging problems in the field of robotics and automation, e.g., multifinger tactile object recognition, multilabel tactile adjective recognition, and multicategory material analysis. The proposed sparse coding model can be used to tackle the challenging visual–tactile fusion recognition problem, and the book develops a series of efficient optimization algorithms to implement the model.

This book is divided into four parts. Part I presents the research background and motivation and introduces the representation and kernel of the concerned tactile and visual modalities. Part II focuses on the tactile perception problem. In Chap. 3, a joint sparse coding method for multifingered tactile fusion task is presented. In Chaps. 4–6, more complicated dictionary learning methods are developed to tackle the difficult tasks of object recognition, tactile adjective property analysis, and material identification. Part III presents more advanced applications of sparse coding and dictionary learning methodology on the heterogeneous visual–tactile fusion problems. Similarly, the joint sparse coding is firstly used to establish the basic framework to tackle the intrinsic problems in visual–tactile fusion in Chap. 7. Chapters 8 and 9 present complicated dictionary learning methods to address the material identification and cross-modal retrieval tasks. Part IV contains Chap. 10, which summarizes this book and presents some prospects. For clear illustration, an outline of the logical dependency among chapters is demonstrated in Fig. 1. Note that we try our best to make each chapter self-contained. Nevertheless, the sparse coding and dictionary learning methods developed in Chaps. 3–9 are always dependent on the kernel representation presented in Chap. 2.

This book is suitable as a reference book for graduate students with a basic knowledge of machine learning as well as professional researchers interested in robotic tactile perception and understanding, and machine learning.

Beijing, China   Huaping Liu
July 2017   Fuchun Sun

Acknowledgements

This book refers to our research work at Department of Computer Science and Technology, Tsinghua University, and State Key Laboratory of Intelligent Technology and Systems, TNLIST, China.

Five years ago, we started looking into the challenging field of robotic tactile perception. Dr. Wei Xiao conducted the first experiment for tactile data acquisition with us under very difficult conditions. With him, we launched the research work and published some preliminary results. Meanwhile, one of our visiting students, Rui Ma, who constructed a more complete tactile dataset, also published our first journal paper on this topic. About three years ago, visiting students Wen Wang and Liuyang Wang carried out the research work on dynamic time sequence classifications. This joint work established a good foundation for the development of object classification based on the tactile sequence. We would like to thank everyone who have participated for their support, dedication, and cooperation.

We would like to sincerely thank our visiting student Jingwei Yang. With her, we were able to explore the idea of using sparse coding for tactile object recognition. In 2015, we completed our first joint paper on solving the problem of tactile classification using joint sparse coding. Since then, we have gradually exploited the advantages of sparse coding in multimodal information processing and have carried out a series of research work on visual and tactile fusion. Visiting students Peng Bai and Fengxue Li also conducted a series of experiments on tactile recognition and provided important support for data acquisition and experimental verification. Our graduate and undergraduate students, Yupei Wu, Yifei Ma, Jiang Lu, and Junyi Che, helped build elegant experimental platforms for tactile perception research. Thanks for their strong support.

In terms of theoretical algorithms, we are particularly grateful to Dr. Minnan Luo and Dr. Wenbing Huang. We are extremely impressed by their strong mathematical knowledge and skills. Their work on sparse coding is a great inspiration to the authors. In addition, our Master students, Mingyi Yuan, Yulong Liu and Yunhui Liu, have successfully applied sparse coding methods to different visual fields, completed excellent Master's theses, and provided critical support for our research methodologies. We also appreciate Hui Zhang, Tao Kong, and Yuan Yuan for their valuable help with deep learning and cyber-physic systems.

We would like to give special thanks to Dr. Bin Fang and Dr. Di Guo, for providing us with cooperation and fruitful discussions in robotic grasp and manipulation. Their deep understanding of tactile perception has provided great insights for the authors. In addition, majority of work they have done has played an important part in accomplishing this book.

In the course of our research, we have obtained a great deal of support from industrial officials. We would like to thank Mr. Liming Huang from Siemens Research, Mrs. Hong Zhang from Intel Research, Mrs. Yan-yan He from P&G Corporation, and Dr. Shan Lu from Shanghai Aerospace Control Technology Institute for their extensive support in our research of tactile perception and visual–tactile fusion.

We would like to express our sincere gratitude to Jie Qin, Yupei Wu, Haibin Fu, Xiaonan Liu, Jing Fang, Liang He, and Ge Gao who have provided immense help with preparation of figures and with the proofreading of the book.

The completion of this book cannot be separated from the strong support of Springer Publishing. We would like to thank our commissioning editors, Lanlan Chang and Jane Li, for their great support.

A great deal of this research was supported by the National Natural Science Foundation of China under the grant U1613212 for a key project "Multi-Modal Fusion Perception and Human-Robot Interaction for Robotic Manipulation," the grant 61673238 for a project "Structured Sparse Coding for Robotic Visual-Tactile Fusion Recognition." This work was also supported partially by the National Natural Science Foundation of China under Grant 91420302 and Grant 61327809.

Finally, on a personal note (HL), I would like to thank my parents and my wife for standing beside me and supporting me throughout my research and writing this book. Special thanks to my little Xinyuan (Harry). During the final stage of writing the book, I didn't have much time to spend with him. I am delighted that he learned how to swim during this period. On a personal note (FS), I would like to thank my parents, wife, and son for supporting my research and writing this book.

Beijing, China   Huaping Liu
July 2017   Fuchun Sun

Contents

Acronyms

ADMM	Alternating Direction Method of Multipliers
BioTacs	Biomimetic Tactile sensors
BPC	Blue Portable Cup
CDC	Coffee Disposable Cup
C-DL	Common Dictionary Learning
CKSC	Concatenation Kernel Sparse Coding
CMOS	Complementary Metal Oxide Semiconductor
DL	Dictionary Learning
DTW	Dynamic Time Warping
EBC	Empty Beer Can
EEG	Electroencephalogram
ELM	Extreme Learning Machine
EMB	Empty Mizone Bottle
EPB	Empty Pocari Bottle
ETC	Empty Tea Can
FBC	Full Beer Can
FMB	Full Mizone Bottle
FPB	Full Pocari Bottle
FSRs	Force Sensing Resistors
FTC	Full Tea Can
GA	Global Alignment
GCDL	Generalized Coupled Dictionary Learning
GPC	Green Portable Cup
HDC	Hard Disposable Cup
HRI	Human–Robot Interaction
ISS	International Space Station
JGKSC	Joint Group Kernel Sparse Coding
JKSC	Joint Kernel Sparse Coding
k-NN	k-Nearest Neighborhood
k-NN-T	k-Nearest Neighborhood with Tactile modality

k-NN-V	k-Nearest Neighborhood with Visual modality
K-RRSS	Kernelized Robust Representation and Structured Sparsity
KSC-T	Kernel Sparse Coding with Tactile modality
KSC-V	Kernel Sparse Coding with Visual modality
LBP	Linear Binary Pattern
LIBSVM	A Library for Support Vector Machine
LS-SVM	Least Squares Support Vector Machine
M2PDL	Multimodal Projective Dictionary pair Learning
MIS	Minimal Invasive Surgery
ML-kNN	Multi-Label kNN
NN	Nearest Neighborhood
PALM	Proximal Alternating Linearization Minimization
PDL	Projective Dictionary pair Learning
PDL-A	Projective Dictionary pair Learning-pixel Averages
PDL-D	Projective Dictionary pair Learning-Depth information
PDL-F	Projective Dictionary pair Learning-Fourier feature
PDL-Gray	Projective Dictionary pair Learning-Gray pixels
PDL-H	Projective Dictionary pair Learning-Haptic information
PDL-LBP	Projective Dictionary pair Learning-Linear Binary Pattern
PDL-RGB	Projective Dictionary pair Learning-RGB information
PDL-V	Projective Dictionary pair Learning-Visual information
PHAC	Penn Haptic Adjective Corpus
PHAC-2	Penn Haptic Adjective Corpus 2
PLC	PLastic Cup
PR2	Personal Robot2
RCovDs	Region Covariance Descriptors
RKHS	Reproducing Kernel Hilbert Space
SCDL	Semi-coupled dictionary learning
SDC	Soft Disposable Cup
S-kNN	Separate k-Nearest Neighborhood
SKSC	Separate Kernel Sparse Coding
SliM2	Supervised coupled dictionary learning with group structures for Multimodal retrieval
SO-DL	Structured Output-associated Dictionary Learning
SPAMS	SPArse Modeling Software
SR-DL	Semantics-Regularized Dictionary Learning
SVM	Support Vector Machine
TD	Toy DRagon
TDO	Toy DOll
TPA	Toy PAnda
TPE	Toy PEnguin
WMCA	Weakly paired Maximum Covariance Analysis

Mathematical Notation

M	The number of the visual training samples
N	The number of the tactile training samples
$\mathbb{T}_i$	The ith tactile training sample
$\mathbb{T}$	Testing tactile sample
$\mathbb{V}_i$	The ith visual training sample
$\mathbb{V}$	Testing visual sample
$\mathfrak{T}$	The set of tactile training samples
$\mathfrak{J}$	The set of visual training samples
$\mathscr{T}$	The manifold in which the tactile sequences lie
$\mathscr{V}$	The manifold in which the visual descriptors lie
$\mathfrak{D}$	Tactile dictionary in the space of $\mathscr{T}$
$\mathfrak{P}$	Visual dictionary in the space of $\mathscr{V}$
$\mathscr{H}_T$	Higher-dimensional (possibly infinite dimensional) inner product space for the tactile modality
$\mathscr{H}_V$	Higher-dimensional (possibly infinite dimensional) inner product space for the visual modality
$\kappa\left(\mathbb{T}_i,\ \mathbb{T}_j\right)$	Kernel function between tactile samples $\mathbb{T}_i$ and $\mathbb{T}_j$
$\kappa\left(\mathbb{V}_i,\ \mathbb{V}_j\right)$	Kernel function between visual samples $\mathbb{V}_i$ and $\mathbb{V}_j$
$\Phi(\cdot)$	Kernel-induced implicit feature mapping for tactile modality
$\Psi(\cdot)$	Kernel-induced implicit feature mapping for visual modality
$\|x\|_0$	The number of the nonzero elements in the vector x
$\|X\|_{row-0}$	The number of the nonzero rows in the matrix X
$\|x\|_1$	The sum of the absolute values of all elements in the vector x
$\|X\|_{2,1}$	The sum of the Euclidean norms of all row vectors in the matrix X
$\|x\|_2$	The Euclidean norm of the vector x
$\|X\|_F$	The Frobenius norm of the matrix X
$\|x\|_\infty$	The maximum values of the absolute values of all elements in the vector x
$\sigma(x)$	Sigmoid activation function for the scalar x
$\mathscr{E}_C$	The set of the elementary C-dimensional vectors

V   All-one matrix with compatible dimensions

I   Identity matrix with compatible dimensions

$\delta^{(c)}$ The characteristic function that selects the coefficients associated with the cth class

Part I
Background

This part of the book comprises two chapters. In Chap. 1, a survey about the tactile object recognition and visual–tactile fusion recognition technology is presented. The technical challenges for tactile perception and visual–tactile fusion understanding are also analyzed in this chapter. Chapter 2 serves as a basis of the whole book, by providing different representations for the tactile and visual modalities.

Chapter 1
Introduction

Abstract For robots, tactile perception is a key function utilized to obtain information from environment. Unlike vision sensors, tactile sensors can directly measure various physical properties of objects and the environment. Similarly, humans also use touch sensory receptors as an important approach to perceive and interact with the environment. In this chapter, a detailed discussion associated with tactile object recognition is presented. Current studies on tactile object recognition are divided into three sub-categories, and detailed analyses are provided. In addition, some advanced topics such as visual–tactile fusion, exploratory procedure, and datasets are discussed.

1.1 Robotic Manipulation and Grasp

The robotic manipulator and the dexterous finger system are most important components for service robots to perform tasks such as heavy domestic work, caring for the elderly, surgical operations, and space or underwater exploration. All of those operations require a manipulation and grasp capability, which remains a challenging problem for intelligent robots. Though many scholars have investigated related problems for several decades [6, 9, 12, 78, 86], the available robotic hand applications are still far from satisfying practical usage. This restricts development of many applications such as electronic commerce, which has benefitted from successful mobile robots. Figuratively, the problem of *Last Mile* can be solved with the outdoor mobile robots; the problem of *Last Foot* can be solved with the indoor mobile robots; and the problem of *Last Inch* must be solved with robotic manipulation and grasp technology. Recently, some major Internet companies have started promoting research on robotic manipulation and grasp. For example, Amazon held the Amazon Picking Challenge (APC)[1] in 2015 (see the left panel of Fig. 1.1[2]) at the 2015 International Conference on Robotics and Automation (ICRA) in Seattle, Washington. After that event, APC

---

[1] https://www.amazonrobotics.com/site/binaries/content/assets/amazonrobotics/pdfs/2015-apc-summary.pdf.

[2] This image is adopted from the website http://robohub.org/team-rbo-from-berlin-wins-amazon-picking-challenge-convincingly/.

© Springer Nature Singapore Pte Ltd. 2018
H. Liu and F. Sun, *Robotic Tactile Perception and Understanding*,
https://doi.org/10.1007/978-981-10-6171-4_1

Fig. 1.1 LEFT: Amazon Picking Challenge which was held at ICRA2015. RIGHT: Robotic Grasping and Manipulation Competition which was held at IROS2016

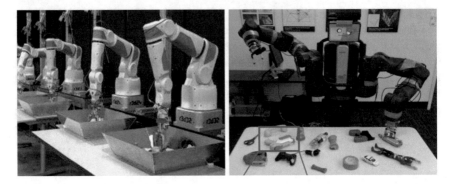

Fig. 1.2 LEFT: Google's collaborative manipulations. Copyright (2016) Sage. Reprinted, with permission, from Ref. [60]. RIGHT: Deep learning robot developed by CMU. Copyright (2016) IEEE. Reprinted, with permission, from Ref. [75]

was held at RoboCup. The goal of the APC is to strengthen ties between the industrial and academic robotic communities in order to promote shared and open solutions to some of the major problems in unstructured automation. In 2016, the Robotic Grasping and Manipulation Competition[3] was held at International Conference on Intelligent Robots and Systems (IROS) in Korea (see the right panel of Fig. 1.1). Google also reported some appealing results on collaborative learning of grasp skills (see the left panel of Fig. 1.2). MIT Technology Review reported on research in a story headlined *Deep-Learning Robot Takes 10 Days to Teach Itself to Grasp* (see the right panel of Fig. 1.2). All of these events show that robotic manipulation and grasp attract considerable attention from both industry and academia.

The technical challenges of manipulation and grasp involve a number of aspects including mechanical structure, hand material, object property, environment perception, and grasp planning. Among them, environment perception is especially difficult compared with industrial robots used for structured environments. In fact, service robots encounter complex, dynamic, and uncertain environments. This requires the robots to perceive and understand its environment in an accurate and timely manner.

---

[3]http://www.rhgm.org/activities/competition_iros2016/competition_iros_summary.pdf.

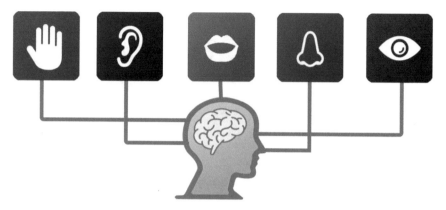

Fig. 1.3 Humans unintentionally integrate the information from visual, auditory, olfactory, gustatory sense, and tactile modalities

For humans, information about the environment can be perceived by looking, listening, tasting, smelling, and touching. After perceiving the environment, humans unintentionally integrate the information from visual, auditory, olfactory, gustatory, and tactile modalities (see Fig. 1.3). It is difficult to say which modality is more important, because humans are accustomed to a multimodal fusion way to understand the environment.

To analyze the importance of different modalities, it is worth to recall an important fact: It is easy to block the visual channel by closing eyes, yet slightly difficult to block the auditory channel by plugging your ears. However, it is almost impossible for a normal person to close his sense of touch. This shows that tactile sensing is a very fundamental perception modality for humans, and touch sensory receptors are used as an important means to perceive and interact with the environment.

Many scholars have conducted various experiments to analyze the role of the touch sense for humans. In the early 1980s, experiments with local anesthesia indicated the importance of humans tactile sensing for a stable grasp [93]. It was found that the applied grip force was critically balanced to optimize motor behavior so that slipping between the skin and the gripped object did not occur and the grip force did not reach exceedingly high values. In [34], an experiment was performed on astronauts at the International Space Station; the vibrotactile cues provided via sense of touch were found to be highly indicative of direction and spatial disorientation. The authors found that artificial touch information in the form of a localized vibration on the torso that indicated down could make orienting in microgravity faster, better, and easier. The importance of the artificial touch information seemed to increase over the initial seven days of staying in microgravity, while the weight of visual information decreased over the same period. In addition, people with impaired tactile sensibility have difficulties with many everyday activities because the brain lacks the information about mechanical contact states needed to plan and control object manipulation tasks.

Touch   Tactile   Haptic

Fig. 1.4 Illustrations of the terms *Touch*, *Tactile*, and *Haptic*

Vision provides only indirect information about such mechanical interactions, and proprioceptive afferents exhibit low sensitivity to mechanical fingertip events [50].

Since tactile sensing plays such important roles for humans, it is practical to equip tactile sensors for robotic grasp tasks. For both humans and robots, tactile sensing is important for interacting with the environment: It is the core sensing used for exploration and manipulation of objects. An effective incorporation of touch sensors on touch-sense-impoverished robots will not only advance research in robotics but will also help us to understand how human interacts with the environment.

Before proceeding, we adopt the results presented in [27], to clarify three terms: *Tactile*, *Touch*, and *Haptic* (see Fig. 1.4).

1. *Tactile* sensing is defined as detection and measurement of contact parameters in a predetermined contact area and subsequent preprocessing of the signals at the taxel level.
2. *Touch* sensing is tactile sensing at single contact point. A representative example is the touchscreen, which has been extensively used in smartphones and iPads.

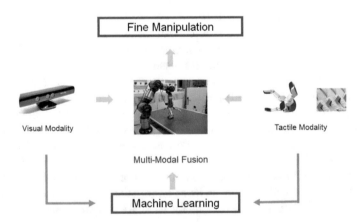

Fig. 1.5 Machine learning-based visual–tactile fusion schemes for robotic manipulation and grasping

3. *Haptics* sensing involves both action and reaction, i.e., two-way transfer of touch information. The haptic system uses significant information about objects and events from both cutaneous and kinesthetic systems

In this book, we strictly follow the above terminologies and focus on the tactile sensing, perception, and understanding problems, but with some abuse of notation.

On the other hand, visual and tactile sensors have become indispensable for robotic fine manipulation. In Fig. 1.5, it is shown that the representative visual–tactile fusion schemes can be established by using advanced machine learning technology.

1.2 Robotic Tactile Perception

At present, many robots are equipped with visual sensors. However, visual sensing is subject to many restrictions in practical applications, such as lighting conditions and occlusions. Tactile sensing is another sensing modality widely used in robotics. Unlike visual sensing, tactile sensors are capable of perceiving some physical properties (e.g., softness/hardness, texture, temperature) of an object directly. Introducing tactile perception to the robot can not only simulate human perception and cognitive mechanisms to a certain extent, but also provide possibilities to satisfy the strong demands for practical robotic applications.

With the development of modern sensors, control, and artificial intelligence technology, extensive research has been conducted on tactile sensors, grasp success prediction [55] and regrasping strategy development [19], and object recognition based on tactile sensing. One early review [58] elaborated the state of the art in tactile sensing and its likely research motivations. It also pointed out the increasing emphasis on understanding of tactile sensing in tasks requiring dexterous manipulation. Broadly speaking, tactile properties refer to any properties measured through contact, including pressure, force, and temperature, while a narrow definition of tactile sensing requires that there must be force measurements involved.

Research on robotic tactile perception has expanded in recent years. Journals, such as *IEEE Transactions on Robotics*, *IEEE Sensors Journal*, and *Robotics and Autonomous Systems*, all published reviews on robotic tactile perception [27, 28, 52]. In addition, *IEEE Transactions on Robotics* released a special issue on the theme of *Robotic Sense of Touch* in 2011 [26]. Furthermore, the journal *IEEE Transactions on Haptics* was officially inaugurated in 2008. Lastly, the conferences ICRA, IROS, and RSS recently initiated a number of topics related to tactile perception. Some representative events are: ICRA2017 workshop on *The Robotic Sense of Touch: From Sensing to Understanding,*[4] RSS2017 workshop on *Tactile Sensing for Manipulation: Hard-*

---

[4]https://roboticsenseoftouchws.wordpress.com/.

ware, Modeling, and Learning,[5] and IROS2017 workshop on *Soft Morphological Design for Haptic Sensation, Interaction and Display.*[6]

Tactile sensors are essential for tactile perception. According to operation principles, tactile sensors can be classified into several types, such as piezoresistive, capacitive, piezoelectric, quantum tunnel effect, optical, barometric, and structure-borne sound. Reference [52] compared the advantages and disadvantages of 28 kinds of tactile sensors in detail, while Ref. [32] developed a multimodal tactile sensor that contained a capacitive sensor array, audio measurement, and proximity perception for recognizing different materials. Although many researchers still use self-developed tactile sensors, commercial tactile sensors are playing an increasingly important role in robotics. The most representative examples are BioTac, PPS, Weiss, and Tekscan.

Tactile perception technology has been widely applied to robotics. For example, Ref. [8] used a three-fingered dexterous hand to catch objects of different shapes. A tactile model built from the hidden Markov model was used to judge object-grasping stability. Additionally, tactile perception technology has also been applied to sliding detection [20], object localization [44, 73], tactile servo [100], and 3D modeling [91]. Here list some representative tactile perception applications on the ground robot, space robots, and marine robots:

1. Ground applications: Ref. [37] proposed a learning algorithm that took haptic sensory signals of a robot obtained while performing actions on food items as input. This robot prepared a salad during 60 sequential robotic experiments, and it made a mistake in only four instances. See the left panel of Fig. 1.6.
2. Space applications: Ref. [40] described the design of a spaceflight-traceable tactile skin suitable for using with robotic manipulators and the algorithms necessary to make use of the skin. See the middle panel of Fig. 1.6.
3. Underwater applications: Ref. [2] developed a deep-sea-capable tactile sensing system, with high spatial and force resolutions. It is the first time to make the underwater haptic exploration possible. It also presented a tactile sensor-based object recognition and localization methodology for structured underwater and deep-sea applications. See the right panel of Fig. 1.6.

Object recognition has always been a key problem in robotics and also important for environment perception. Therefore, how to make use of tactile information to realize object recognition draws wide attention from researchers, and tactile object recognition has become a hot research topic. However, tactile sensor data acquisition mechanisms differ from each other and different grasping movements in tactile information acquisition also affect data characteristics. Therefore, no well-established method for data collection and classification was established. To help address this problem, Ref. [52] divided tactile object recognition research into three major categories: tactile object identification, texture recognition, and contact pattern recognition. In this chapter, we use different guidelines based on a tactile exploratory

---

[5]https://sites.google.com/view/rss17ts/overview.

[6]https://sites.google.com/site/iros17softhaptic/.

Fig. 1.6 Some representative examples of tactile applications. Left: Ground. Copyright (2016) IEEE. Reprinted, with permission, from Ref. [37]. Middle: Space. Copyright (2012) IEEE. Reprinted, with permission, from Ref. [40], Right: Underwater. Copyright (2015) Wiley. Used with permission from Ref. [2]

Fig. 1.7 Three kinds of representative objects which were usually used for tactile recognition research. Left: rigid objects. Copyright (2015) IEEE. Reprinted, with permission, from Ref. [66]. Middle: textured material. Copyright (2015) IEEE. Reprinted, with permission, from Ref. [83]. Right: deformable objects. Reprinted from Ref. [33], with permission from Elsevier

procedure that can be used to differentiate the shape of rigid objects, texture of material surfaces, and deformation of soft objects. Typical examples of these objects are metal parts, clothes, and fruits, respectively. Figure 1.7 shows some representative objects extracted from research papers illustrating these three kinds of tasks. For rigid object recognition, shape information is primarily used. Objects for texture recognition generally have standard and regular shapes, so it is important to investigate their surface properties for recognition. In contrast, deformable objects are primarily recognized by their stiffness and damping characteristics.

Besides manipulation and grasp, there are a number of fields which can benefit from the tactile perception.

1. Material evaluations: Material property is important for a product. The BioTac Toccare™ carefully recreates the same interaction as the human hand touching a material. As a result, it can acquire data that mimics the human perception of touch. The measurements of material tested are of the 15 dimensions of touch.
2. Physical human–robot interaction: Tactile recognition could open up applications for touch-based interaction in areas such as human–robot interaction. The detection of human touch can be important for safe robot operation around humans and furthermore may contribute to robot behavior execution [5]. In order to enable

artificial social agents such as robots to understand human touch input, automatic recognition of different types of touch is needed. In Ref. [45], the authors investigated the potential for deep learning for classifying affective touch on robotic skin in a social setting.

3. Online shopping: The tactile information exchange problem is more significant in the case of Internet shopping, which is more risky than traditional shopping due to the lack of opportunity to physically examine the product and lack of personal contact [53]. In the clothing and textile category, touch is quite relevant, as it plays a dual role in evaluating physical attributes of the product, such as texture. Reference [59] pointed out that that one of the five most important reasons for not purchasing online was an inability to touch the merchandise.

In this chapter, the current studies on tactile object recognition are divided into three sub-categories with detailed discussions. In addition, some advanced topics such as visual–tactile fusion, exploratory procedure, and datasets are discussed. Note that in [27], tactile sensing was classified with respect to some criteria such as the sensing principle, location of the sensor, and task to be performed, while this work focuses on extrinsic tactile sensing according to the above classification.

The rest of this chapter is organized as follows: Sect. 1.3 analyzes the exploratory procedure for tactile information acquisition. In Sects. 1.4–1.6, the applications of the tactile sensor for perceiving shape, stiffness, and texture are discussed. Section 1.7 is about visual–tactile fusion. Section 1.8 provides information about some datasets. Finally, Sect. 1.9 presents a summary.

1.3   Tactile Exploratory Procedure

Since tactile signals can only be obtained by contacting and touching, the exploratory procedure for collecting tactile data is very important. Generally speaking, recognizing shape requires contacting and grasping the object; recognizing materials requires the material to slide along the surface of the robot; and recognizing deformability requires squeezing the object. However, there does not exist a unified strategy for the exploratory procedure. According to the findings of experimental psychology [57], six kinds of actions illustrated in Fig. 1.8 are performed by humans in order to explore objects:

1. Pressing the object to determine its softness,
2. Lateral sliding along the object to perceive surface texture,
3. Static contact with the objects to measure temperature or heat conductivity,
4. Enclosure with an object to determine its global shape and volume,
5. Lifting the object to determine its weight, and
6. Following the contour of the object to perceived its local shape.

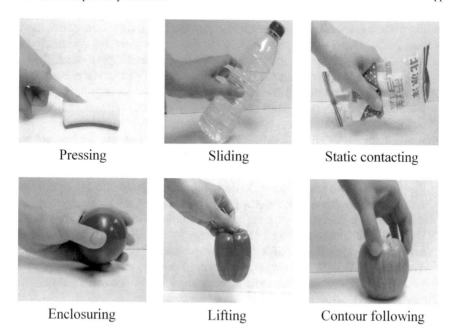

Pressing	Sliding	Static contacting
Enclosuring	Lifting	Contour following

Fig. 1.8 Six kinds of representative exploratory actions

The above actions can be imitated by the robotic manipulator to perform tactile exploration. In the existing work, the main exploratory procedures can be roughly classified as the following categories:

1. Passive mode: In this case, the robotic manipulator is fixed and the human operator hands over the object to the manipulator. The robotic hand mounted on the manipulator blindly grasps the object and performs actions such as press and squeeze. For example, in [21], the human operator grasped the bottle and put it in the space between the two-finger hand, and then, a press action was performed to obtain tactile sequences. Such a passive mode is very popular in recognition tasks for textured materials. Because of the diversity of the materials, various exploratory procedures are combined together to obtain sufficient tactile information. Both the work in [22, 83] took five different exploratory procedures for such tasks.

2. Semi-active mode: In this case, objects are usually fixed in some place. The manipulator detects and approaches the object according to some prescribed trajectory and performs exploratory procedures. Since the approach procedure utilizes a closed-loop control strategy, there exist uncertainties on the grasp point. The exploratory procedures, however, are designed beforehand. Due to the grasp

uncertainties, relative motion between object and fingers, the semi-active mode may produce more noisy tactile signals. However, such a strategy is closer to the human's grasp strategy. A representative work can be found in [84], which divided the procedure into three stages: (1) open fingers according to some preshape; (2) move the fingers according to some planned path until it contacts the object; (3) perform exploratory procedures such as press or squeeze until some termination conditions are satisfied.

3. Active mode: This strategy exhibits strong flexibility because the manipulator finds the object and explores it autonomously. There exist many challenges when adopting this strategy, and no unified method has ever been presented. Reference [82] adopted the decision theory to design the active grasp strategy to increase recognition performance. Reference [74] developed the tactile alignment method using the object surface contour information. Furthermore, Ref. [95] adopted the Bayesian inference to develop the exploratory procedure, while Ref. [37] resorted to the learning technology and designed an exploratory procedure for cutting food. Very recently, Ref. [97] developed methods to adaptively select a sequence of wrist poses that achieved accurate tactile object recognition by enclosure grasps.

The above discussions disclose that different exploratory procedures should be performed to recognize the object's shape, stiffness, and texture. It is difficult, if not impossible, to recognize all properties of an object using one single tactile exploratory procedure. Therefore, it is natural to classify the existing work on tactile object recognition according to the action of tactile exploratory procedures. The following three sections will discuss how to use the tactile sensor to perceive the object's shape, texture, and deformability. Besides, it should be noted that Ref. [87] implemented tactile object identification and feature extraction techniques on data acquired during a single, unplanned grasp with a simple, underactuated robot hand equipped with inexpensive barometric pressure sensors. The proposed method in [87] does not require object exploration, regrasping, grasp-release, or force modulation and works for arbitrary object start positions and orientations.

1.4   Tactile Perception for Shape

Shape classification of rigid objects using tactile signals has a long history. For example, Ref. [3] used touch point cloud data to fit the quadratic surface model and further realized the tactile shape recognition. Reference [80] described the process of object recognition using a mobile robot equipped with eight tentacle tactile sensors. While moving, a tentacle tactile sensor can not only scan and instantly record the shape of objects, but also recognize, catch, and move the object according to internal programs. After analyzing the tactile information of grasped objects, the least square fitting method and circle fitting method were used to classify and recognize objects. Conversely, Ref. [49] proposed the Gaussian process classification method for sparse tactile point cloud. Generally, a single grasp can only perceive the shape of the part that is in contact with the tactile sensor, so it can only handle the situation where objects have simple shapes. Recently, Ref. [63] described the local shape of objects by extracting the covariance matrix of the tactile array signal. Most of the existing work can only deal with objects with simple shape.

When the tactile data are regarded as a low-resolution gray image, image processing and computer vision technologies can be used to extract features from the tactile array signal and classify different shapes. As aforementioned, tactile sensors can only perceive limited parts of objects, so the information from different parts of the object is expected to be obtained through multiple grasps. A bag-of-words (BoW) model can then be constructed for tactile signals. Based on the BoW feature, a naive Bayes classifier can be trained to classify the objects. However, this method requires a manipulator to grasp an object by many times to collect tactile information from different parts. Furthermore, the direct use of tactile image data introduces a lot of noises. To avoid these problems, [74] used the SIFT feature to deal with the tactile image and relaxed restrictions on the position and orientation of objects. Reference [71] applied this method to the task of sliding detection. Tactile sensors collect tactile signals through direct contact. However, since the position of objects may change during contact, directly applying feature extraction methods in image processing may cause some problems. To address this, Ref. [66] proposed Tactile-SIFT, a new descriptor suitable for tactile image processing, and it was used to construct a BoW model. Figure 1.9 lists some of the aforementioned experimental objects for tactile shape recognition. These objects usually have obvious shape features, and some are even specially designed for algorithm verification (see the first row of the left column in Fig. 1.9). Very recently, [99] presented a new descriptor, which was invariant to object movement and simple to construct, using only the relative geometry of points on the object surface, for tactile 3D object classification. It is important to note that object recognition does not only rely on tactile sensors. In reality, visual sensors have

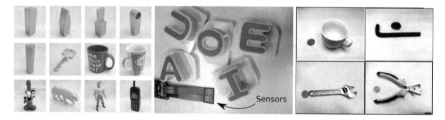

Fig. 1.9 The representative objects used for shape-based tactile object recognition. Left: [2009] IEEE. Reprinted, with permission, from Ref. [82]. Middle: [2011] IEEE. Reprinted, with permission, from Ref. [74]. Right: [2015] IEEE. Reprinted, with permission, from Ref. [66]

already been widely used in this task. In turn, exploring how to combine visual and tactile sensing in order to accurately recognize different objects is worthy of further research.

1.5   Tactile Perception for Texture

Texture information reflects the distribution characteristics of microstructures on the surface of an object. Classification for the object's material can be determined by surface texture features. Tactile sensors can perceive a lot of material information that visual sensors have difficulties to perceive. Extensive research has focused on tactile material recognition. Classifying the material texture usually requires actions such as scraping, sliding, and rubbing to obtain vibration signals. Therefore, it is necessary to consider characteristics of time series. The most intuitive solution is to employ signal processing methods. For example, Ref. [83] recognized 20 different textures using five scraping actions; Ref. [41] recognized eight different textured disks; Ref. [79] recognized 15 kinds of surface materials; and Ref. [48] identified eight surface textures by simulating human behaviors through multiple contacts and implementing a majority voting. Conversely, Ref. [29] directly used the slope and peak of the tactile time series to develop a perception model based on the nonparametric Bayesian method and used it to recognize 28 different disks. Additionally, Ref. [22] learned 25 haptic adjectives for textured materials. All of these works extracted features using the discrete Fourier transform or other frequency domain analysis tools. From another viewpoint, Ref. [88] pointed out the similarity between tactile and speech signals and resorted to the Mel-frequency cepstral coefficients, which are commonly used in audio processing to extract features. Common methods for classification include the nearest neighbor classifier, support vector machine (SVM) [31, 83], and Gaussian process [88]. One example of using the SVM classifier is seen in [17]. In this study, magnetic flux obtained three-dimension tactile values and treated the covariance matrix of these values as features to classify eight texture materials by SVM. More recently, Ref. [7] developed a deep learning method for robust material classification with tactile skins. Figures 1.10, 1.11, and 1.12 show some representative examples of experimental objects for texture recognition and corresponding operation scenes. Until now, most of the existing work focuses on regular textured objects, and complicated natural textured objects have received very little attention.

Texture materials usually belong to surface characteristics and, as such, can also be perceived by visual sensors. Compared with visual sensors, tactile sensors obtain finer texture characteristics and also yield additional information through vibration and sliding. However, most current texture recognition tasks are limited to simple object shapes. For objects with complex shapes, further work is required to investigate how to design reasonable contact actions and use tactile information for analysis.

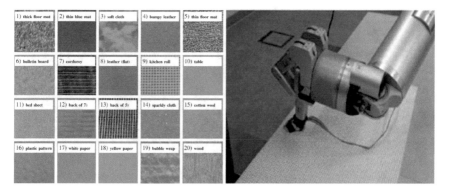

Fig. 1.10 Representative textured objects used for texture-based tactile recognition. [2011] IEEE. Reprinted, with permission, from Ref. [83]

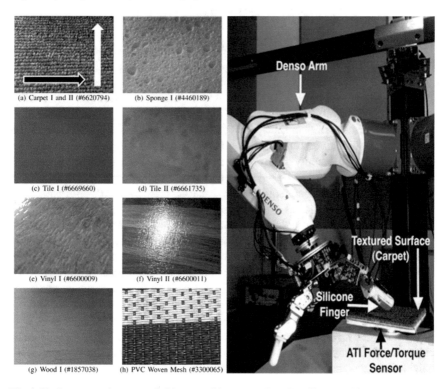

Fig. 1.11 Representative textured objects used for texture-based tactile recognition. [2011] IEEE. Reprinted, with permission, from Ref. [48]

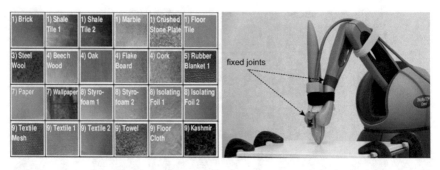

Fig. 1.12 Representative textured objects used for texture-based tactile recognition. [2014] IEEE. Reprinted, with permission, from Ref. [88]

1.6 Tactile Perception for Deformable Objects

Compared with tactile recognition based on shape and texture, object recognition for deformable objects pays more attention to surface characteristics and the internal state of the object, which cannot be directly obtained by normal visual sensors. Because of the complexity of object deformation, it is difficult to describe the deformation mechanism with a unified model.

Based on changes of one-dimension force on the fingertip, Ref. [21] proposed a simple and useful method for tactile feature extraction and designed a classification algorithm to classify empty and full bottles. This resulted in a method that could perceive the internal state of an object by touching. For the five-finger iCub robotic hand, Ref. [84] used the Gaussian process to extract features from tactile sequences and proposed an incremental object recognition method. It was used to identify soft toys, hard books, and bottles and cans containing various amounts of liquid. Ref. [33] described a self-designed tactile sensor with 64 tactile sensing modules arranged in an 8×8 grid. This sensor was attached to the Schunk2 and Schunk3 fingers, which were used to grasp various objects to build a tactile dataset. After the data collection process, distance was measured using dynamic time warping and the nearest neighborhood classifier was used to classify objects. The aforementioned works primarily used hands with two, three, or five fingers; each finger is able to collect data. However, most of these works only concatenated data from different fingers through simple splicing or counting statistics, which pay more attention to individual fingers rather than the relationship between fingers.

Figures 1.13, 1.14, and 1.15 provide literature examples of experimental objects and their corresponding operation scenarios for the identification of tactile deformation. Objects used in these studies are common household objects, such as fruits, or containers such as cans and bottles. Furthermore, the operation patterns of these objects differ from each other. All these factors make object recognition challenging. To address this, Ref. [68] proposed a spatiotemporal unsupervised feature learning method that made full use of the correlation information from tactile sequences

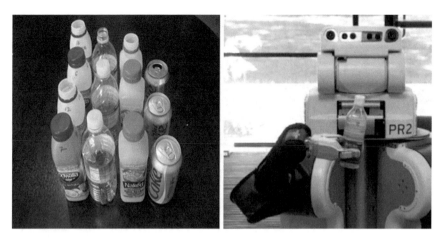

Fig. 1.13 Representative objects used for deformation-based tactile recognition. [2011] IEEE. Reprinted, with permission, from Ref. [21]

Fig. 1.14 Representative objects used for deformation-based tactile recognition. Reprinted from Ref. [33], with permission from Elsevier

in both time and space domains. The method was validated on different datasets [33, 84]. Another study [37] considered the deformation of food and designed operations with knives and forks to obtain tactile information. After training, 12 different foods were successfully recognized. On the other hand, Ref. [62] used a soft manipulator and simplified the grasp process. A random forest classifier was designed based on deformation and rigidity. Reference [95] integrated force, oscillation, and temperature signals from a BioTac sensor to deal with both texture and deformation recognition. In Ref. [16], a randomized tiling convolutional networks in a hierarchical fusion strategy was developed for tactile object recognition.

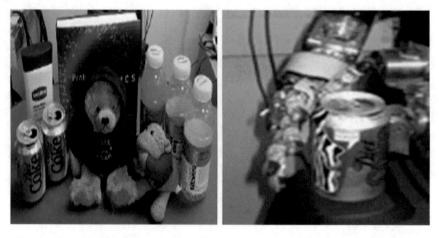

Fig. 1.15 Representative objects used for deformation-based tactile recognition. [2014] IEEE. Reprinted, with permission, from Ref. [84]

Most of the aforementioned works used tactile sensors integrated on fingers and grasped objects with the precise grasp. However, many manipulators also have tactile sensors on their palm. This inspired some scholars to grasp objects with a power grasp. For example, Refs. [72, 81] used this grasp to recognize multiple objects based on a single-layer neural network and deep learning technology. Reference [67] also used this power grasp strategy to classify 16 different objects. Figures 1.16, 1.17, and 1.18 list the experimental objects and grasp sceneries used in these works. A future trend is to combine the two grasp methods together to obtain better performance.

1. Eggplant 2. Orange 3. Cup 4. Cup with handle 5. Can

6. Salt 7. Bottle 8. Star fruit 9. Pear 10. Amicelli

Fig. 1.16 Representative objects used for the power grasp strategy. [2012] IEEE. Reprinted, with permission, from Ref. [72]

Fig. 1.17 Representative objects used for the power grasp strategy. [2014] IEEE. Reprinted, with permission, from Ref. [81]

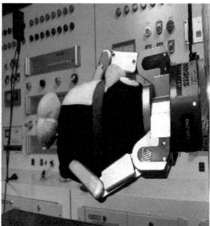

Fig. 1.18 Representative objects used for the power grasp strategy. Reprinted from Ref. [67], with permission of Springer

1.7 Visual–Tactile Fusion for Object Recognition

Though tactile sensing is important, Ref. [92] provided evidences that tactile signals were highly variable despite good repeatability in grasping conditions. It is also pointed out that using a simple machine learning algorithm, grasp outcome prediction based purely on tactile sensors was not reliable enough for real-world responsibilities.

Therefore, to achieve fine operations, robots are usually equipped with a variety of sensors. If all sensors only perceive and understand the surrounding environment with independent methods for different modalities, the intrinsic relationship between different modalities is cut off, which severely reduces the intelligence of the perception action. Therefore, in order to determine the object's location and attribute information, the multimodal (e.g., visual and tactile modalities) fusion theory and methods should be developed. The problem of visual–tactile fusion for perception has attracted the attention of many robotic researchers. The internationally renowned academic conference Robotics Science and Systems 2015 specifically organized a workshop named *Learning for Visual and Tactile Interaction*.

Visual and tactile modalities are quite different from each other. Firstly, the format, frequency, and range of object information are different. Tactile sensing obtains information about objects when it continuously touches the object, while the visual modality can simultaneously obtain multiple different features of an object at a distance. Furthermore, some features can only be obtained by one single perceptual mode. For example, the color of an object can only be obtained visually, while the texture, hardness, and temperature of a surface can be more naturally obtained through tactile sensing. In addition, asynchronous information obtained from two modalities and different perception ranges brings a great challenge to multimodal fusion.

There are various methods for visual and tactile fusion, and some technologies allow for tactile information to be partly obtained through visual perception. For example, Ref. [69] used a microcamera to obtain object surface images and then used optical flow to detect sliding, while Refs. [4, 24, 61] used cameras to detect changes in object shape to obtain additional tactile information. None of these works were based on visual–tactile fusion.

The application of visual–tactile fusion is quite extensive. Reference [85] reported experimental results in using both visual and tactile information for manipulator grasping and pointed out that with the introduction of tactile information more precise results can be obtained. Reference [13] realized location of polyhedron by integrating visual and tactile information. Reference [46] used visual images and tactile signals for 3D reconstruction. In [11], the visual image was first used for rough modeling, and then the tactile signals were used for fine-tuning. The grasp stability learning using visual–tactile fusion was investigated in [8]. Dense mapping was recently developed in [10], which assumed that the visually similar scene should have similar tactile characteristics. In [76], the author developed a system that integrates the visual, tactile, and force to perform the task of complicated opening doors. Reference [65] investigated the correspondence between visual and tactile features. In [43], tactile and visual data was integrated using auto-encoders for stable reinforcement learning. Very recently, Ref. [98] proposed to integrate tactile and visual sensing to predict task-compatible grasp regions for manipulation. Reference [47] developed an object-tracking framework that fuses point cloud information from an RGB-D camera with tactile information from a GelSight contact sensor. See Fig. 1.19 for the illustrations.

As for object recognition, which is the focus of this book, few work has been published. Generally speaking, the visual modality can be used to deal with color and shape, while tactile modality is good at dealing with stiffness and temperature. For surface material, both visual modality and tactile modality work. However, the former is good at a coarse level, while the latter is good at a fine level. Reference [94] presented a detailed explanation of this problem. An early work was proposed by [54],

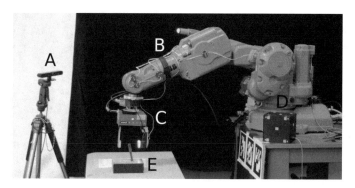

Fig. 1.19 The setup used in experiments developed in [47] consists of an Asus Xtion RGB-D camera (A) observing a 6-DOF ABB IRB-140 arm (B). The end effector is a Schunk WSG-50 parallel gripper with a GelSight-enabled custom set of fingers (C). A cube with attached optical markers (D), and a small screwdriver and rectangular holster (E) are used as manipulators. [2017] IEEE. Reprinted, with permission, from Ref. [47]

which focused on utilizing visual information to help tactile feature extraction. In that work, the authors discovered an important problem which indicates that visual data and tactile data are weakly paired. In addition, they just used the tactile information for classification, with visual information just used for training. In [90], a new framework for object classification and grasp planning using visual and tactile sensing was established.

Very recently, Refs. [36, 101] utilized a deep learning method for the joint learning of visual and tactile information. All of these above works dealt with textured material only. For deformable objects, Ref. [39] presented an interesting work that tried to tell the internal state of a container. The author used a fixed Kinect camera to capture the object in order to detect deformability, and then, the tactile signals were introduced to analyze the internal state. However, this method requires the 3D model of the object, and therefore, it is difficult to be extended to unfamiliar objects. In Fig. 1.20, some representative data collection scenes or the algorithm architectures are listed, which were adopted in the corresponding references. Currently, substantial challenges remain due to the gap between different perception modalities.

In addition to the multimodal fusion, the cross-modal recognition using visual and tactile information is also appealing. In [35], the author proposed a framework to deal with cross-modal visuo-tactile object recognition, which means that the object recognition algorithm is trained only with visual data and is able to recognize objects leveraging only tactile perception. The proposed architecture is listed in Fig. 1.21. Reference [96] sought to associate information from vision and touch by jointly training deep networks across the three modalities. Through the networks, each input, regardless of modality, generated an embedding vector that records the fabric's physical property. By comparing the embedding, this system was able to look at a fabric image and predict feeling, and vice versa.

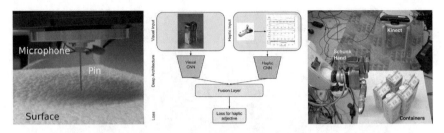

Fig. 1.20 Some experimental scenes of algorithm architectures of the visual–tactile fusion work. Left: [2011] IEEE. Reprinted, with permission, from Ref. [54]. Middle: [2016] IEEE. Reprinted, with permission, from Ref. [36]. Right: [2014] IEEE. Reprinted, with permission, from Ref. [39]

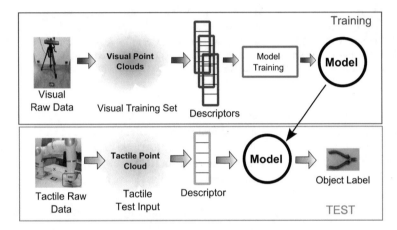

Fig. 1.21 Cross-modal recognition concept: training pipeline (top) and execution pipeline (bottom). [2017] IEEE. Reprinted, with permission, from Ref. [35]

1.8   Public Datasets

Currently, there are a number of visual object recognition datasets developed as benchmarks. Some of them could be used for robotic applications, such as the 300 objects datasets developed in [56]. As a comparison, the construction work of tactile object datasets is still in a preliminary stage. Most of the existing work uses their own developed small-scale datasets and is not released for public use, which prevents comparisons under the same standards. Some representative datasets are summarized below.

1.8.1   Tactile Dataset

In [38], the authors utilized multiple types of fingers to complete grasp simulation. They generated the grasp pose for each object and constructed the famous Columbia

Grasp Database. Furthermore, they utilized GraspIt!, which is a simulation tool [70], to produce the tactile feedback for each grasp pose, and established a set of complete simulation tactile datasets. Reference [30] used such datasets for learning grasp stability.

Reference [9] utilized the RobWorkSim tool to develop the simulation tactile dataset SDS. This dataset includes the tactile signals for five types of grasp cases. In addition, they established SD-5 using the Schunk fingers to collect the practical tactile signals for five objects. SDS and SD-5 are used for grasp stability analysis and learning.

For textured materials, the GRASP group at University of Pennsylvania released Penn Haptic Texture Toolkit (HaTT) [25], which includes 100 materials. In [88], the authors introduced a haptic texture database which allows for a systematic analysis of feature candidates. The publicly available database includes recorded accelerations measured during controlled and well-defined texture scans, as well as uncontrolled human freehand texture explorations for 43 different textures.

In Ref. [33], some various tactile datasets were presented. The tactile signals were collected by using the developed flexible tactile sensor. Seven deformable fruits (grape, kiwi, lime, mushroom, orange, plum, and tomato) were grasped by the Schunk Parallel gripper and the obtained tactile signals form the dataset SPr-7. For ten other various household objects, both rigid and deformable, some were similar in shape and size. The set of objects consisted of a rubber ball, balsam bottle, rubber duck, empty plastic bottle, full plastic bottle, bad orange, fresh orange, juggling ball, tape roll, and a small block of wood. They used the Schunk Parallel gripper to establish the dataset SPr-10. In addition, they used a three-finger hand to collect the new dataset SD-10, using the same objects. Reference [84] constructed the ten-object iCub dataset which were collected using five-finger hand. It seems that existing datasets are small-scale due to the high cost of collection. Very recently, Ref. [18] developed a BioTac grasp stability dataset.

1.8.2 Visual–Tactile Fusion Datasets

Since the study on visual–tactile fusion recognition has only been for a short time, the dataset is in its infant stage. Reference [54] provided a small-scale dataset which includes both image and tactile signals. The tactile signals were obtained by sliding the pin on the materials. In HaTT [25], although the textured images were provided, they did not focus on the problem of object recognition, but the texture synthesis used both tactile and image information.

Very recently, Refs. [36, 101] developed deep learning methods for visual–tactile fusion. Both datasets are collected for textured materials. The Portable Robotic Optical/Tactile ObservatioNPACKage (PROTON) is a new hand-held visuo-haptic sensing system that records surface interactions [15] (See Fig. 1.22). The long-term research goal of PROTON project is to collect a large dataset of matched visuo-haptic

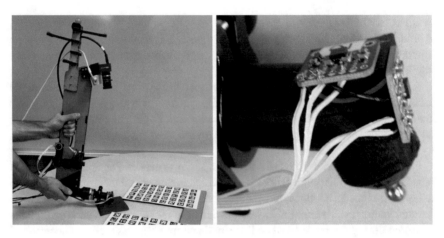

Fig. 1.22 Left: Proton Pack. Right: End effector. [2017] AAAI. Reprinted, with permission, from Ref. [15]

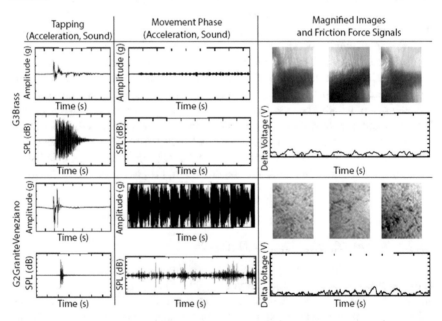

Fig. 1.23 Examples of the image, friction force, sound, and acceleration signals for two surfaces (brass and granite). SPL stands for sound pressure level. [2017] IEEE. Reprinted, with permission, from Ref. [89]

surface data for use by robots in applications such as grasping unfamiliar objects and walking or driving over unknown terrain.

Since different sensors can be used to capture different modalities of properties about one surface, combining the collected measurement information is a better

Fig. 1.24 Recording procedure, exemplarily shown for an operator. First, a surface image is captured using the camera preview. Secondly, the recording device impacts the surface. Thereafter, an operator may arbitrarily move the tool over the surface. [2017] IEEE. Reprinted, with permission, from Ref. [89]

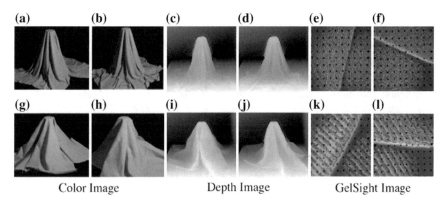

Fig. 1.25 Three modalities of the fabric data. For the visual information, the fabrics are draped from a cylinder in natural state; for the tactile information, a human holds the GelSight sensor and presses on a fold on the fabric. [2017] IEEE. Reprinted, with permission, from Ref. [96]

strategy to improve categorization performance. Also, recent advances in robotics make it possible for robots to interact with environments and hence acquire multimodal measurement information for environment understanding. Very recently, Ref. [88] presented an approach for tool-mediated surface classification that combined multiple signals and released the TUM dataset for research purposes. Figure 1.23 shows typical sound, acceleration, and image signals, captured by performing impacting and moving, respectively. The measurement stylus is a free-to-wield object with a stainless-steel tool-tip, shown in Fig. 1.24. The data collection is performed on 108 surface material instances.

Reference [96] collected a dataset for fabric perception that consists of visual images (color and depth), GelSight videos, and human labeling of properties. The dataset contains 118 fabrics, including apparel fabrics like broadcloth, polyester, knit, satin; bedding fabrics like terry and fleece; and functional fabrics like burlap, curtain cloth, oilcloth. See Fig. 1.25 for the details.

1.9 Summary

In summary, tactile information and visual–tactile fusion information are very important in the process of robot operations and are also the focus of research in the field
of robot perception. However, research work in this area faces many challenges at
present. The specific summary is as follows:

1. Although object recognition based on tactile information has achieved great
   progress and many research results on recognition based on shape, texture, and
   deformation have been published, there remains a long road toward practical
   application. In the meantime, the recognition of deformable objects has become
   a main direction of tactile object recognition because of the combination of surface characteristics and the internal state of the object. Machine learning has
   become the mainstream method of tactile object recognition. At present, the
   reported method includes nearest neighbor classification, SVM, decision tree,
   hidden Markov model, Gaussian process, and Bayesian learning. The application
   of deep learning in tactile signal processing has also begun. However, how to
   achieve a more efficient and accurate classification by effectively extracting the
   tactile features of ordinary objects is still a challenging problem. Recently, we
   are excited to witness that some complicated machine learning methods such as
   transfer learning [51] and one-shot learning [1] were used for tactile information
   processing.
2. Overall, the detection method is crucial for tactile perception. The exploratory
   procedure acts as a key ingredient for tactile sensing. However, the relevant theoretical basis for it is still insufficient. Current research designed the detection process based on the artificial experience, and this remains underdeveloped regarding
   the active detection mode.
3. Visual–tactile fusion can provide more information for object recognition, but in
   practical applications, two important problems are how to mine the correlation
   properties of tactile and visual information, and how to learn joint expression of
   them. Research in this area is at an early phase. Visual–tactile fusion and other
   multimodal perception technologies provide more extensive and comprehensive
   information for robots to observe and understand the environment and then operate
   better, and they are of great significance toward improving robots' performance.
4. Both tactile object recognition and visual–tactile fusion object recognition are
   facing the challenge of the lack of large-scale datasets. Lack of data samples will
   restrict the application of some machine learning methods (such as deep learning) and does not permit a thorough performance evaluation of various methods.
   Theory and algorithm research and the construction of an effective dataset are
   the focus of future research in this area. From current publicly reported papers,
   we can see that visual and tactile fusion object recognition dataset has attracted
   considerable attention from various institutes and universities including the Max
   Planck Institute [54], University of Pennsylvania [14], University of California
   Berkeley [36], Technical University of Munich [101], Massachusetts Institute of
   Technology [96], Tsinghua University [64], and Waseda University [81].

To tackle the challenges in tactile perception and the visual–tactile fusion, we establish a unified sparse coding and dictionary learning framework, which forms the main contents of this book. In this book, a set of structured sparse coding models are developed to address the issues of dynamic tactile sensing. We then show that the proposed framework is effective in improving the performance of multifingered tactile object recognition, multilabel tactile adjective recognition, and multicategory material analysis, which are all challenging practical tasks in the fields of robotics and automation. The proposed sparse coding model can also tackle the challenging visual–tactile fusion recognition problem, and the book develops a series of efficient optimization algorithms to implement the model.

It should be noted that the sparse coding method has not received the deserved attention in the tactile recognition fields. Here, we list some highly-related work which elegantly adopted the sparse coding for tactile information processing. Reference [68] proposed a new tactile descriptor named spatiotemporal hierarchical matching pursuit which was based on the concept of unsupervised hierarchical feature learning realized using sparse coding. Reference [77] established a method to find an approximated sparse representation of the obtained tactile signal spectrograms that captures high-level features from the data. In [23], the grasp stability assessment was performed through unsupervised feature learning of tactile images. Very recently, Ref. [42] developed a tactile sensing technique based on compressed sensing, which simultaneously performed data sampling and compression with recovery guarantees. This method has been successfully applied to reduce hardware complexity and data transmission, while allowing fast, accurate reconstruction of the full-resolution tactile signal. However, all of those work focuses on the feature learning stage for the tactile signal, while the methods developed in this book directly address the object recognition problems.

References

1. Abderrahmane, Z., Ganesh, G., Cherubini, A., Crosnier, A.: Zero-shot object recognition based on haptic attributes (2017)
2. Aggarwal, A., Kampmann, P., Lemburg, J., Kirchner, F.: Haptic object recognition in underwater and deep-sea environments. J. Field Robot. **32**(1), 167–185 (2015)
3. Allen, P.K., Roberts, K.S.: Haptic object recognition using a multi-fingered dextrous hand. In: Robotics and Automation, 1989. Proceedings., 1989 IEEE International Conference on, pp. 342–347 (1989)
4. Alt, N., Steinbach, E.: Navigation and manipulation planning using a visuo-haptic sensor on a mobile platform. IEEE Trans. Instrum. Meas. **63**(11), 2570–2582 (2014)
5. Argall, B.D., Billard, A.G.: A survey of tactile human-robot interactions. Robot. Auton. Syst. **58**(10), 1159–1176 (2010)
6. Asif, U., Bennamoun, M., Sohel, F.A.: Rgb-d object recognition and grasp detection using hierarchical cascaded forests. IEEE Trans, Robot (2017)
7. Baishya, S.S., Bäuml, B.: Robust material classification with a tactile skin using deep learning. In: Intelligent Robots and Systems (IROS), 2016 IEEE/RSJ International Conference on, pp. 8–15 (2016)

8. Bekiroglu, Y., Detry, R., Kragic, D.: Learning tactile characterizations of object-and pose-specific grasps. In: Intelligent Robots and Systems (IROS), 2011 IEEE/RSJ International Conference on, pp. 1554–1560 (2011)
9. Bekiroglu, Y., Laaksonen, J., Jorgensen, J.A., Kyrki, V., Kragic, D.: Assessing grasp stability based on learning and haptic data. IEEE Trans. Robot. **27**(3), 616–629 (2011)
10. Bhattacharjee, T., Shenoi, A.A., Park, D., Rehg, J.M., Kemp, C.C.: Combining tactile sensing and vision for rapid haptic mapping. In: Intelligent Robots and Systems (IROS), 2015 IEEE/RSJ International Conference on, pp. 1200–1207 (2015)
11. Bjorkman, M., Bekiroglu, Y., Hogman, V., Kragic, D.: Enhancing visual perception of shape through tactile glances. In: Intelligent Robots and Systems (IROS), 2013 IEEE/RSJ International Conference on, pp. 3180–3186 (2013)
12. Bohg, J., Morales, A., Asfour, T., Kragic, D.: Data-driven grasp synthesisła survey. IEEE Trans. Robot. **30**(2), 289–309 (2014)
13. Boshra, M., Zhang, H.: Localizing a polyhedral object in a robot hand by integrating visual and tactile data. Pattern Recognit. **33**(3), 483–501 (2000)
14. Burka, A., Hu, S., Helgeson, S., Krishnan, S., Gao, Y., Hendricks, L.A., Darrell, T., Kuchenbecker, K.J.: Proton: A visuo-haptic data acquisition system for robotic learning of surface properties. In: Multisensor Fusion and Integration for Intelligent Systems (MFI), 2016 IEEE International Conference on, pp. 58–65 (2016)
15. Burka, A., Kuchenbecker, K.J.: How much haptic surface data is enough? (2017)
16. Cao, L., Kotagiri, R., Sun, F., Li, H., Huang, W., Aye, Z.M.M.: Efficient spatio-temporal tactile object recognition with randomized tiling convolutional networks in a hierarchical fusion strategy. In: Proceedings of the Thirtieth AAAI Conference on Artificial Intelligence, pp. 3337–3345. AAAI Press (2016)
17. Chathuranga, D.S., Wang, Z., Noh, Y., Nanayakkara, T., Hirai, S.: Robust real time material classification algorithm using soft three axis tactile sensor: evaluation of the algorithm. In: Intelligent Robots and Systems (IROS), 2015 IEEE/RSJ International Conference on, pp. 2093–2098 (2015)
18. Chebotar, Y., Hausman, K., Su, Z., Molchanov, A., Kroemer, O., Sukhatme, G., Schaal, S.: Bigs: Biotac grasp stability dataset. In: ICRA 2016 Workshop on Grasping and Manipulation Datasets (2016)
19. Chebotar, Y., Hausman, K., Su, Z., Sukhatme, G.S., Schaal, S.: Self-supervised regrasping using spatio-temporal tactile features and reinforcement learning. In: Intelligent Robots and Systems (IROS), 2016 IEEE/RSJ International Conference on, pp. 1960–1966. IEEE (2016)
20. Cheng, Y., Su, C., Jia, Y., Xi, N.: Data correlation approach for slippage detection in robotic manipulations using tactile sensor array. In: Intelligent Robots and Systems (IROS), 2015 IEEE/RSJ International Conference on, pp. 2717–2722 (2015)
21. Chitta, S., Sturm, J., Piccoli, M., Burgard, W.: Tactile sensing for mobile manipulation. IEEE Trans. Robot. **27**(3), 558–568 (2011)
22. Chu, V., McMahon, I., Riano, L., McDonald, C.G., He, Q., Perez-Tejada, J.M., Arrigo, M., Darrell, T., Kuchenbecker, K.J.: Robotic learning of haptic adjectives through physical interaction. Robot. Auton. Syst. **63**, 279–292 (2015)
23. Cockburn, D., Roberge, J.P., Le, T.H.L., Maslyczyk, A., Duchaine, V.: Grasp stability assessment through unsupervised feature learning of tactile images. In: Robotics and Automation (ICRA), 2017 IEEE International Conference on. IEEE (2017)
24. Corradi, T., Hall, P., Iravani, P.: Bayesian tactile object recognition: learning and recognising objects using a new inexpensive tactile sensor. In: Robotics and Automation (ICRA), 2015 IEEE International Conference on, pp. 3909–3914 (2015)
25. Culbertson, H., Lopez Delgado, J.J., Kuchenbecker, K.J.: The penn haptic texture toolkit for modeling, rendering, and evaluating haptic virtual textures (2014)
26. Dahiya, R.S., Metta, G., Cannata, G., Valle, M.: Guest editorial special issue on robotic sense of touch. IEEE Trans. Robot. **27**(3), 385–388 (2011)
27. Dahiya, R.S., Metta, G., Valle, M., Sandini, G.: Tactile sensingłfrom humans to humanoids. IEEE Trans. Robot. **26**(1), 1–20 (2010)

28. Dahiya, R.S., Mittendorfer, P., Valle, M., Cheng, G., Lumelsky, V.J.: Directions toward effective utilization of tactile skin: a review. IEEE Sens. J. **13**(11), 4121–4138 (2013)
29. Dallaire, P., Giguère, P., Émond, D., Chaib-Draa, B.: Autonomous tactile perception: a combined improved sensing and bayesian nonparametric approach. Robot. Auton. Syst. **62**(4), 422–435 (2014)
30. Dang, H.: Stable and semantic robotic grasping using tactile feedback (2013)
31. Decherchi, S., Gastaldo, P., Dahiya, R.S., Valle, M., Zunino, R.: Tactile-data classification of contact materials using computational intelligence. IEEE Trans. Robot. **27**(3), 635–639 (2011)
32. Denei, S., Maiolino, P., Baglini, E., Cannata, G.: On the development of a tactile sensor for fabric manipulation and classification for industrial applications. In: Intelligent Robots and Systems (IROS), 2015 IEEE/RSJ International Conference on, pp. 5081–5086 (2015)
33. Drimus, A., Kootstra, G., Bilberg, A., Kragic, D.: Design of a flexible tactile sensor for classification of rigid and deformable objects. Robot. Auton. Syst. **62**(1), 3–15 (2014)
34. van Erp, J.B., van Veen, H.A.: Touch down: the effect of artificial touch cues on orientation in microgravity. Neurosci. Lett. **404**(1), 78–82 (2006)
35. Falco, P., Lu, S., Cirillo, A., Natale, C., Pirozzi, S., Lee, D.: Cross-modal visuo-tactile object recognition using robotic active exploration
36. Gao, Y., Hendricks, L.A., Kuchenbecker, K.J., Darrell, T.: Deep learning for tactile understanding from visual and haptic data. In: Robotics and Automation (ICRA), 2016 IEEE International Conference on, pp. 536–543 (2016)
37. Gemici, M.C., Saxena, A.: Learning haptic representation for manipulating deformable food objects. In: Intelligent Robots and Systems (IROS 2014), 2014 IEEE/RSJ International Conference on, pp. 638–645 (2014)
38. Goldfeder, C., Ciocarlie, M., Dang, H., Allen, P.K.: The columbia grasp database. In: Robotics and Automation, 2009. ICRA'09. IEEE International Conference on, pp. 1710–1716 (2009)
39. Güler, P., Bekiroglu, Y., Gratal, X., Pauwels, K., Kragic, D.: What's in the container? classifying object contents from vision and touch. In: Intelligent Robots and Systems (IROS 2014), 2014 IEEE/RSJ International Conference on, pp. 3961–3968 (2014)
40. Henshaw, C.G.: Touch sensing for space robotics. Aerospace Conference, 2012 IEEE, pp. 1–13 (2012)
41. Heyneman, B., Cutkosky, M.R.: Biologically inspired tactile classification of object-hand and object-world interactions. In: Robotics and Biomimetics (ROBIO), 2012 IEEE International Conference on, pp. 167–173 (2012)
42. Hollis, B., Patterson, S., Trinkle, J.: Compressed sensing for scalable robotic tactile skins (2017). arXiv:1705.05247
43. van Hoof, H., Chen, N., Karl, M., van der Smagt, P., Peters, J.: Stable reinforcement learning with autoencoders for tactile and visual data. In: Intelligent Robots and Systems (IROS), 2016 IEEE/RSJ International Conference on, pp. 3928–3934. IEEE (2016)
44. Hsiao, K., Kaelbling, L., Lozano-Pérez, T.: Task-driven tactile exploration (2010)
45. Hughes, D., Krauthammer, A., Correll, N.: Recognizing social touch gestures using recurrent and convolutional neural networks. In: Robotics and Automation (ICRA), 2017 IEEE International Conference on. IEEE (2017)
46. Ilonen, J., Bohg, J., Kyrki, V.: Fusing visual and tactile sensing for 3-d object reconstruction while grasping. In: Robotics and Automation (ICRA), 2013 IEEE International Conference on, pp. 3547–3554 (2013)
47. Izatt, G., Mirano, G., Adelson, E., Tedrake, R.: Tracking objects with point clouds from vision and touch
48. Jamali, N., Sammut, C.: Majority voting: Material classification by tactile sensing using surface texture. IEEE Trans. Robot. **27**(3), 508–521 (2011)
49. Jin, M., Gu, H., Fan, S., Zhang, Y., Liu, H.: Object shape recognition approach for sparse point clouds from tactile exploration. In: Robotics and Biomimetics (ROBIO), 2013 IEEE International Conference on, pp. 558–562 (2013)

50. Johansson, R.S., Flanagan, J.R.: Coding and use of tactile signals from the fingertips in object manipulation tasks. Nat. Rev. Neurosci. **10**(5), 345–359 (2009)
51. Kaboli, M., Walker, R., Cheng, G.: Re-using prior tactile experience by robotic hands to discriminate in-hand objects via texture properties. In: Robotics and Automation (ICRA), 2016 IEEE International Conference on, pp. 2242–2247. IEEE (2016)
52. Kappassov, Z., Corrales, J.A., Perdereau, V.: Tactile sensing in dexterous robot hands. Robot. Auton. Syst. **74**, 195–220 (2015)
53. Kim, J., Forsythe, S.: Adoption of sensory enabling technology for online apparel shopping. Eur. J. Mark. **43**(9/10), 1101–1120 (2009)
54. Kroemer, O., Lampert, C.H., Peters, J.: Learning dynamic tactile sensing with robust vision-based training. IEEE Trans. Robot. **27**(3), 545–557 (2011)
55. Krug, R., Lilienthal, A.J., Kragic, D., Bekiroglu, Y.: Analytic grasp success prediction with tactile feedback. In: Robotics and Automation (ICRA), 2016 IEEE International Conference on, pp. 165–171. IEEE (2016)
56. Lai, K., Bo, L., Ren, X., Fox, D.: A large-scale hierarchical multi-view rgb-d object dataset. In: Robotics and Automation (ICRA), 2011 IEEE International Conference on, pp. 1817–1824 (2011)
57. Lederman, S.J., Klatzky, R.L.: Hand movements: a window into haptic object recognition. Cogn. Psychol. **19**(3), 342–368 (1987)
58. Lee, M.H., Nicholls, H.R.: Review article tactile sensing for mechatronicsła state of the art survey. Mechatronics **9**(1), 1–31 (1999)
59. Lester, D.H., Forman, A.M., Loyd, D.: Internet shopping and buying behavior of college students. Serv. Mark. Q. **27**(2), 123–138 (2006)
60. Levine, S., Pastor, P., Krizhevsky, A., Ibarz, J., Quillen, D.: Learning hand-eye coordination for robotic grasping with deep learning and large-scale data collection. In: The International Journal of Robotics Research, p. 0278364917710318 (2016)
61. Li, R., Adelson, E.H.: Sensing and recognizing surface textures using a gelsight sensor. In: Proceedings of the IEEE Conference on Computer Vision and Pattern Recognition, pp. 1241–1247 (2013)
62. Liarokapis, M.V., Calli, B., Spiers, A.J., Dollar, A.M.: Unplanned, model-free, single grasp object classification with underactuated hands and force sensors. In: Intelligent Robots and Systems (IROS), 2015 IEEE/RSJ International Conference on, pp. 5073–5080 (2015)
63. Liu, H., Song, X., Nanayakkara, T., Seneviratne, L.D., Althoefer, K.: A computationally fast algorithm for local contact shape and pose classification using a tactile array sensor. In: Robotics and Automation (ICRA), 2012 IEEE International Conference on, pp. 1410–1415 (2012)
64. Liu, H., Yu, Y., Sun, F., Gu, J.: Visual-tactile fusion for object recognition. IEEE Trans. Autom. Sci. Eng. **14**(2), 996–1008 (2017)
65. Luo, S., Mou, W., Althoefer, K., Liu, H.: Localizing the object contact through matching tactile features with visual map. In: Robotics and Automation (ICRA), 2015 IEEE International Conference on, pp. 3903–3908 (2015)
66. Luo, S., Mou, W., Althoefer, K., Liu, H.: Novel tactile-sift descriptor for object shape recognition. IEEE Sens. J. **15**(9), 5001–5009 (2015)
67. Ma, R., Liu, H., Sun, F., Yang, Q., Gao, M.: Linear dynamic system method for tactile object classification. Sci. China Inf. Sci. **57**(12), 1–11 (2014)
68. Madry, M., Bo, L., Kragic, D., Fox, D.: St-hmp: unsupervised spatio-temporal feature learning for tactile data. In: Robotics and Automation (ICRA), 2014 IEEE International Conference on, pp. 2262–2269 (2014)
69. Maldonado, A., Alvarez, H., Beetz, M.: Improving robot manipulation through fingertip perception. In: Intelligent Robots and Systems (IROS), 2012 IEEE/RSJ International Conference on, pp. 2947–2954 (2012)
70. Miller, A.T., Allen, P.K.: Graspit! a versatile simulator for robotic grasping. IEEE Robot. Autom. Mag. **11**(4), 110–122 (2004)

71. Nagatani, T., Noda, A., Hirai, S., et al.: What can be inferred from a tactile arrayed sensor in autonomous in-hand manipulation? In: Automation Science and Engineering (CASE), 2012 IEEE International Conference on, pp. 461–468 (2012)
72. Navarro, S.E., Gorges, N., Wörn, H., Schill, J., Asfour, T., Dillmann, R.: Haptic object recognition for multi-fingered robot hands. In: Haptics Symposium (HAPTICS), 2012 IEEE, pp. 497–502 (2012)
73. Petrovskaya, A., Khatib, O.: Global localization of objects via touch. IEEE Trans. Rob. 27(3), 569–585 (2011)
74. Pezzementi, Z., Plaku, E., Reyda, C., Hager, G.D.: Tactile-object recognition from appearance information. IEEE Trans. Rob. 27(3), 473–487 (2011)
75. Pinto, L., Gupta, A.: Supersizing self-supervision: Learning to grasp from 50k tries and 700 robot hours. In: Robotics and Automation (ICRA), 2016 IEEE International Conference on, pp. 3406–3413. IEEE (2016)
76. Prats, M., Sanz, P.J., Del Pobil, A.P.: Vision-tactile-force integration and robot physical interaction. In: Robotics and Automation, 2009. ICRA'09. IEEE International Conference on, pp. 3975–3980 (2009)
77. Roberge, J.P., Rispal, S., Wong, T., Duchaine, V.: Unsupervised feature learning for classifying dynamic tactile events using sparse coding. In: Robotics and Automation (ICRA), 2016 IEEE International Conference on, pp. 2675–2681. IEEE (2016)
78. Romano, J.M., Hsiao, K., Niemeyer, G., Chitta, S., Kuchenbecker, K.J.: Human-inspired robotic grasp control with tactile sensing. IEEE Trans. Robot. 27(6), 1067–1079 (2011)
79. Romano, J.M., Kuchenbecker, K.J.: Methods for robotic tool-mediated haptic surface recognition. In: Haptics Symposium (HAPTICS), 2014 IEEE, pp. 49–56 (2014)
80. Russell, R.A., Wijaya, J.A.: Object location and recognition using whisker sensors. In: Australasian Conference on Robotics and Automation, pp. 761–768 (2003)
81. Schmitz, A., Bansho, Y., Noda, K., Iwata, H., Ogata, T., Sugano, S.: Tactile object recognition using deep learning and dropout. In: Humanoid Robots (Humanoids), 2014 14th IEEE-RAS International Conference on, pp. 1044–1050 (2014)
82. Schneider, A., Sturm, J., Stachniss, C., Reisert, M., Burkhardt, H., Burgard, W.: Object identification with tactile sensors using bag-of-features. In: Intelligent Robots and Systems, 2009. IROS 2009. IEEE/RSJ International Conference on, pp. 243–248 (2009)
83. Sinapov, J., Sukhoy, V., Sahai, R., Stoytchev, A.: Vibrotactile recognition and categorization of surfaces by a humanoid robot. IEEE Trans. Robot. 27(3), 488–497 (2011)
84. Soh, H., Demiris, Y.: Incrementally learning objects by touch: Online discriminative and generative models for tactile-based recognition. IEEE Trans. Haptics 7(4), 512–525 (2014)
85. Son, J.S., Howe, R., Wang, J., Hager, G.D.: Preliminary results on grasping with vision and touch. In: Intelligent Robots and Systems'96, IROS96, Proceedings of the 1996 IEEE/RSJ International Conference on, vol. 3, pp. 1068–1075 (1996)
86. Song, D., Ek, C.H., Huebner, K., Kragic, D.: Task-based robot grasp planning using probabilistic inference. IEEE Trans. Robot. 31(3), 546–561 (2015)
87. Spiers, A.J., Liarokapis, M.V., Calli, B., Dollar, A.M.: Single-grasp object classification and feature extraction with simple robot hands and tactile sensors. IEEE Trans. Haptics 9(2), 207–220 (2016)
88. Strese, M., Lee, J.Y., Schuwerk, C., Han, Q., Kim, H.G., Steinbach, E.: A haptic texture database for tool-mediated texture recognition and classification. In: Haptic, Audio and Visual Environments and Games (HAVE), 2014 IEEE International Symposium on, pp. 118–123 (2014)
89. Strese, M., Schuwerk, C., Iepure, A., Steinbach, E.: Multimodal feature-based surface material classification. IEEE Trans, Haptics (2017)
90. Sun, F., Liu, C., Huang, W., Zhang, J.: Object classification and grasp planning using visual and tactile sensing. IEEE Trans. Syst. Man Cybern. Syst. 46(7), 969–979 (2016)
91. Taira, R., Saga, S., Okatani, T., Deguchi, K.: 3d reconstruction of reflective surface on reflection type tactile sensor using constraints of geometrical optics. In: SICE Annual Conference 2010, Proceedings of, pp. 3144–3149 (2010)

92. Wan, Q., Adams, R.P., Howe, R.D.: Variability and predictability in tactile sensing during grasping. In: Robotics and Automation (ICRA), 2016 IEEE International Conference on, pp. 158–164. IEEE (2016)
93. Westling, G., Johansson, R.: Factors influencing the force control during precision grip. Exp. Brain Res. **53**(2), 277–284 (1984)
94. Woods, A.T., Newell, F.N.: Visual, haptic and cross-modal recognition of objects and scenes. J. Physiol. Paris **98**(1), 147–159 (2004)
95. Xu, D., Loeb, G.E., Fishel, J.A.: Tactile identification of objects using bayesian exploration. In: Robotics and Automation (ICRA), 2013 IEEE International Conference on, pp. 3056–3061 (2013)
96. Yuan, W., Wang, S., Dong, S., Adelson, E.: Connecting look and feel: associating the visual and tactile properties of physical materials (2017). arXiv:1704.03822
97. Zhang, M.M., Atanasov, N., Daniilidis, K.: Active tactile object recognition by monte carlo tree search (2017). arXiv:1703.00095
98. Zhang, M.M., Detry, R., Larry, M., Kostas, D.: Tactile-vision integration for task-compatible fine-part manipulation. In: Robotics: Science and Systems (RSS) Workshop on Revisiting Contact C Turning a Problem into a Solution (2017)
99. Zhang, M.M., Kennedy, M.D., Hsieh, M.A., Daniilidis, K.: A triangle histogram for object classification by tactile sensing. In: Intelligent Robots and Systems (IROS), 2016 IEEE/RSJ International Conference on, pp. 4931–4938. IEEE (2016)
100. Zhang, Y.F., Liu, H.: Tactile sensor based varying contact point manipulation strategy for dexterous robot hand manipulating unknown objects. In: Intelligent Robots and Systems (IROS), 2012 IEEE/RSJ International Conference on, pp. 4756–4761 (2012)
101. Zheng, H., Fang, L., Ji, M., Strese, M., Özer, Y., Steinbach, E.: Deep learning for surface material classification using haptic and visual information. IEEE Trans. Multimed. **18**(12), 2407–2416 (2016)

Chapter 2
Representation of Tactile and Visual Modalities

Abstract Representation is the prerequisite of the perception and understanding. In this chapter, the representation methods for the concerned tactile and visual modalities are introduced. The tactile samples are regarded as multivariate time sequences and the dynamic time warping distances are employed to evaluate differences between tactile samples. Further, the canonical time warping distance is introduced to incorporate the spatial layout information of the tactile array. Since the induced kernels cannot be guaranteed to be positive definite, the more complicated global alignment kernel is used. For the visual modality, a popular covariance descriptor and the corresponding Log-Euclidean kernel are introduced.

2.1 Tactile Modality Representation

In this book, two types of tactile sensors are investigated under the proposed unified framework. This section, therefore, focuses on how to represent the tactile signals.

The first type of tactile signals is collected with the BarrettHand[1] (see Fig. 2.1), which has three fingers, labeled as Finger 1, Finger 2, and Finger 3. Finger 1 and Finger 2 rotate synchronously and symmetrically about the base joint in a spreading action. The "spread' motion around the palm allows an "on-the-fly" grasp reconfiguration to adapt to varying target object sizes, shapes, and orientations. Aside from the spreading motion, each of the three fingers on the BarrettHand features two joints driven by a single DC brushless servomotor. Using the fingers together allows the BarrettHand to "grasp" a wide variety of objects securely. Each tactile sensor array contains 24 sensor cells arranged in 3 columns and 8 rows. The main specifications of the BarrettHand are summarized in Table 2.1. More data collection details can be found in [14].

The second type of tactile signals is collected with SynTouch[2] Biomimetic haptic sensors (BioTac), which is shown in Fig. 2.2. Such sensors can be mounted on a number of robotic fingers. In this book, the publicly available Penn Haptic Adjective

---

[1]http://www.barrett.com/products-hand.htm

[2]https://www.syntouchinc.com/sensor-technology/

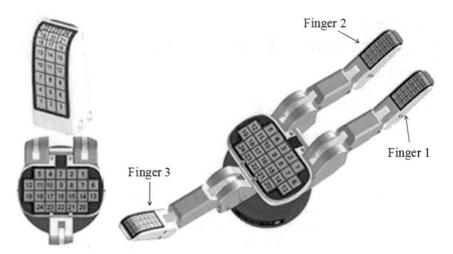

Fig. 2.1 Tactile sensors of BarrettHand

Table 2.1 BarrettHand Specifications

Tactile sensor	Element type	24 capacitive cells per sensor pad
	Range	$10N/cm^2$
	Resolution	$0.01N/cell$
Range of Motion	Finger base joint	140°
	Finger joint	45°
	Finger Spread	180°
Kinematics	Total fingers	3
	Total hand axes	8
	Total hand motors	4

Corpus 2 (PHAC-2) dataset is used, which was originally developed in [4]. Each object is explored by a pair of BioTac sensors, which are mounted on the gripper of a Willow Garage Personal Robot2 (PR2). Each object is felt with four exploratory procedures. The BioTac sensor generates five types of signals: low-frequency fluid pressure, high-frequency fluid vibrations, core temperature, core temperature change, and 19 electrode impedance which are spatially distributed across the sensor. Although the joint positions and gripper velocity and acceleration information are available, they are not used for classifying the tactile signals.

Fig. 2.2 BioTac sensors.
This figure is adopted from
the website https://www.
syntouchinc.com/sensor-
technology/

2.1.1 Tactile Sequence

Formally, it is assumed that the number of the fingers is N_F. At each time step, the tactile data is collected from the multiple sensor cells in each finger. By reshaping the matrix as into a $d^{(f)}$-dimensional vector for the f th finger, a $d^{(f)}$-dimensional dynamic tactile sequence is obtained; See Fig. 2.3 for illustration. Table 2.2 shows the details about the two tactile sensors.

The measurable space of interested tactile sequence signals is denoted by $\mathcal{T}$. Since it is expected to utilize the dynamic features which try to model the process the entire tactile signal changes over time, the i th dynamic tactile sequence $\mathbb{T}_i^{(f)} \in \mathcal{T}$ for the f th finger is represented as

$$\mathbb{T}_i^{(f)} = [\mathbb{T}_{i,1}^{(f)}, \mathbb{T}_{i,2}^{(f)}, \cdots, \mathbb{T}_{i,T_i}^{(f)}], \tag{2.1}$$

where $\mathbb{T}_{i,t}^{(f)} \in \mathbb{R}^{d^{(f)}}$ for $t = 1, 2, \cdots, T_i$, and T_i is the number of the sampled time instants for this sequence. For the same sequence, the lengths corresponding to different fingers should be equal. That is to say, T_i is independent of f. However, the

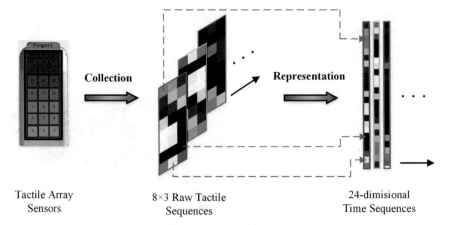

Fig. 2.3 Illustration of the tactile sequence representation for one finger of BarrettHand

Table 2.2 Details about the sensors

Tactile Sensors	The number of fingers N_F	Dimensions
BarrettHand	3	$d^{(1)} = d^{(2)} = d^{(3)} = 24$
BioTac	2	$d^{(1)} = d^{(2)} = 19$

lengths for different fingers are different from sequence to sequence, i.e., T_i maybe not equal to T_j for $i \neq j$.

For the multifingered hand, there are two ways to deal with the obtained tactile measurements. The first one is to regard each finger independently (see the middle row of Fig. 2.4). For this setting, an effective fusion strategy should be developed to combine the information provided by each finger. In Figs. 2.5 and 2.6, some representative tactile sequence samples which are collected by the BarrettHand and BioTac sensors are demonstrated respectively.

The second one is to combine all the measurements of the fingers. Concretely speaking, at each time step, the tactile data from the $d^{(f)}$ sensor cells in each finger is collected. The $d^{(f)}$-dimensional dynamic tactile sequences $\mathbb{T}_i^{(f)} \in R^{d^{(f)} \times T_i}$ are obtained for the fth finger. Finally, the N_F sequences are concatenated into one single sequence

$$\mathbb{T}_i = \begin{bmatrix} \mathbb{T}_i^{(1)} \\ \vdots \\ \mathbb{T}_i^{(N_F)} \end{bmatrix} \in R^{d \times T_i},$$

where $d = \sum_{f=1}^{N_F} d^{(f)}$. The effect is shown in the bottom row of Fig. 2.4 for illustration.

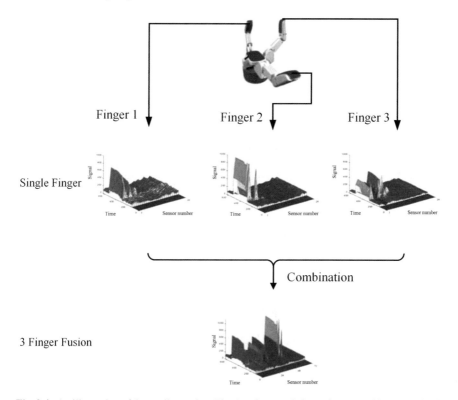

Finger 1   Finger 2   Finger 3

Single Finger

Combination

3 Finger Fusion

Fig. 2.4 An illustration of the tactile sensing. The data from each fingertip are combined as a single matrix measurement by concatenating all of them

2.1.2 *Dynamic Time Warping Distance*

A popular and effective method for comparing the time sequences is the Dynamic Time Warping (DTW) distance, which employs the dynamic programming paradigm to compute the alignment between two time sequences and allows similar shapes to match, even if they are out of phase in time. See Fig. 2.7 for a simple illustration. The DTW determines the alignment that "warps" one time sequence onto another, so the distance can be used as a basis for determining the similarity between the time sequences. The details can be found in [9] and [15]. Below is a brief introduction to DTW.

Suppose there are two tactile sequences $\mathbb{T}_i$ and $\mathbb{T}_j$ of the length T_i and T_j, which can be represented as

$$\mathbb{T}_i = [\mathbb{T}_{i,1}, \mathbb{T}_{i,2}, \cdots, \mathbb{T}_{i,T_i}], \quad \mathbb{T}_j = [\mathbb{T}_{j,1}, \mathbb{T}_{j,2}, \cdots, \mathbb{T}_{j,T_j}], \qquad (2.2)$$

where $\mathbb{T}_{i,t} \in R^d$ and $\mathbb{T}_{j,t} \in R^d$. DTW tries to solve the following optimization problem

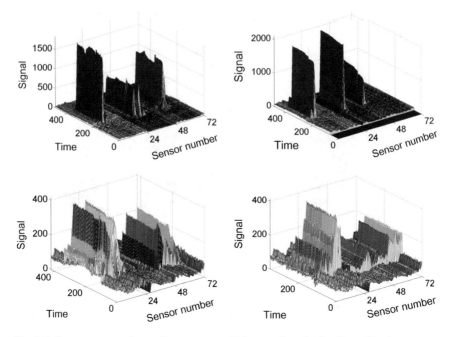

Fig. 2.5 Some representative tactile sequences which are collected using BarrettHand

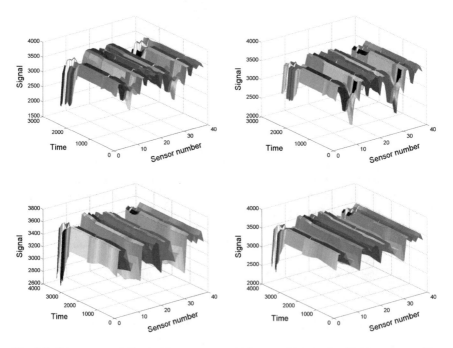

Fig. 2.6 Some representative tactile sequences which are collected using BioTac sensors. The samples are adopted from PHAC-2 dataset [4]

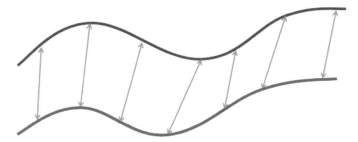

Fig. 2.7 Illustration of the dynamic time warping method. The two sequences which exhibit different lengths can be aligned by the arrowed lines

$$d_{DTW}(\mathbb{T}_i, \mathbb{T}_j) = \min_{\mathbf{P},K} \sum_{k=1}^{K} ||\mathbb{T}_{i,\mathbf{P}_{1,k}} - \mathbb{T}_{j,\mathbf{P}_{2,k}}||_2, \tag{2.3}$$

where $\mathbf{P} \in R^{2 \times K}$ is the mapping matrix, and K is the number of steps needed to align both signals. Denote the k-column of $\mathbf{P}$ as $\mathbf{p}_k$, then the constraints on the variable matrix $\mathbf{P}$ can be described as:

1. $\mathbf{P}_{1,k} \in \{1, 2, \cdots, T_i\}$, and $\mathbf{P}_{2,k} \in \{1, 2, \cdots, T_j\}$.
2. Boundary condition: $\mathbf{p}_1 = [1, 1]^T$, $\mathbf{p}_K = [T_i, T_j]^T$.
3. Continuity: $\mathbf{0} \preccurlyeq \mathbf{p}_{k+1} - \mathbf{p}_k \preccurlyeq \mathbf{1}$ for $k = 1, 2, \cdots, K - 1$.
4. Monotonicity: $\mathbf{p}_{k_1} - \mathbf{p}_{k_2} \preccurlyeq 0$ for $k_1 \preccurlyeq k_2$.

The value of K is naturally subject to the constraints

$$\max(T_i, T_j) \leq K \leq T_i + T_j - 1.$$

The optimization problem (2.3) can be equivalently rewritten as [15]

$$\min_{\mathbf{Z},\mathbf{Y}} ||\mathbb{T}_i\mathbf{Z}^T - \mathbb{T}_j\mathbf{Y}^T||_F, \tag{2.4}$$

where $\mathbf{Z} \in \{0, 1\}^{K \times T_i}$ and $\mathbf{Y} \in \{0, 1\}^{K \times T_j}$ are binary selection matrices that need to be inferred to align $\mathbb{T}_i$ and $\mathbb{T}_j$.

DTW only provides the alignment along the temporal line but neglects the spatial alignment. Since the tactile sequence may be a combination of multifingered tactile sequences. In practice, the hand may grasp the object from different angles, and therefore admits different spatial relation in the tactile sequence. To obtain a more accurate metric, the Canonical Time Warping (CTW) method proposed in [15] can be adopted. CTW essentially solves the following optimization problem:

$$d_{CTW}(\mathbb{T}_i, \mathbb{T}_j) = \min_{\mathbf{Z},\mathbf{Y},\mathbf{U},\mathbf{V}} ||\mathbf{U}\mathbb{T}_i\mathbf{Z}^T - \mathbf{V}\mathbb{T}_j\mathbf{Y}^T||_F, \tag{2.5}$$

where $\mathbf{U} \in R^{d \times d}$ and $\mathbf{V} \in R^{d \times d}$ parameterize the spatial warping by projecting the sequence into the same coordinate system. The following constraints:

1. $\mathbb{T}_i \mathbf{Z}^T \mathbf{1} = \mathbf{0}, \mathbb{T}_j \mathbf{Y}^T \mathbf{1} = \mathbf{0}$
2. $\mathbf{U}^T \mathbb{T}_i \mathbf{Z}^T \mathbf{Z} \mathbb{T}_i^T \mathbf{U} = \mathbf{V}^T \mathbb{T}_j \mathbf{Y}^T \mathbf{Y} \mathbb{T}_j^T \mathbf{V}^T = \mathbf{I}$
3. $\mathbf{U}^T \mathbb{T}_i \mathbf{Z}^T \mathbf{Y} \mathbb{T}_j^T \mathbf{V}$ is a diagonal matrix

are introduced to ensure the invariance to translation, rotation, and scaling. The optimization problem (2.5) is nonconvex, and we have to alternate between solving $\mathbf{Z}$, $\mathbf{Y}$ using DTW and $\mathbf{U}, \mathbf{V}$ using Canonical Component Analysis (CCA). The algorithm details can be found in [15].

It shows that CTW is an extension of Canonical Correspondence Analysis (CCA) and DTW, used to align two tactile sequences $\mathbb{T}_i$ and $\mathbb{T}_j$ in space and time, where CCA applies a linear transformation to the rows (features), while DTW applies binary transformation to the columns (time).

Using the above-mentioned d_{CTW} and d_{CTW} distances, the corresponding DTW kernel and CTW kernels can be easily constructed as

$$\kappa_{DTW}(\mathbb{T}_i, \mathbb{T}_j) = e^{-\gamma d_{DTW}^2(\mathbb{T}_i, \mathbb{T}_j)}$$

and

$$\kappa_{CTW}(\mathbb{T}_i, \mathbb{T}_j) = e^{-\gamma d_{CTW}^2(\mathbb{T}_i, \mathbb{T}_j)}$$

respectively, where γ is the adjusting parameter.

However, it is well known that DTW is not a true metric and it is difficult to construct the positive-definite kernel from DTW distance [3]. In some previous work such as [3], some extra modifications were always required to guarantee the positive definiteness of the DTW kernel matrix. Such a processing introduced unexpected effects for the final performance. To this end, the Global Alignment(GA) kernel which was proposed in [5] is employed. It is introduced in the following section.

2.1.3   Global Alignment Kernel

For the two tactile sequences $\mathbb{T}_i$ and $\mathbb{T}_j$, an alignment π is denoted to be a pair of increasing integral vectors (π_i, π_j) of length $|\pi|$ such that

$$1 = \pi_i(1) \leq \cdots \pi_i(|\pi|) = T_i$$

and

$$1 = \pi_j(1) \leq \cdots \pi_j(|\pi|) = T_j,$$

with unitary increments and no simultaneous repetitions. Since the two tactile sequences have $T_i + T_j$ points and they are matched at least at one point of time, it is easy to find $|\pi| \leq T_i + T_j - 1$.

The alignment cost of $\mathbb{T}_i$ and $\mathbb{T}_j$ is defined under the alignment strategy π as

$$\text{COST}_{\mathbb{T}_i, \mathbb{T}_j}(\pi) = \sum_{t=1}^{|\pi|} \psi(\mathbb{T}_{i,\pi_i(t)}, \mathbb{T}_{j,\pi_j(t)}), \qquad (2.6)$$

where $\psi(\cdot, \cdot)$ is used to denote the local divergence that measures the discrepancy between the two vectors. According to the suggestions in [5], the following local divergence is used

$$\psi(\boldsymbol{u}, \boldsymbol{v}) = \frac{1}{2\sigma^2} \|\boldsymbol{u} - \boldsymbol{v}\|_2^2 + \log(2 - e^{-\frac{\|\boldsymbol{u}-\boldsymbol{v}\|^2}{2\sigma^2}}), \qquad (2.7)$$

where σ is a parameter which should be determined by the users.

The GA kernel assumes that the minimum value of alignments may be sensitive to peculiarities of the time series and intends to take advantage of all alignments weighted exponentially. It is defined as the sum of exponentiated and sign changed costs of the individual alignments:

$$\kappa_{GA}(\mathbb{T}_i, \mathbb{T}_j) = \sum_{\pi \in \Pi(t_i, t_j)} e^{-\text{COST}_{\mathbb{T}_i, \mathbb{T}_j}(\pi)}, \qquad (2.8)$$

where $\Pi(t_i, t_j)$ denotes the set of all alignments between two time sequences of length t_i and t_j. It has been argued that κ_{GA} runs over the whole spectrum of the costs and gives rise to a smoother measure than the minimum of the costs, i.e., the DTW distance. It has also been shown that this kernel is positive definite provided that $\frac{e^{-\psi}}{1+e^{-\psi}}$ is positive definite [5]. However, the time cost of calculating GA kernel is significantly higher than that of DTW kernel.

In this book, the above kernels are alternatively adopted for different robotic hands. The details will be given in the subsequent chapters.

2.2 Visual Modality Representation

Since this book also investigates how to use visual information to improve tactile perception and understanding, a brief introduction about the visual modality representation is useful.

How to efficiently extract discriminative feature from an object using visual modality and accurately classify that object is an unsolved and challenging problem. A major concern in visual modality representation is the lack of a competent similarity criterion that captures both statistical and spatial properties; most approaches depend either on color distributions or structural models. Many different representations, from aggregated statistics to appearance models, have been used for object recognition. Histograms are popular representations of nonparametric density, but they disregard the spatial arrangement of feature values. Moreover, they do not scale to higher dimensions due to exponential size and sparsity. Appearance models map the image features onto a fixed size window. Since the dimensionality is a polynomial in the number of features and window size, only a relatively small number of features can be used. To overcome the shortcomings of the existing approaches, the authors in [12] proposed a covariance matrix representation to describe the object windows and used this approach for detection and classification. After then such descriptors have been extensively used for many domains including tracking [11, 13], text localization [7], action recognition [8], material recognition [6].

Motivated by its success, the covariance descriptors are computed, which encapsulate features (position, intensity, edge, etc.) over the entire image of an object. This results in a symmetric positive-definite matrix that embodies the object. The details are introduced as follows.

For a given rectangular region which includes M_r rows and M_c columns, let $\mathbf{f}_{xy}(x = 1, \cdots, M_r, y = 1, \cdots, M_c)$ be the feature vectors inside this region for each pixel. The feature vector $\mathbf{f}_{xy}$ can be constructed using two types of mappings: spatial attributes obtained from pixel coordinate values, and appearance attributes, i.e., intensity, gradient. These features may be associated directly to the pixel coordinates. A typical feature vector representation is given by

$$\mathbf{f}_{xy} = [x, y, I(x, y), |I_x(x, y)|, |I_y(x, y)|]^T, \qquad (2.9)$$

where x, y are pixel coordinates, $I(x, y)$ is the intensity values; and $I_x(x, y)$, $I_y(x, y)$ are the intensity derivatives of the grayscale images.

The covariance feature of a region can therefore be calculated as

$$\mathbb{C} = \frac{1}{M_r M_c - 1} \sum_{x=1}^{M_r} \sum_{y=1}^{M_c} (\mathbf{f}_{xy} - \boldsymbol{\mu})(\mathbf{f}_{xy} - \boldsymbol{\mu})^T, \qquad (2.10)$$

where $\boldsymbol{\mu}$ is the vector of the means of the corresponding features for the points within this region. The covariance matrix is a symmetric matrix where its diagonal entries represent the variance of each feature and the nondiagonal entries represent their respective correlations. Figure 2.8 shows an illustration regarding the descriptor construction procedure.

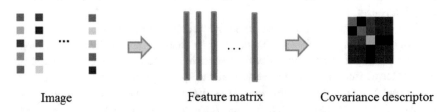

Image   Feature matrix   Covariance descriptor

Fig. 2.8 Construction procedure of the covariance descriptor

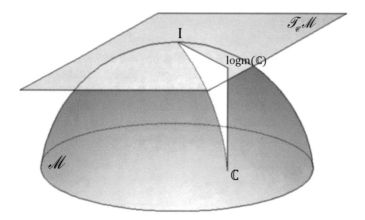

Fig. 2.9 Tactile manifold $\mathcal{M}$ and the corresponding local tangent space $\mathcal{T}_{\mathbb{C}}\mathcal{M}$ at **I**. The logarithmic map $\text{logm}(\cdot)$ projects the matrix $\mathbb{C}$ into the tangent space

Since the covariance descriptors occupy a space that spans a Riemannian manifold [1, 2], the correct manipulation of these matrices relies on a special branch of differential geometry, namely the Riemannian geometry. The proposed method consists in taking into account the Riemannian geometry of the space of covariance matrices. Indeed at each point of the manifold $\mathcal{M}$, a scalar product can be defined in the associated tangent space $\mathcal{T}_{\mathbb{C}}\mathcal{M}$. This tangent space is Euclidean and locally homomorphic to the manifold and Riemannian distance computations in the manifold can be well approximated by Euclidean distance computations in the tangent space. See Fig. 2.9 for illustration.

To this end, the reference point is fixed as the identify matrix, and the logarithmic map[3] is used to projects locally all covariance matrices onto the tangent plane by:

$$\mathbb{C}_i \rightarrow \text{logm}(\mathbb{C}_i).$$

and construct the Log-Euclidean kernel as

$$\kappa_{COV}(\mathbb{C}_i, \mathbb{C}_j) = trace(\text{logm}(\mathbb{C}_i)\text{logm}(\mathbb{C}_j))$$

More details and discussions for computer vision applications can be found in [1] and [10].

---

[3]If $\mathbb{C} = \mathbf{U}\Lambda\mathbf{U}^T$ is the eigen-decomposition of the positive-definite matrix $\mathbb{C}$, then its matrix logarithm can be written as $\text{logm}(\mathbb{C}) = \mathbf{U}\log\Lambda\mathbf{U}^T$, where $\log\Lambda$ is the diagonal matrix whose entries contain the logarithm of the eigenvalues.

2.3   Summary

This chapter provides some off-the-shelf distance and kernel representation for the tactile and visual modalities. Such kernels serve as the basis of the tactile perception and understanding. However, it should be noted that the concrete kernel forms are just used for the algorithm developed. In fact, any other appropriate kernels can be incorporated into the proposed perception and understanding framework.

References

1. Arsigny, V., Fillard, P., Pennec, X., Ayache, N.: Geometric means in a novel vector space structure on symmetric positive-definite matrices. SIAM J. Matrix Anal. Appl. **29**(1), 328–347 (2007)
2. Barachant, A., Bonnet, S., Congedo, M., Jutten, C.: Classification of covariance matrices using a riemannian-based kernel for BCI applications. Neurocomputing **112**, 172–178 (2013)
3. Chen, Z., Zuo, W., Hu, Q., Lin, L.: Kernel sparse representation for time series classification. Inf. Sci. **292**, 15–26 (2015)
4. Chu, V., McMahon, I., Riano, L., McDonald, C.G., He, Q., Perez-Tejada, J.M., Arrigo, M., Darrell, T., Kuchenbecker, K.J.: Robotic learning of haptic adjectives through physical interaction. Robot. Auton. Syst. **63**, 279–292 (2015)
5. Cuturi, M.: Fast global alignment kernels. In: Proceedings of the 28th international conference on machine learning (ICML-11), pp. 929–936. (2011)
6. Harandi, M., Salzmann, M.: Riemannian coding and dictionary learning: Kernels to the rescue. In: Proceedings of the IEEE Conference on Computer Vision and Pattern Recognition, pp. 3926–3935. (2015)
7. Huang, W., Lin, Z., Yang, J., Wang, J.: Text localization in natural images using stroke feature transform and text covariance descriptors. In: Proceedings of the IEEE International Conference on Computer Vision, pp. 1241–1248. (2013)
8. Hussein, M.E., Torki, M., Gowayyed, M.A., El-Saban, M.: Human action recognition using a temporal hierarchy of covariance descriptors on 3D joint locations. IJCAI **13**, 2466–2472 (2013)
9. Keogh, E.: Exact indexing of dynamic time warping. In: Proceedings of the 28th international conference on Very Large Data Bases, pp. 406–417. (2002)
10. Li, P., Wang, Q., Zuo, W., Zhang, L.: Log-euclidean kernels for sparse representation and dictionary learning. In: Proceedings of the IEEE International Conference on Computer Vision, pp. 1601–1608. (2013)
11. Liu, H., Sun, F.: Fusion tracking in color and infrared images using sequential belief propagation. IEEE International Conference on Robotics and Automation, ICRA **2008**, 2259–2264 (2008)
12. Tuzel, O., Porikli, F., Meer, P.: Region covariance: A fast descriptor for detection and classification. Comput. Vis.-ECCV **2006**, 589–600 (2006)
13. Wang, S., Zhang, L., Liang, Y., Pan, Q.: Semi-coupled dictionary learning with applications to image super-resolution and photo-sketch synthesis. In: IEEE Conference on Computer Vision and Pattern Recognition (CVPR), pp. 2216–2223. (2012)
14. Xiao, W., Sun, F., Liu, H., He, C.: Dexterous robotic-hand grasp learning using piecewise linear dynamic systems model. In: Foundations and Practical Applications of Cognitive Systems and Information Processing pp. 845–855. (2014)
15. Zhou, F., Torre, F.: Canonical time warping for alignment of human behavior. In: Advances in Neural Information Processing Systems, pp. 2286–2294. (2009)

Part II
Tactile Perception

This part of the book focuses on the tactile perception problems. It comprises four chapters. Chapter 3 tackles the multifingered tactile object recognition problem using joint sparse coding and shows the potential power of sparse coding to tackle the fusion problems. In Chaps. 4–6, more complicated dictionary learning technologies are developed for structured sparse coding methods. Such methods are used to tackle the tactile adjective properties analysis and material identification problems. Those chapters show that many intrinsic difficult problems, such as multifinger fusion, multilabel classification, and multitask recognition, can be naturally dealt with under the unified sparse coding and dictionary learning framework.

Chapter 3
Tactile Object Recognition Using Joint Sparse Coding

Abstract In this chapter, the investigated tactile data is regarded as time sequences, of which dissimilarity can be evaluated by the popular dynamic time warping method. A kernel sparse coding method is therefore developed to address the tactile data representation and classification problem. However, the naive use of sparse coding neglects the intrinsic relation between individual fingers, which simultaneously contact the object. To tackle this problem, a joint kernel sparse coding model is proposed to solve the multi-finger tactile sequence classification task. In this model, the intrinsic relations between fingers are explicitly taken into account using the joint sparse coding, which encourages all of the coding vectors to share the same sparsity support pattern. The experimental results show that the joint sparse coding achieves better performance than conventional sparse coding.

3.1 Introduction

Tactile object recognition is one of the key tasks for robotic tactile perception. As mentioned previously, in most existing work on tactile sensing, the grasping hand usually has several (typically 2–3) fingers. Existing models do not exploit the intrinsic relations between fingers, instead the tactile sequences are concatenated into a single matrix. In this book, the BarrettHand platform, which has three fingers with tactile sensors, will be used to investigate the intrinsic relations between fingers for grasp analysis and tactile sequence classification.

On the other hand, it is a challenge to integrate the tactile sequences from separate fingers, and a joint kernel sparse coding method is developed to address this issue. Variations and extensions of sparse representation have been employed in many classification tasks, such as object recognition [13, 23], action recognition [5, 18], video summarization [14], object tracking [17, 19]. Although sparse coding is effective in many fields, its usefulness in time series applications is limited because time series do not usually lie in the Euclidean space [10]; thus, the conventional sparse coding for vector spaces is not appropriate. Kernel sparse coding has been proposed to address this problem. By using a suitably designed kernel, the linear sparse coding can be extended to the nonlinear case [4]. Recently, Ref. [15] developed an effective robust dictionary learning method for kernel sparse coding.

In this chapter, a joint kernel sparse coding method is developed to explicitly model the intrinsic relations between individual fingers. A set of tactile sequences that explicitly include the individual finger information is collected to validate the effectiveness of the proposed method. The experimental results demonstrate good performance of joint kernel sparse coding method on fusing the tactile sequences.

The rest of this chapter is organized as follows: Sects. 3.2 and 3.3 present the kernel sparse coding and the joint kernel sparse coding methods, respectively. Section 3.4 gives the experimental results. Finally, the conclusions are given in Sect. 3.5.

3.2 Kernel Sparse Coding

Linear sparse coding methods usually do not work on tactile sequences because they do not lie in Euclidean space. To address this issue, the kernel trick can be employed.

Assume C classes of objects, which admit N tactile training samples

$$\mathfrak{T} = \{\mathbb{T}_i\}_{i=1}^N \subset \mathscr{T},$$

where $\mathscr{T}$ represents the manifold in which the tactile sequences lie. If mapping the training samples into higher-dimensional space by proper mapping functions, the performance is expected to be improved. The linearity in feature space corresponds to the nonlinearity in the original space. To this end, it is denoted

$$\Phi(\cdot) : \mathscr{T} \to \mathscr{H}_T$$

to be the implicit nonlinear mappings from $\mathscr{T}$ into higher-dimensional (possibly infinite-dimensional) inner product space $\mathscr{H}_T$. An illustration can be found in Fig. 3.1. The mapping function is associated with some kernel

$$\kappa(\mathbb{T}_i, \mathbb{T}_j) = \Phi^T(\mathbb{T}_i)\Phi(\mathbb{T}_j),$$

which can be explicitly represented as DTW or CTW kernels [24]. or other appropriate kernel forms.

The given N training samples are then arranged as columns of a matrix

$$\Phi(\mathfrak{T}) = [\Phi(\mathbb{T}_1)\ \Phi(\mathbb{T}_2)\ \cdots\ \Phi(\mathbb{T}_N)],$$

which is called as a dictionary in the higher-dimensional space. Given sufficient training samples, any new (test) sample $\mathbb{T}$ will lie approximately in the linear span

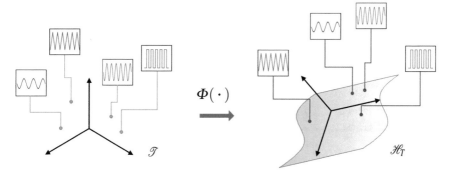

Fig. 3.1 Illustration of the kernel method for tactile samples. In the original tactile space $\mathcal{T}$, two tactile sequences with the same label may be far apart. The mapping function $\Phi(\cdot) : \mathcal{T} \to \mathcal{H}_T$ transforms all of the samples into a new feature space $\mathcal{H}_T$. In the transformed space, the two tactile sequences with the same label may be close

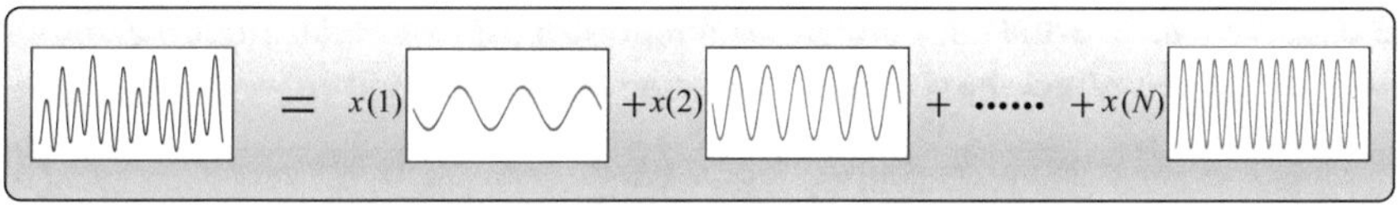

Fig. 3.2 Illustration of the linear reconstruction. The test sample shown in the left can be linearly reconstructed by the training samples which are shown in the right of the equality sign. The symbols $x(1), \cdots , x(N)$ are the reconstruction coefficients

of the training samples with the same label (see Fig. 3.2 for illustration). That is to say, it is expected that there exists a vector $x \in R^N$ which satisfies:

$$\Phi(\mathbb{T}) = \Phi(\mathfrak{T})x.$$

To obtain the value of x, the optimization problem can be formulated as:

$$\min_{x} ||\Phi(\mathbb{T}) - \Phi(\mathfrak{T})x||_F^2. \tag{3.1}$$

The reconstruction term $||\Phi(\mathbb{T}) - \Phi(\mathfrak{T})x||_F^2$ can be represented as

$$trace\{(\Phi(\mathbb{T}) - \Phi(\mathfrak{T})x)^T (\Phi(\mathbb{T}) - \Phi(\mathfrak{T})x)\}$$
$$= \kappa(\mathbb{T}, \mathbb{T}) - 2\kappa^T(\mathbb{T}, \mathfrak{T})x + x^T \kappa(\mathfrak{T}, \mathfrak{T})x, \tag{3.2}$$

where

$$\kappa(\mathbb{T}, \mathfrak{T}) = \begin{bmatrix} \kappa(\mathbb{T}, \mathbb{T}_1) \\ \kappa(\mathbb{T}, \mathbb{T}_2) \\ \vdots \\ \kappa(\mathbb{T}, \mathbb{T}_N) \end{bmatrix} \in R^N$$

and

$$\kappa(\mathfrak{T}, \mathfrak{T}) = \begin{bmatrix} \kappa(\mathbb{T}_1, \mathbb{T}_1) & \kappa(\mathbb{T}_1, \mathbb{T}_2) & \cdots & \kappa(\mathbb{T}_1, \mathbb{T}_N) \\ \kappa(\mathbb{T}_2, \mathbb{T}_1) & \kappa(\mathbb{T}_2, \mathbb{T}_2) & \cdots & \kappa(\mathbb{T}_2, \mathbb{T}_N) \\ \vdots & \vdots & \ddots & \vdots \\ \kappa(\mathbb{T}_N, \mathbb{T}_1) & \kappa(\mathbb{T}_N, \mathbb{T}_2) & \cdots & \kappa(\mathbb{T}_N, \mathbb{T}_N) \end{bmatrix} \in R^{N \times N}.$$

Since the term $\kappa(\mathbb{T}, \mathbb{T})$ is a constant, the optimization problem in (3.1) can be transformed as

$$\min_{x} \quad -2\kappa^T(\mathbb{T}, \mathfrak{T})x + x^T \kappa(\mathfrak{T}, \mathfrak{T})x \tag{3.3}$$

which admits the analytic solution as

$$x = \kappa(\mathfrak{T}, \mathfrak{T})^{-1}\kappa(\mathbb{T}, \mathfrak{T}).$$

Though the kernel matrix $\kappa(\mathfrak{T}, \mathfrak{T})$ usually is invertible, the above solution may be ill-conditioned. To avoid this problem, a common trick is to introduce a regularization term $||x||_2$ to construct the so-called ridge regression problem:

$$\min_{x} ||\Phi(\mathbb{T}) - \Phi(\mathfrak{T})x||_F^2 + \lambda ||x||_2^2. \tag{3.4}$$

where λ is the penalty parameter. This problem produces the analytic solution as

$$x = (\kappa(\mathfrak{T}, \mathfrak{T}) + \lambda I)^{-1}\kappa(\mathbb{T}, \mathfrak{T}).$$

where I is an identity matrix with appropriate dimensions.

Nevertheless, the solution x provides little information about our tactile object recognition. That is to say, there is no any strategy to encourage x to be discriminative. This motivates us to impose other constraints on x.

In practice, if there are tactile training samples about objects *Apple*, *Bottle*, *Cup* and *Book*, then the testing sample of *Apple* should be linearly represented by the samples corresponding to the training samples of *Apple*, but not the training samples of *Bottle*, *Cup* and *Book*. That is to say, the element of the expected x should be

$$x(i) = \begin{cases} no - zero & \text{If } \mathbb{T} \text{ and } \mathbb{T}_i \text{ belong to the same object class} \\ 0 & \text{Otherwise} \end{cases}$$

Therefore, when the number of the class is large, the sparsity of x is naturally encouraged. See Fig. 3.3 for illustrations. If the obtained solution of x is sparse, it is highly possibly that the activated elements of x correspond to the true object label. Therefore, the sparsity provides strong support for the discrimination. Motivated by this point, the following kernel sparse coding problem can be formulated.

$$\begin{aligned} \min_{x} & ||\Phi(\mathbb{T}) - \Phi(\mathfrak{T})x||_F^2 \\ \text{s.t.} & \quad ||x||_0 \leq S \end{aligned} \tag{3.5}$$

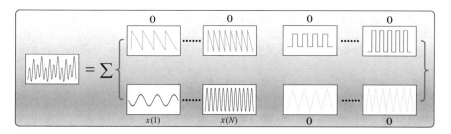

Fig. 3.3 Illustration of the sparse reconstruction. If all of the training samples are involved into the reconstruction, it is expected that only the samples with the same label are assigned nonzero reconstruction coefficients. The reconstruction coefficients for other training samples should be zero. The whole reconstruction vector is therefore sparse

where $||x||_0$ calculates the number of the nonzero elements in x and S is used to control the sparsity. An alternative form of the above optimization problem is

$$\min_{x} ||\Phi(\mathbb{T}) - \Phi(\mathfrak{T})x||_F^2 + \lambda||x||_0, \tag{3.6}$$

where λ is the penalty parameter. However, the relation between the values of S and λ is complicated.

The optimization problems in (3.5) and (3.6) explicitly introduce the sparsity prior to the objective function, and therefore, the obtained solution may be expected to be sparse and discriminative. Unfortunately, this optimization problem is non-convex and NP-hard. It is rather difficult to develop the optimization algorithm, and many scholars resort to adopt some alternatives to approximate it. Among the alternatives, the l_1-norm is rather popular, since [7] pointed that *for most large underdetermined systems of linear equations the minimal l_1-norm solution is also the sparsest solution.* Principally, the l_1-norm $||x||_1$ calculates the sum of all of the absolute values of x and therefore the newly formulated optimization problem

$$\min_{x} ||\Phi(\mathbb{T}) - \Phi(\mathfrak{T})x||_F^2 + \lambda||x||_1, \tag{3.7}$$

where λ is the penalty parameter, is convex, and easy to solve.

More details about the relationship between l_0 and l_1-norms can be found in [5, 7]. Although Eq. (3.4) is highly similar to Eq. (3.7), their intrinsic difference is rather significant:

1. The optimization problem (3.7) may produce sparse solution, while (3.4) cannot achieve this point.
2. The l_1 penalty term in (3.7) is non-differentiable, and it cannot admit analytical solution, while l_2 penalty term in (3.4) is differentiable and it naturally admits analytical solution,

According to the above-mentioned property of the kernel function, the optimization problem (3.7) can be reformulated as

$$\min_{x} \; - 2\kappa^T(\mathbb{T}, \mathfrak{T})x + x^T \kappa(\mathfrak{T}, \mathfrak{T})x + \lambda ||x||_1. \tag{3.8}$$

The kernel trick obviates the need for the mapping function to be of the form $\Phi(\cdot)$, rather, only the kernel functions are required.

After obtaining the value of x, the most important thing is to perform the classification according to the sparse solution x. To this end, the symbol $\delta^{(c)}$ is introduced as the characteristic function that selects the coefficients associated with the cth class. That is to say, the ith element in $\delta^{(c)}(x) \in R^N$ is defined as

$$\delta^{(c)}(x)(i) = \begin{cases} x(i) & \text{If } \mathbb{T}_i \text{ belongs to the c } - \text{ th object} \\ 0 & \text{Otherwise} \end{cases}$$

Then the test sample $\mathbb{T}$ is classified according to the residue

$$r^{(c)} = -2\kappa^T(\mathbb{T}, \mathfrak{T})\delta^{(c)}(x) + \delta^{(c)}(x)^T \kappa(\mathfrak{T}, \mathfrak{T})\delta^{(c)}(x). \tag{3.9}$$

The test sample is then assigned to the class that gives the smallest reconstruction error. Thus, the label is given by

$$c^* = \underset{c \in \{1, \cdots, C\}}{\arg \min} \; r^{(c)}. \tag{3.10}$$

The above classification procedure seems a little complicated than some conventional classifier design methods. In the following sections and chapters, we will systematically show the advantages of the sparse coding on the fusion of multi-finger information, multitask classification, and multimodal recognition.

3.3   Joint Kernel Sparse Coding

The above-mentioned kernel sparse coding method uses the kernel to realize the coding of the single-finger tactile sequence. To achieve tactile sequence classification in practice, however, the hand usually has multiple fingers. Each finger represents a different view and provides a different tactile sequence. How the intrinsic relation among those fingers can be exploited is important for object recognition using tactile measurements.

Formally, if N_F fingers are used, the training sample set for the fth finger can be formulated as

$$\mathfrak{T}^{(f)} = \{\mathbb{T}_i^{(f)}\}_{i=1}^N,$$

where $\mathbb{T}_i^{(f)}$ is the ith tactile sample collected from the the fth finger. Similarly, the fth dictionary can be constructed as

$$\Phi(\mathbb{T}^{(f)}) = [\Phi(\mathbb{T}_1^{(f)})\ \Phi(\mathbb{T}_2^{(f)}) \cdots \Phi(\mathbb{T}_N^{(f)})].$$

Consider the test sequence

$$\mathbb{T} = \{\mathbb{T}^{(1)}, \mathbb{T}^{(2)}, \cdots, \mathbb{T}^{(N_F)}\},$$

where $\mathbb{T}^{(f)}$ is the sequence which is obtained by the fth finger and $f = 1, 2, \cdots, N_F$. Finding the sparse representations is equivalent to solving the following problems:

$$\begin{cases} \min_{x^{(1)}} ||\Phi(\mathbb{T}^{(1)}) - \Phi(\mathfrak{T}^{(1)})x^{(1)}||_F^2 + \lambda||x^{(1)}||_1 \\ \min_{x^{(2)}} ||\Phi(\mathbb{T}^{(2)}) - \Phi(\mathfrak{T}^{(2)})x^{(2)}||_F^2 + \lambda||x^{(2)}||_1 \\ \qquad\qquad \vdots \\ \min_{x^{(N_F)}} ||\Phi(\mathbb{T}^{(N_F)}) - \Phi(\mathfrak{T}^{(N_F)})x^{(N_F)}||_F^2 + \lambda||x^{(N_F)}||_1, \end{cases} \qquad (3.11)$$

where $x^{(f)} \in \mathbb{R}^N$ for $f = 1, 2, \cdots, N_F$ is the coding coefficient vector for the fth finger.

After solving the above problems, the combined residue corresponding to each finger can be calculated as

$$r^{(c)} = \sum_{f=1}^{N_F} \{-2\kappa^T(\mathbb{T}^{(f)}, \mathfrak{T}^{(f)})\delta^{(c)}(x^{(f)}) + x^{(f)^T}\kappa(\mathfrak{T}^{(f)}, \mathfrak{T}^{(f)})\delta^{(c)}(x^{(f)})\}. \quad (3.12)$$

Finally, the label of the test sequence is given by (3.10).

Since all of the fingers are used to grasp the same object, there exist intrinsic constraint relations on the coding vectors $x^{(1)}, x^{(2)}, \cdots$, and $x^{(N_F)}$. The above optimization procedure, however, neglects the intrinsic relation between different fingers and allows each finger modality to independently give the optimal solution. This approach is termed as separate kernel sparse coding (SKSC) method.

A naive way of combining multi-finger data is to concatenate all vectors into one single vector which acts as input of the framework, ignoring the characteristics of specific modalities. This is equivalent to requiring that all of the coding vectors to be equal. That is to say,

$$x^{(1)} = x^{(2)} = \cdots = x^{(N_F)}. \qquad (3.13)$$

Conceptually, this is equivalent to concatenating all of the fingers into one finger and solving a single sparse optimization problem. For convenience, this method is

termed as concatenation kernel sparse coding (CKSC). The optimization problem is
then transformed as

$$\min_{x} \sum_{f=1}^{N_F} ||\Phi(\mathbb{T}^{(f)}) - \Phi(\mathfrak{T}^{(f)})x||_2^2 + \lambda ||x||_1, \quad (3.14)$$

where x is the common coding vector.

This approach is limited because information sources with different statistical
properties are mixed in a simplistic manner. The performance is not satisfactory, as
it may lead to over-fitting or fail to learn associations between fingers with different
underlying statistics.

In fact, each of the different modalities must have its own independent coding
vector based only on the modality's own data. To address this problem, there need
to be a trade-off between SKSC and CKSC. Motivated by the success of joint sparse
coding [9, 22], one can regard each finger as being an independent sensor, and thus
code the fingers separately. The intrinsic relation is expressed by the sparsity support
pattern. An illustration can be found in Fig. 3.4.

The method is to require the separate coding vectors to share a common sparsity
pattern, but allow them to have different values. Thus,

$$Sp(x^{(1)}) = Sp(x^{(2)}) = \cdots = Sp(x^{(N_F)}),$$

where $Sp(x)$ represents the sparsity pattern vector of the vector x. The length of
$Sp(x)$ is the same as that of x. If the ith element of x is zero, then the ith element of
$Sp(x)$ is zero; otherwise, the ith element of $Sp(x)$ is set to 1. That is to say,

$$Sp(x)(i) = \begin{cases} 1 & x(i) \neq 0 \\ 0 & x(i) = 0 \end{cases}$$

From this definition, it can be seen that the sparsity pattern vector stores the information about its pattern in the vector x. This pattern is essential for a sparse coding
vector.

The above problem can be further transformed into the problem requiring the
combined matrix

$$X = [x^{(1)} \ x^{(2)} \ \cdots \ x^{(N_F)}] \in \mathbb{R}^{N \times N_F}$$

to be row-sparse. Consequently, each column vector $x^{(f)}$ is sparse and the sparsity
pattern of $x^{(1)}, x^{(2)}, \cdots, x^{(N_F)}$ are shared by them.

Solving row-sparsity optimization is a NP problem, and the $l_{2,1}$-norm is resorted
for its approximate solution. The $l_{2,1}$-norm of X calculates the sum of the l_2-norm
of each row. That is to say,

$$||X||_{2,1} = \sum_{n=1}^{N} ||X(n, :)||_2 \quad (3.15)$$

where $X(n, :)$ represents the nth row of X.

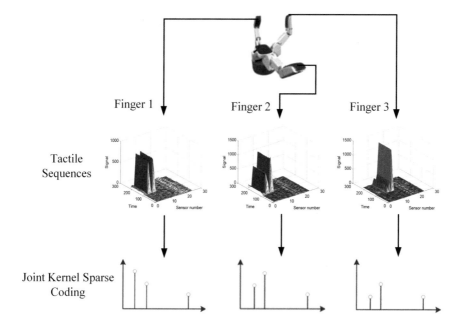

Fig. 3.4 Illustration of the tactile sequence classification with joint kernel sparse representation. For a given object, the tactile sequences of the three fingers are recorded. Next, each finger sequence is represented as a linear combination of the corresponding training sequences, in a joint kernel sparse way across all fingers

By penalizing the sum of l_2-norms of the rows of coefficients associated with each coding vector across different fingers, similar sparse patterns for all fingers are encouraged.

Thus, the optimization problem becomes:

$$\min_{X} \sum_{f=1}^{N_F} ||\Phi(\mathbb{T}^{(f)}) - \Phi(\mathfrak{T}^{(f)})x^{(f)}||_F^2 + \lambda||X||_{2,1}. \qquad (3.16)$$

and this method is termed as Joint Kernel Sparse Coding (JKSC), which preserves the intrinsic relation between fingers.

The above optimization problems can be solved effectively using existing software, such as CVX package [3] or SPAM software [21].

The core contribution of this work is the kernel sparse coding method for tactile object recognition. Especially, the joint kernel sparse coding method is developed to exploit the intrinsic relation among fingers. Undoubtedly, this method also provides an effective strategy for other applications of tactile measurements. A straightforward extension is the grasp stability assessment, which is one of the most important tasks of the tactile sensors on the robot hand [6, 11]. In [1, 2, 20], the grasp stability analysis problem has been thoroughly studied and a popular method is to re-formulate it as a two-class classification problem. In this regard, the introduced kernel sparse coding methods can be used for the grasp stability assessment. The role of the intrinsic relation between fingers to the grasp stability is worthy of deep investigation, and the proposed joint coding strategy may provide a feasible method to achieve it. Further, how to simultaneously perform object recognition and grasp stability analysis is more appealing. Tackling such a problem may reveal more intrinsic relation between object and grasp pose.

3.4   Experimental Results

In this section, the collected dataset for validation of the introduced joint kernel sparse coding method is described. In addition, the experimental results on datasets which are publicly available are also presented.

3.4.1   Data Collection

The robot used for gathering data and carrying out the experiments is a Schunk manipulator equipped with a BarrettHand having tactile sensors. The experiment is performed with the tactile sensors mounted on the fingertips of the robot hand, as shown in Fig. 3.5. The objects are placed in a fixed position on a table, and the trajectory planning of the manipulator was performed offline. The data collection procedure is similar to the active perception workflow in [8], as a static reading of tactile information is not sufficient to classify the object under inspection. To this end, the manipulator explores the objects using a palpation procedure. During this activity, the tactile sensors are stimulated with a sequence of tactile measurements. Next, the sequence is classified to recognize which object is palpated. As the tactile

Fig. 3.5   The experimental setup. The manipulator explores the objects using a palpation procedure. [2016] IEEE. Reprinted, with permission, from Ref. [12]

sensor outputs zero when the sensor is not touching an object, one can determine the start of a palpation event when the tactile sensor input is above a specified threshold. The event ends when the tactile sensors do not report any significant change. As the execution time varies with each operation, the length of each tactile sequence varies. Finally, all measurements are normalized to the sensor's maximum response.

The hand is used to grasp five differently shaped bottles with water and without water. In Fig. 3.6, the photos of the bottles are listed. The lower row shows the five bottles full of water (denoted as *Af*, *Bf*, *Cf*, *Df*, and *Ef*), and the upper row shows the corresponding empty bottles (denoted as *Ae*, *Be*, *Ce*, *De*, and *Ee*). It is obvious that their visual appearances are very similar. The difference between empty bottle and full bottle partially comes from the fact that the bottles are made of plastic which is easy to deformation, and the tactile information is useful in determining deformation properties of bottles. Figure 3.7 shows the tactile sequences which are produced by Finger 1 for the objects *Ae*, *Ce*, *Af* and *Cf*. Although it is difficult to discriminate the bottles by visual appearance, especially between the full state and the empty state of the same bottle, their tactile sequences do differ.

During data collection, each bottle was randomly placed in the table and grasped 20 times by the three fingers of the dexterous hands. Each grasp action lasted 8.2–18 s. The sampling period was 0.04 s, and therefore, the length of the obtained sequence was 205–450. Using these settings, a challenging 10-object dataset is constructed, which included 200 tactile sequence samples.

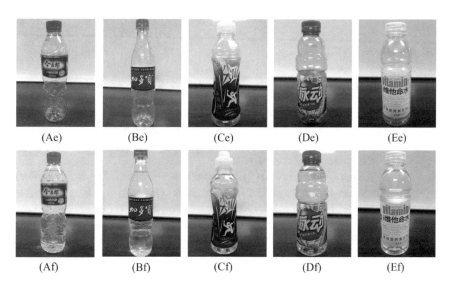

(Ae)	(Be)	(Ce)	(De)	(Ee)

(Af)	(Bf)	(Cf)	(Df)	(Ef)

Fig. 3.6 Experimental objects. The first row shows the five empty bottles (which are labeled as *Ae*, *Be*, *Ce*, *De*, and *Ee*). The second row shows the five bottles full of water (*Af*, *Bf*, *Cf*, *Df*, and *Ef*). [2016] IEEE. Reprinted, with permission, from Ref. [12]

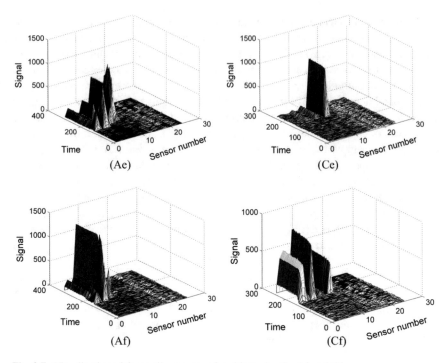

Fig. 3.7 Visualization of the tactile sequence for objects *Ae*, *Ce*, *Af*, and *Cf*

3.4.2   Result Analysis

For performance evaluation, the following methods are compared:

1. Nearest Neighborhood (NN) Method. This method uses the concatenation feature and the DTW distance to search for the nearest training sample. Subsequently, the label of this training sample is assigned to the test sample. This approach serves as the baseline for comparison.
2. Separate Kernel Sparse Coding (SKSC) Method. This method separately solves the optimization problems in (3.11) and uses Eq. (3.12) to calculate the fusion residue.
3. Concatenation Kernel Sparse Coding (CKSC) Method. This method adopts the constraints (3.13) and solves the optimization problem (3.14) and uses Eq. (3.12) to calculate the fusion residue.
4. Joint Kernel Sparse Coding (JKSC) Method. This method solves the joint sparse optimization problem (3.16) and uses Eq. (3.12) to calculate the fusion residue.

Of the above methods, NN, CKSC, and JKSC consider the intrinsic relation between fingers. NN and CKSC use the concatenation feature and impose strict requirements on the relation, while JKSC only requires the common sparsity pattern and has a relaxed requirement. SKSC does not account for the intrinsic relation.

Fig. 3.8 Recognition
accuracy of the four methods
versus data split ratio on the
10-object data sets

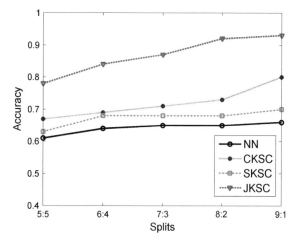

The comparisons are performed for five split cases: training/testing $= 5/5, 6/4,$ $7/3, 8/2,$ and $9/1$. For each split case, the dataset is randomly split as training set and testing test for 10 trials, and the averaged recognition accuracies are reported. Figure 3.8 shows the accuracy of the five cases. The accuracy is defined as the ratio of the number of the correctly classified testing samples and the number of all testing samples. The proposed JKSC method consistently outperforms the other methods. The SKSC method, which neglects the intrinsic relations between fingers, performs slightly better than NN but worse than JKSC and CKSC methods. From those results, the following observations are obtained:

1. The sparse coding methods, SKSC, CKSC, and JKSC, perform better than NN. Thus, the kernel sparse coding strategy is indeed an effective method for improving the classification performance.
2. CKSC and JKSC perform better than SKSC. Therefore, the intrinsic relation between fingers plays an important role in the classifier design.
3. JKSC performs consistently better than CKSC. This demonstrates that the joint sparse coding strategy, which encourages the common sparsity pattern, is more effective than methods that encourage the common coding vector, which is a stricter requirement.

Further, the influence of the parameter λ is analyzed for the 9/1 split case. The averaged recognition accuracies are reported under the different values of λ. In Fig. 3.9, the classification accuracy versus the value of λ are demonstrated. The best results are achieved for $\lambda = 0.1$. This indicates that both the reconstruction error term and the sparsity term play important roles in the classification.

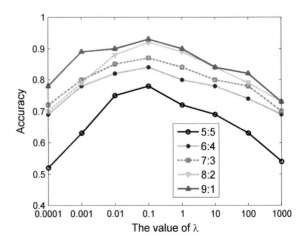

Fig. 3.9 Recognition accuracy versus the value of λ for five split ratios

In Figs. 3.10, 3.11, 3.12, and 3.13, the confusion matrices for the 9/1 split case is presented. By comparing the confusion matrices of the four classifiers, it is found that the objects *Bf*, *Df*, and *Ef* can easily be classified using the proposed JKSC method. Furthermore, for the same bottle, the empty state and the full state are also classified successfully.

In Figs. 3.14, 3.15, and 3.16, an example is given to show the difference between the various sparse coding strategies. The test sample belongs to the 6th class object(*Cf*). The SKSC method gives three different coding vectors $x^{(1)}$, $x^{(2)}$, and $x^{(3)}$. The results are given in Fig. 3.14, where the green bar indicates the correct class. This result shows that the three fingers give different results, and the interpretability is weak. In fact, this method classifies this sample as the 4th class, which is indicated as a red line on the horizontal axis. For the CKSC method, the results of which are shown in Fig. 3.15, there is only a single coding vector. From the results, it can be seen that the atoms corresponding to the 4th class (*Bf*) are activated and are thus still incorrect. In the JKSC method, of which results are shown in Fig. 3.16, the three tactile sequences obtained from individual fingers are separately coded with a common sparsity pattern and the results are more robust. The result for Finger 1 is slightly incorrect, but the results for Fingers 2 and 3 are correct, and therefore, the fused results are also correct.

Before closing this subsection, a brief analysis is made about the time–costs. Please note that all of the compared methods do not require training phase, and therefore, it only concerns the time–cost of the test phase only. The main time–cost is dominated by two stages: (1) The DTW calculation. The DTW distances or kernels should be calculated between the test sample and all of the training samples. (2) The sparse coding. This stage is not required by NN. The time–costs of other calculations such as sorting and residue calculation are omitted. In Table 3.1, it demonstrates

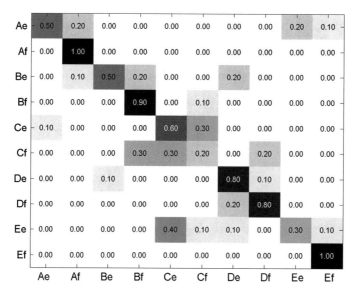

Fig. 3.10 Confusion matrices for NN method

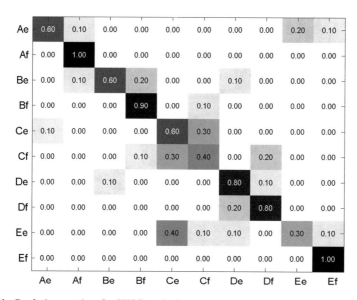

Fig. 3.11 Confusion matrices for SKSC method

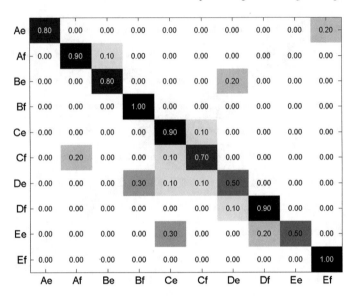

Fig. 3.12 Confusion matrices for CKSC method

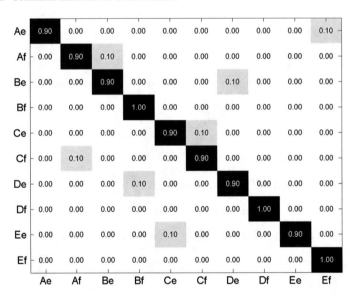

Fig. 3.13 Confusion matrices for JKSC method

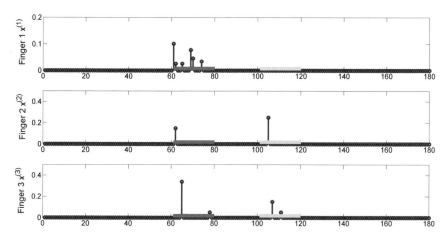

Fig. 3.14 An illustration of the SKSC coding strategies. In all training sample sets, atoms 1–18 belong to the first class, atoms 19–36 belong to the second class, and so on. The horizontal axis corresponds to the atoms of the training sample set. The overlaid red line indicates the 4th class and the green line indicates the 6th class

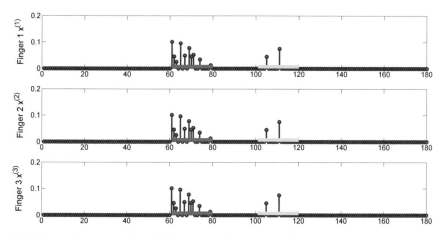

Fig. 3.15 An illustration of the CKSC sparse coding strategies. In all training sample sets, atoms 1–18 belong to the first class, atoms 19–36 belong to the second class, and so on. The horizontal axis corresponds to the atoms of the training sample set. The overlaid red line indicates the 4th class and the green line indicates the 6th class

the averaged test time using an un-optimized MATLAB program on PC platform (3.4 GHz CPU, 16 G Memory) for the two stages. From those results, the following observations are concluded:

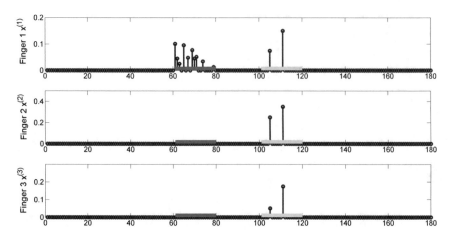

Fig. 3.16 An illustration of the JKSC sparse coding strategies. In all training sample sets, atoms 1–18 belong to the first class, atoms 19–36 belong to the second class, and so on. The horizontal axis corresponds to the atoms of the training sample set. The overlaid red line indicates the 4th class and the green line indicates the 6th class

1. Compared with the DTW calculation, the sparse coding optimization in SKSC, CKSC, and JKSC does not introduce too much time–cost.
2. The time–cost of DTW in SKSC and JKSC is smaller than that of NN and CKSC. The reason is that NN and CKSC use the concatenated feature with 72 dimensions, while SKSC and JKSC use three 24-dimensional feature for DTW calculation. The latter two require less time–cost.
3. CKSC requires to solve one single kernel sparse coding problem, while SKSC requires to solve three independent kernel sparse coding problems. Therefore, the coding time–cost of SKSC is significantly larger than that of CKSC. In addition, JKSC requires to solve three independent sparse coding problems with one extra joint sparsity constraint. Therefore, it is less efficient due to the involvement of joint sparse optimization.

Due to the MATLAB implementation, such results are far away from the real-time application. In addition to implementing the algorithm using C program, the time efficiency can also be improved from several aspects. On one hand, the kernel dictionary learning [16] can be utilized to reduce the size of dictionary. On the other hand, there are many emerging methods to speed up the sparse optimization, which can be used to reduce the time–cost. Finally, the DTW calculation, which forms the bottleneck, can be accelerated using some parallel computing devices.

Table 3.1 Averaged time–cost comparison in seconds

Method	DTW	Sparse coding	Total
NN	1.5028	–	1.5028
SKSC	1.1818	0.6019	1.7837
CKSC	1.5224	0.2874	1.8098
JKSC	1.1745	0.7425	1.9170

3.4.3 Results for the Public Dataset

In the above subsection, the three-fingered BarrettHand is adopted for experimental validation. However, the proposed method can easily be adapted for use with other types of multi-fingered hands. To show the flexibility of the proposed method, some public available datasets are employed for validation. In those datasets, the number of fingers is limited to two. This does not cause any difficulties when using the proposed method.

The adopted datasets include Schunk Parallel dataset with 10 objects (SPr-10) and the Schunk Parallel dataset with seven objects (SPr-7) [8]. The two datasets were generated from the same set of household objects of complex shape presented in Fig. 3.17, using the flexible piezoresistive rubber tactile sensors. In Table 3.2, the information about those datasets is listed. For more details about these datasets, please see [8, 20].

Fig. 3.17 The grasped objects in the public datasets. LEFT: SPr-10, RIGHT: SPr-7. Please note that although the left figure shows only 9 objects, there are 10 object instances in SPr-10. The reason is the authors of [8] collected the tactile data using the bottle with two statuses: empty and full. Reprinted from Ref. [8], with permission from Elsevier

Table 3.2 Summary about the two public datasets

Datasets	♯Fingers	♯Dimensions	♯Objects	♯Samples
SPr-7	2	Total 128	7	70
SPr-10	2	Total 128	10	100

Unfortunately, SPr-10 and SPr-7 do not explicitly include the separate finger information. This prevents us from testing the proposed method. Instead, after analyzing the data collection procedure, it is assumed that the presented data is a concatenation of a two-finger sequence (From Figs. 3.18 and 3.19, it can be seen that the data exhibits an obvious two-finger effect). According to this assumption, each frame of the sequence is manually divided into two 64-dimensional parts to virtually correspond to different fingers. This setting serves to validate the proposed method. In Table 3.3, the average classification results are presented for the four methods over 10 random splits. The split ratio of the training and testing sample is 9:1. The results show that JKSC performs better than SKSC and CKSC. Figure 3.20 shows the recognition accuracies versus the parameter λ. It shows that the best performance is obtained when λ is between $[0.01, 0.1]$.

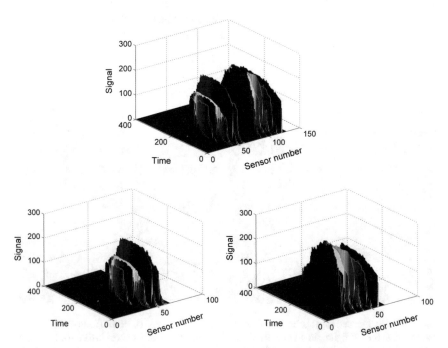

Fig. 3.18 Visualization of the tactile sequence of SPr-7. The top panel shows the original 128-dimensional tactile sequence, and the bottom panel shows the virtual two-finger sequences which are obtained by dividing the original tactile sequence into two 64-dimensional tactile sequences

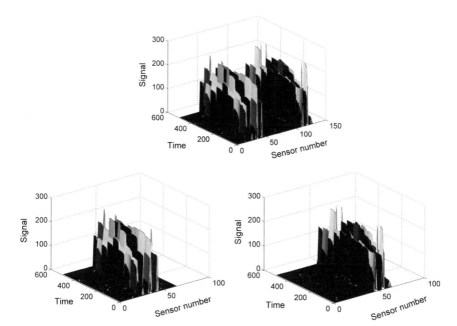

Fig. 3.19 Visualization of the tactile sequence of SPr-10. The top panel shows the original 128-dimensional tactile sequence, and the bottom panel shows the virtual two-finger sequences which are obtained by dividing the original tactile sequence into two 64-dimensional tactile sequences

Table 3.3 Recognition accuracies of the four methods using the public datasets SPr-7 and SPr-10

Datesets	NN (%)	SKSC (%)	CKSC (%)	**JKSC (%)**
SPr-7	87.15	86.12	88.57	**93.43**
SPr-10	79.00	81.10	85.43	**91.34**

It is worth noting that recently some more advanced and more complicated classification methods can achieve even better performance on these two datasets [20]. Notwithstanding, it is still unclear how to incorporate the intrinsic relation between fingers into the existing work. This book considers the sparse coding methods only and focuses on showing the effectiveness of JKSC in terms of its simplicity and effectiveness. If a more sophisticated kernel is adopted, better performance may be obtained, but this remains the future work. In addition, the information of the joint angles also plays important roles to deal with the pose changing problem.

3.5   Summary

In practical robotic manipulation, the hand usually has multiple fingers. Each finger represents a different view and provides a different tactile sequence. Therefore, a

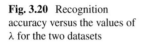

Fig. 3.20 Recognition accuracy versus the values of λ for the two datasets

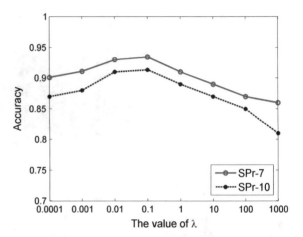

hypothesis is made that there exist some intrinsic relation which helps to improve the tactile object recognition performance. To validate this hypothesis, the recognition framework of joint kernel sparse coding is developed, which exploits the intrinsic relation among fingers and encourages different coding vectors to share the same sparsity support. That is to say, each finger is regarded as an independent sensor, and thus code the fingers separately. The intrinsic relation is expressed by the sparse support pattern. The experimental results on three datasets show that the proposed coding method can elegantly take the advantage of having multiple fingers to improve recognition performance and it outperforms the conventional sparse coding methods including SKSC and CKSC. This validates the hypothesis that the intrinsic relation among those fingers plays an important role for object recognition using tactile measurements.

Since the proposed joint coding strategy provides a general idea to exploit the intrinsic relation among fingers, it can be used for more sophisticated cases by incorporating the carefully designed feature descriptors or kernels.

References

1. Bekiroglu, Y., Kragic, D., Kyrki, V.: Learning grasp stability based on tactile data and HMMs. In: RO-MAN, 2010 IEEE, pp. 132–137 (2010)
2. Bekiroglu, Y., Laaksonen, J., Jorgensen, J.A., Kyrki, V., Kragic, D.: Assessing grasp stability based on learning and haptic data. IEEE Trans. Rob. **27**(3), 616–629 (2011)
3. Boyd, S., Vandenberghe, L.: Convex optimization (2004)
4. Chen, Z., Zuo, W., Hu, Q., Lin, L.: Kernel sparse representation for time series classification. Inf. Sci. **292**, 15–26 (2015)
5. Cheng, H., Liu, Z., Hou, L., Yang, J.: Sparsity-induced similarity measure and its applications. IEEE Trans. Circuits Syst. Video Technol. **26**(4), 613–626 (2016)
6. Dang, H., Allen, P.K.: Learning grasp stability. In: 2012 IEEE International Conference on Robotics and Automation (ICRA), pp. 2392–2397 (2012)

7. Donoho, D.L.: For most large underdetermined systems of linear equations the minimal l_1-norm solution is also the sparsest solution. Commun. Pure Appl. Math. **59**(6), 797–829 (2006)
8. Drimus, A., Kootstra, G., Bilberg, A., Kragic, D.: Design of a flexible tactile sensor for classification of rigid and deformable objects. Rob. Autonomous Syst. **62**(1), 3–15 (2014)
9. Hu, W., Li, W., Zhang, X., Maybank, S.: Single and multiple object tracking using a multi-feature joint sparse representation. IEEE Trans. Pattern Anal. Mach. Intell. **37**(4), 816–833 (2015)
10. Huang, W., Sun, F., Cao, L., Zhao, D., Liu, H., Harandi, M.: Sparse coding and dictionary learning with linear dynamical systems. In: Proceedings of the IEEE Conference on Computer Vision and Pattern Recognition, pp. 3938–3947 (2016)
11. Kappler, D., Bohg, J., Schaal, S.: Leveraging big data for grasp planning. In: 2015 IEEE International Conference on Robotics and Automation (ICRA), pp. 4304–4311 (2015)
12. Liu, H., Guo, D., Sun, F.: Object recognition using tactile measurements: kernel sparse coding methods. IEEE Trans. Instrum. Meas. **65**(3), 656–665 (2016)
13. Liu, H., Liu, Y., Sun, F.: Traffic sign recognition using group sparse coding. Inf. Sci. **266**, 75–89 (2014)
14. Liu, H., Liu, Y., Yu, Y., Sun, F.: Diversified key-frame selection using structured $l_{2,1}$ optimization. IEEE Trans. Industr. Inf. **10**(3), 1736–1745 (2014)
15. Liu, H., Qin, J., Cheng, H., Sun, F.: Robust kernel dictionary learning using a whole sequence convergent algorithm. In: IJCAI, vol. 1, p. 5 (2015)
16. Liu, H., Qin, J., Cheng, H., Sun, F.: Robust kernel dictionary learning using a whole sequence convergent algorithm. IJCAI **1**(2), 5 (2015)
17. Liu, H., Sun, F.: Fusion tracking in color and infrared images using joint sparse representation. Sci. China Inf. Sci. **55**(3), 590–599 (2012)
18. Liu, H., Yuan, M., Sun, F.: RGB-D action recognition using linear coding. Neurocomputing **149**, 79–85 (2015)
19. Liu, H., Yuan, M., Sun, F., Zhang, J.: Spatial neighborhood-constrained linear coding for visual object tracking. IEEE Trans. Industr. Inf. **10**(1), 469–480 (2014)
20. Madry, M., Bo, L., Kragic, D., Fox, D.: ST-HMP: Unsupervised spatio-temporal feature learning for tactile data. In: 2014 IEEE International Conference on Robotics and Automation (ICRA), pp. 2262–2269 (2014)
21. Mairal, J., Bach, F., Ponce, J., et al.: Sparse modeling for image and vision processing. Foundations Trends® Comput. Graphics Vis. **8**(2-3), 85–283 (2014)
22. Shekhar, S., Patel, V.M., Nasrabadi, N.M., Chellappa, R.: Joint sparse representation for robust multimodal biometrics recognition. IEEE Trans. Pattern Anal. Mach. Intell. **36**(1), 113–126 (2014)
23. Wright, J., Yang, A.Y., Ganesh, A., Sastry, S.S., Ma, Y.: Robust face recognition via sparse representation. IEEE Trans. Pattern Anal. Mach. Intell. **31**(2), 210–227 (2009)
24. Zhou, F., Torre, F.: Canonical time warping for alignment of human behavior. In: Advances in Neural Information Processing Systems, pp. 2286–2294 (2009)

Chapter 4
Tactile Object Recognition Using Supervised Dictionary Learning

Abstract This chapter addresses the tactile object recognition problem by developing an extreme kernel sparse learning methodology. This method combines the advantages of extreme learning machine (ELM) and kernel sparse learning by simultaneously addressing the dictionary learning and the classifier design problems. Furthermore, to tackle the intrinsic difficulties which are introduced by the *Representer Theorem*, a reduced kernel dictionary learning method is developed by introducing row-sparsity constraint. A globally convergent algorithm is developed to solve the optimization problem, and the theoretical proof is provided. Finally, extensive experimental validations on some public available tactile sequence datasets show the advantages of the proposed method.

4.1 Introduction

The previous chapters investigate the utility of the intrinsic relations between fingers for tactile object recognition. To exploit these relations, a joint kernel sparse coding method is developed to fuse the tactile sequences from separate fingers. However, this work regards all of the training samples as the dictionary and does not investigate the dictionary learning problem. This limits the application in more practical scenarios. If the training samples are mapped into a higher-dimensional feature space by a proper mapping function, and the dictionary is learned in this feature space, a better linear representation can be expected. In [9], the dictionary learning problem was tackled by gradient descent over the basis set in the input space directly. To compute the gradient, a specific kernel function such as the Gaussian kernel had to be employed. Similarly, Refs. [11] and [19] addressed the dictionary learning problem on symmetry-positive-definite (SPD) manifold, using Stein kernel and Log-Euclidean kernel, respectively. In addition, Ref. [29] investigated the online dictionary learning on SPD manifold. All of those work deal with specified kernel and can limit their applicability considerably. In [12], a nonlinear generalization of sparse coding and dictionary learning on manifold was proposed. This method is not based on kernel and requires an extra affine constraint on the coding coefficients, which may be unexpected in practice. Reference [20] revealed that the dictionary

© Springer Nature Singapore Pte Ltd. 2018
H. Liu and F. Sun, *Robotic Tactile Perception and Understanding*,
https://doi.org/10.1007/978-981-10-6171-4_4

optimization only needs inner products of samples, and this property can be used to kernelize linear sparse coding. Recently, some scholars proposed more principled kernel dictionary learning method [1, 17, 21, 26]. In [6], the kernel sparse coding for time series was established. Those methods are based on the basic conclusion that the dictionary atoms in the feature space can be linearly reconstructed by the samples in the feature space. As a result, the complicated dictionary learning problem in feature space is formulated as the rather simpler search of a coefficient matrix.

The extreme sparse learning framework [24] combined the idea of dictionary learning with the nonlinear classifier and achieved excellent performance in facial emotion recognition. Furthermore, a kernel extension of the framework was developed to incorporate the advantages of kernel ELM. A significant limitation of [24] is that the nonlinear learning is introduced in the ELM classifier design, but not the dictionary learning. Therefore, such a model cannot be used to deal with tactile sequence signals which do not lie in Euclidean space.

The goal of this chapter is to establish a supervised kernel dictionary learning for more complicated tactile object recognition. A joint learning framework which combines the ELM and kernel dictionary learning for tactile object recognition is developed. By introducing row-sparsity constraint to reduce the time-cost and storage burdens, a reduced kernel dictionary learning method is developed. Such a method addresses the intrinsic difficulty lies in the existing kernel dictionary learning methods which adopt the *Representer Theorem*. Also, a globally convergent algorithm to solve the proposed extreme kernel sparse learning problem is developed and the theoretical proof about the convergence is given. Extensive experimental validations are performed on some public available tactile sequence datasets and show the advantages of the proposed method.

The rest of this chapter is organized as follows: Sect. 4.2 formulates the tactile dictionary learning problem. Section 4.3 gives a brief introduction to the ELM. Sections 4.4 and 4.5 present the proposed extreme kernel dictionary learning model and the reduced version, respectively. In Sects. 4.6 and 4.7, the optimization algorithm and the convergence proof are given, respectively. Section 4.8 shows the experimental results. Finally, the conclusions are given in Sect. 4.8.

4.2   Tactile Dictionary Learning

The problem of tactile object recognition can be formulated as: Given a set of N training tactile sequences $\mathfrak{T} = \{\mathbb{T}_i\}_{i=1}^N \subset \mathscr{T}$ and their corresponding label $z_i \in \{1, 2, \cdots, C\}$, where C is the class number of the objects, the task is to design a classifier that determines the label of a newly arrived tactile sequence $\mathbb{T} \in \mathscr{T}$.

The previous chapters consider using $\mathfrak{T}$ to sparsely represent the test sample $\mathbb{T}$. The sparse coding method exhibits great advantages in classification and multifinger fusion. However, it also exhibits nonnegligible disadvantages:

1. It regards the whole training sample set as the fixed dictionary; this lazy method incurs significant time and storage costs.
2. The obtained coding vector is independent of the task. That is to, no matter what task is concerned, the obtained coding vectors are the same.
3. The class label information, which is available at training stage, is not fully exploited.

Dictionary learning, which learns a compact dictionary from the training samples, is an effective strategy to tackle those problem. Since the tactile sequences do not lie in the Euclidean space, a suitable coding strategy should be developed to effectively represent them. The coding is closely dependent on the dictionary which should be learned from the training samples. The task of tactile dictionary learning tries to obtain a compact dictionary

$$\mathcal{D} = [d_1, ..., d_K],$$

where $K < N$ is the size of the dictionary, and $d_k \in \mathcal{H}_T$ for $k = 1, 2, \cdots, K$. Such a dictionary should effectively summarize the whole training set $\{\mathbb{T}_i\}_{i=1}^N$ and provides a good basis for sparse coding in the implicit feature space.

By denoting $\Phi(\mathfrak{T}) = [\Phi(\mathbb{T}_1), \cdots, \Phi(\mathbb{T}_N)]$, the kernel dictionary learning problem can be formulated as:

$$\begin{aligned} \min_{\mathcal{D},X} \quad & ||\Phi(\mathfrak{T}) - \mathcal{D}X||_F^2, \\ \text{s.t.} \quad & ||x_i||_0 \le S \text{ for } i = 1, 2, \cdots, N \\ & ||d_k||_2 = 1 \text{ for } k = 1, 2, \cdots, K, \end{aligned} \quad (4.1)$$

where $X = [x_1, x_2, \cdots, x_N] \in \mathbb{R}^{K \times N}$ is the sparse coding matrix and the parameter S is used to control the sparsity.

After getting the sparse code x_i for the original sample $\mathbb{T}_i$, the reconstruction error method adopted in the previous chapter can no longer be used to classify the testing sample. The reason is that there is no class structure in the dictionary. Instead, conventional classifier can be used for classification. The most simple method is to adopt a linear classifier which solves the following optimization problem:

$$\min_{w} \sum_{i=1}^{N} (w^T x_i - z_i)^2 \quad (4.2)$$

where $w \in R^K$ is the classifier parameter vector.

Assume the obtained solutions of the dictionary in (4.1) and (4.2) are $\mathcal{D}^*$ and the classifier vector is w^*, respectively, then one can use them for classifing unseen testing samples. During the testing stage, for the testing sample $\mathbb{T} \in \mathcal{T}$, its coding vectors can be obtained by solving

$$\begin{aligned} \min_{x} \quad & ||\Phi(\mathbb{T}) - \mathcal{D}^*x||_2^2, \\ \text{s.t.} \quad & ||x||_0 \le S \end{aligned} \quad (4.3)$$

and obtain its label according to

$$c^* = \arg\min_{c \in \{1, \cdots, C\}} |w^{*T}x - c|. \tag{4.4}$$

However, such a method exhibits an obvious disadvantage that the dictionary learning stage and the classifier learning stage are independent, which limits the performance of the dictionary. A better solution is to jointly learn the dictionary and the classifier, i.e., introducing the discriminative capability into the dictionary learning. This leads to the following discriminate dictionary learning problem:

$$\min_{\mathcal{D}, X} \ \rho||\Phi(\mathfrak{T}) - \mathcal{D}X||_F^2 + \sum_{i=1}^{N}(w^T x_i - z_i)^2$$
$$\text{s.t.} \quad ||x_i||_0 \leq S \ \text{for} \ i = 1, 2, \cdots, N \tag{4.5}$$
$$||d_k||_2 = 1 \ \text{for} \ k = 1, 2, \cdots, K,$$

where ρ is the penalty parameter.

Generally speaking, the work on dictionary learning can be coarsely divided into two categories: unsupervised and supervised. The latter exploits the label information, while the former does not. Nevertheless, almost all of the supervised dictionary learning methods adopted linear classifier to construct the supervised term. An important reason is lacking efficient learning algorithm when the nonlinear classifier is incorporated. Very recently, a breakthrough occurs in [24], which exploited the advantages of extreme learning machine (ELM) to construct an extreme sparse learning method. The following sections will briefly recall the basic principle of ELM and then develop a new supervised dictionary learning method for tactile object recognition (Fig. 4.1).

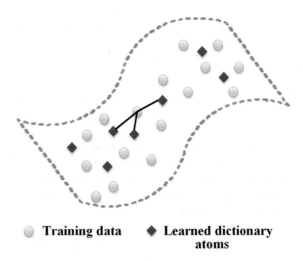

Fig. 4.1 Illustration of the tactile dictionary learning. In the transformed feature space, each training sample can be sparsely reconstructed by the atoms of the learned dictionary

◯ **Training data**   ◆ **Learned dictionary atoms**

4.3 Extreme Learning Machines

The basic idea of ELM is to develop a neural network with random weights to get new feature representations. The original ELM can only deal with vector-form feature descriptor, so the training sample set is denoted as $\{x_i\}$ for $i = 1, 2, \cdots, N$, where $x_i \in \mathbb{R}^K$ is the K-dimensional feature vector and N is the number of the training samples.

According to the core idea of ELM, the hidden layer activation function is denoted as

$$h_l(x_i) = \sigma(\boldsymbol{\beta}_l^T x_i + b_l) \quad \text{for } l = 1, 2, \cdots, L$$

where L is the number of hidden nodes. The parameters $\boldsymbol{\beta}_l \in \mathbb{R}^L$ and $b_l \in \mathbb{R}$ are randomly determined according to specified probability distribution, and

$$\sigma(u) = \frac{1}{1 + e^{-u}}$$

is the sigmoid activation function.

Further, the label vector is constructed as

$$z = [z_1, z_2, \cdots, z_N]^T \in \mathbb{R}^N$$

and the following matrix is used to represent the hidden output matrix

$$H(X) = \begin{bmatrix} h_1(x_1) & h_2(x_1) & \cdots & h_L(x_1) \\ h_1(x_2) & h_2(x_2) & \cdots & h_L(x_2) \\ \vdots & \vdots & \ddots & \vdots \\ h_1(x_N) & h_2(x_N) & \cdots & h_L(x_N) \end{bmatrix} \in \mathbb{R}^{N \times L},$$

and ELM seeks a solution to solve the following optimization problem

$$\min_{w} \ \|H(X)w - z\|_2^2 + \gamma \|w\|_2^2, \tag{4.6}$$

where $w \in \mathbb{R}^L$ is ELM classifier parameter and γ is a regularization parameter.

The above procedure, though has shown powerful capability and has extensive applications, can only deal with the features with vector forms. For nonvector form such as the tactile sequences, the kernel ELM (K-ELM) may be utilized by developing a suitably designed kernel.

ELM originally invented by [15] has become an effective learning algorithm for various tasks [5, 25, 27, 28]. By working on a simple structure named single-hidden layer feed-forward neural networks and randomly applying computational hidden nodes, ELM requires fewer optimization constraints in comparison to SVM [14] and provides a good generalization and a highly accurate learning solution for both classification and regression problems. In [8], ELM was used for tactile object recognition and showed promising results. Though kernel ELM can be used to deal with the tactile sequence, by using the suitably designed kernel [2, 13, 16], it does not exploit more discriminative information.

Another method is to extract the vector-form feature from the original samples and then use ELM for classification. For example, our previous work in [22] utilized the linear dynamic system to model the time sequence and use bag-of-systems model to obtain the vector-form feature descriptors. Obvious, both of the above two methods fix the feature extractor before the classifier design. Therefore, the feature design and the classifier design stages are independent. This often results in sub-optimal results. This section will try to address the key problem of how to design the coding vectors for the original tactile samples. The coding vector can then be suitable for the ELM classification.

4.4 Extreme Kernel Sparse Learning

In Fig. 4.2, the joint learning framework of the proposed extreme kernel sparse learning method is present. From this figure, it can be seen clearly that the tactile sample is represented as a coding vector, which serves as the input vector for the ELM classifier. The core problem is how to jointly optimize them for better performance. To solve this problem, the kernel dictionary learning method is employed. It is briefly introduced as follows.

By combing the objective functions in (4.6) and (4.5), the extreme kernel sparse learning problem can be formulated as

$$
\min_{\mathfrak{D}, X, w} \ ||H(X)w - z||_2^2 + \rho||\Phi(\mathfrak{T}) - \mathfrak{D}X||_F^2 + \gamma||w||_2^2,
$$
$$
\text{s.t.} \ \ ||x_i||_0 \leq S \ \text{ for } \ i = 1, 2, \cdots, N \tag{4.7}
$$
$$
||d_k||_2 = 1 \ \text{ for } \ k = 1, 2, \cdots, K.
$$

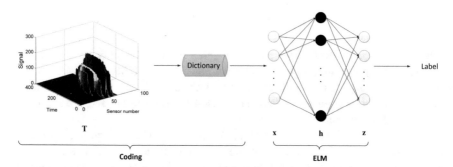

Fig. 4.2 The joint learning framework of the proposed extreme kernel sparse learning. The tactile sequence $\mathbb{T}$ is coded into the vector **x**, which is used for the input of ELM. The gray circle represents the hidden node, and the red circle represents the output node

The regularization parameter ρ is used to control the importance of the reconstruction error, and γ is used to avoid too large solution for $\boldsymbol{w}$.

The core difference between the model (4.7) and the model given in [24] lies in the second term. In fact, the model in [24] dealt with vector space only. The kernel trick adopted in [24] was just used for ELM learning, but not dictionary learning. Therefore, it cannot be used to deal with the tactile sequences which do not lie in Euclidean space. In addition, in the model (4.7)), the sparsity is characterized by the zero norm, which is more straightforward than the 1-norm used in [24].

However, the optimization problem in Eq. (4.7) cannot be directly solved since the mapping $\Phi(\cdot)$ may not be explicitly represented. Fortunately, the kernel trick provides an effective method to avoid dealing with the mapping $\Phi(\cdot)$ [10, 11]. Nevertheless, the dictionary learning problem is still nontrivial since the dictionary atoms $\boldsymbol{d}_k$ lies in the implicit feature space. For general cases of kernels, Refs. [11, 26] utilized the *Representer Theorem*, which indicates that the element $\boldsymbol{d}_k$ in dictionary $\mathfrak{D}$ can be represented by a linear combination of the training samples (see Fig. 4.3 for the illustration), i.e.,

$$\Phi(\boldsymbol{d}_k) = \sum_{i=1}^{N} \Phi(\mathbb{T}_i)a_{i,k} = \Phi(\mathfrak{T})\boldsymbol{a}_k$$

for $k = 1, 2, \cdots, K$, where $a_{i,k}$ is the reconstruction coefficient and $\boldsymbol{a}_k = [a_{1,k}, a_{2,k}, \cdots, a_{N,k}]^T$.

The above equation can be written as the following compact form:

$$\mathfrak{D} = \Phi(\mathfrak{T})A, \tag{4.8}$$

where $A = [\boldsymbol{a}_1, \boldsymbol{a}_2, \cdots, \boldsymbol{a}_K] \in \mathbb{R}^{N \times K}$ is the reconstruction matrix. This means that the dictionary atoms can be linearly reconstructed by all of the training samples in the

Fig. 4.3 Illustration of the tactile dictionary reconstruction. In the transformed feature space, each atom in the dictionary can be linearly reconstructed by all of the training samples

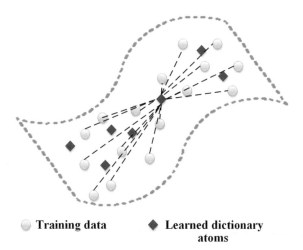

○ **Training data**   ◆ **Learned dictionary atoms**

feature space. Therefore, the kernel dictionary learning problem can be reformulated as

$$\min_{A,X,w} \quad ||H(X)w - z||_2^2 + \rho||\Phi(\mathfrak{T}) - \Phi(\mathfrak{T})AX||_F^2 + \gamma||w||_2^2,$$
$$\text{s.t.} \quad ||x_i||_0 \leq S \quad \text{for} \quad i = 1, 2, \cdots, N \qquad (4.9)$$
$$||\Phi(\mathfrak{T})a_k||_2 = 1 \quad \text{for} \quad k = 1, 2, \cdots, K.$$

By this formulation, it is found that the original data matrix $\Phi(\mathfrak{T})$ is compressed as a reduced dictionary $\mathfrak{D} = \Phi(\mathfrak{T})A$ and each sample $\mathbb{T}_i \in \mathscr{T}$ is represented as K-dimensional sparse vector $x_i \in \mathbb{R}^K$.

The optimization model in (4.9) provides a great advantage since it does not search the dictionary atoms in the feature space, but only calculates the coefficient matrix A. Therefore, this formulation can be used for any type of kernel functions.

Nevertheless, this method suffers from one intrinsic drawback, which occurs in the test phase. Considering a test sample $\mathbb{T} \in \mathscr{T}$ and representing it using the learned dictionary $\mathfrak{D} = \Phi(\mathfrak{T})A$, one can usually search the coding vector x which satisfies $||x||_0 \leq S$ to minimize

$$||\Phi(\mathbb{T}) - \Phi(\mathfrak{T})Ax||_2^2.$$

Note that this reconstruction error term can be equivalently represented as

$$\Phi^T(\mathbb{T})\Phi(\mathbb{T}) - 2\Phi^T(\mathbb{T})\Phi(\mathfrak{T})Ax + x^T A^T \Phi^T(\mathfrak{T})\Phi(\mathfrak{T})Ax. \qquad (4.10)$$

The calculation of $\Phi^T(\mathbb{T})\Phi(\mathfrak{T})$ should be transformed as calculating

$$\kappa(\mathbb{T}, \mathbb{T}_1), \kappa(\mathbb{T}, \mathbb{T}_2), \cdots, \kappa(\mathbb{T}, \mathbb{T}_N).$$

This implies that all of the training samples $\{\mathbb{T}_i\}_{i=1}^N$ have to be stored and used for the sparse coding of test samples. This contradicts the intrinsic compression meaning of dictionary learning, which tries to learn a compact dictionary to approximately represent all of the training samples. According to the idea of dictionary learning, once the dictionary is learned, the training samples which are used to learn the dictionary can be discarded and only the dictionary itself is preserved for further use. However, this is impossible in the above-mentioned kernel dictionary learning framework. The intrinsic reason is that the *Representer Theorem* uses all of training samples to reconstruct the dictionary atoms in the feature space. It seems as if $\Phi(\mathfrak{T})A$ formed a compressed version of $\Phi(\mathfrak{T})$ since $K < N$. However, $\Phi(\mathfrak{T})A$ cannot be explicitly calculated and it has to resort kernel function to calculate $\Phi^T(\mathbb{T})\Phi(\mathfrak{T})A$ and $x^T A^T \Phi^T(\mathfrak{T})\Phi(\mathfrak{T})Ax$. In this sense, it is unavoidable to calculate the kernel functions between the test sample and all of the training samples. The dictionary $\Phi(\mathfrak{T})A$ does summarize the dataset but does not reduce the data storage requirements at all.

4.5 Reduced Extreme Kernel Sparse Learning

To address the efficacy problem incurred by the kernel, the requirement that the dictionary atoms should be reconstructed by all of the training samples need be relaxed, and then the number of training samples which contribute to reconstruct the dictionary atoms in the feature space should be reduced. To this end, few of the training samples are selected and the scale of the problem is reduced. The selection strategy can be various. For example, the random selection strategy or k-means clustering method can be used. For convenience, the selected training samples are called as prototypes (Fig. 4.4).

Assuming that P is the parameter which represents the expected number of selected prototypes, the indices of the selected prototypes are denoted as $i_1, i_2, \cdots, i_P$, then the reduced sample matrix can be constructed in the feature space as

$$\Phi(\tilde{\mathfrak{T}}) = [\Phi(\mathbb{T}_{i_1}), \cdots, \Phi(\mathbb{T}_{i_P})].$$

Thus, the following reduced optimization problem is constructed

$$\begin{aligned}
\min_{\tilde{A}, X, w} \quad & ||H(X)w - z||_2^2 + \rho||\Phi(\tilde{\mathfrak{T}}) - \Phi(\tilde{\mathfrak{T}})\tilde{A}X||_F^2 + \gamma||w||_2^2 \\
\text{s.t.} \quad & ||x_i||_0 \le S \text{ for } i = 1, 2, \cdots, N \\
& ||\Phi(\tilde{\mathfrak{T}})\tilde{a}_k||_2 = 1 \text{ for } k = 1, 2, \cdots, K,
\end{aligned} \tag{4.11}$$

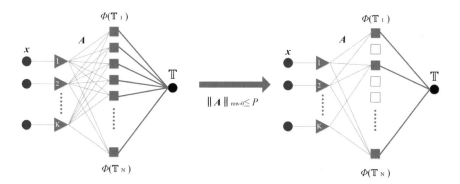

Fig. 4.4 An illustration of the reduced strategy. The red circle represents the test sample in the feature space. The blue squares represent the training samples in the feature space. The blue lines represent the kernel functions between the test sample and the training samples. In addition, the triangles are used to represent the dictionary atoms and the yellow circles are used to represent the coding vector. LEFT: The Extreme Kernel Sparse Learning; RIGHT: The Reduced Extreme Kernel Sparse Learning. This figure shows the principle of the reduced strategy is to remove most of the kernel functions between the test sample and the training samples by constraining the row-sparsity of A. In the right panel, the removed training samples are marked with the empty squares

where $\tilde{a}_k$ is the kth column of $\tilde{A} \in \mathbb{R}^{P \times K}$, which is the reduced reconstruction matrix. In this case, if the task is to consider a test sample $\mathbb{T}$ and want to represent it using the learned dictionary, then what need to do is searching the sparse coding vector x satisfying $||x||_0 \leq S$ to minimize

$$||\Phi(\mathbb{T}) - \Phi(\tilde{\mathfrak{T}})\tilde{A}x||_2^2.$$

It can be seen from this that the storage and time cost are reduced since only P training samples are involved in this optimization.

Nevertheless, it is easy to observe that the above strategies share a common drawback, i.e., the prototype selection procedure and the dictionary learning procedure are performed separately, and therefore, it is difficult to develop the intrinsic relation between the two procedures. Instead of selecting prototypes beforehand from training samples, one can treat them as target variables to be optimized in the optimization framework. This not only allows more flexibility for prototype selection, but more importantly enables further performance improvements. Since it is unknown which samples should be selected to reconstruct the dictionary, the sparsity regularization is resorted to tackle this problem. It is achieved by penalizing the number of the nonzero rows in the matrix A. Concretely speaking, $\Phi(\mathfrak{T})A$ is still used to represent the dictionary $\mathbb{D}$, but the row-sparsity is imposed on the matrix A to ensure that only a few training samples are actually used to reconstruct the dictionary. By denoting $||A||_{\text{row}-0}$ as the number of the nonzero rows in A, the optimization problem can be constructed as

$$
\begin{aligned}
\min_{A, X, w} \quad & ||H(X)w - z||_2^2 + \rho||\Phi(\mathfrak{T}) - \Phi(\mathfrak{T})AX||_F^2 + \gamma||w||_2^2 \\
\text{s.t.} \quad & ||x_i||_0 \leq S \text{ for } i = 1, 2, \cdots, N \\
& ||\Phi(\mathfrak{T})a_k||_2 = 1 \text{ for } k = 1, 2, \cdots, K, \\
& ||A||_{\text{row}-0} \leq P.
\end{aligned}
\tag{4.12}
$$

It is noted that P takes value from the interval $[1, N]$. If $P = N$, then the model (4.12) reduces to (4.9). Regarding the row-sparsity term $||A||_{\text{row}-0}$, no approximation (neither convex nor nonconvex approximation) is used.

After completing the training stage by solving (4.12), the obtained solutions is denoted as X^*, A^* and w^*. Further, the indexes of the nonzero rows are denoted in A^* as $i_1^*, i_2^*, \cdots, i_P^*$. Then the nonzero rows in A^* can be extracted to form a reduced matrix $\tilde{A}^* \in \mathbb{R}^{P \times K}$. Compared to the optimization problem in (4.11), this method simultaneously performs the prototype selection and kernel dictionary learning.

By denoting

$$\Phi(\tilde{\mathfrak{T}}^*) = [\Phi(\mathbb{T}_{i_1^*}), \cdots, \Phi(\mathbb{T}_{i_P^*})]$$

as the reduced sample matrix in the feature space, it is easy to get

$$\Phi(\tilde{\mathbb{T}})A^* = \Phi(\tilde{\mathbb{T}}^*)\tilde{A}^*.$$

As a result, for classifying a test sample $\mathbb{T} \in \mathscr{T}$, the following sparse coding optimization problem can be solved.

$$
\begin{aligned}
&\min_{\boldsymbol{x}} \ ||\Phi(\mathbb{T}) - \Phi(\tilde{\mathbb{T}}^*)\tilde{\boldsymbol{A}}^* \boldsymbol{x}||_2^2 \\
&\text{s.t.} \ \ ||\boldsymbol{x}||_0 \leq S
\end{aligned}
\tag{4.13}
$$

Using the obtained coding vector $\boldsymbol{x}^*$, the label c^* can be obtained as:

$$
c^* = \arg\min_{c \in \{1, \cdots, C\}} |H(\boldsymbol{x}^*)\boldsymbol{w}^* - c|.
\tag{4.14}
$$

4.6   Optimization Algorithm

The optimization problem in Eq. (4.12) is obviously nonconvex and nonsmooth. Following [3, 4], the proximal alternating linearization minimization (PALM) algorithm is used to solve it. A great advantage of PALM is that it can be used to solve nonconvex problem and produces solution with Cauchy convergence. Therefore, it is a whole sequence convergent algorithm. The core of this algorithm is, for each block of coordinate, one gradient step is performed on the smooth part, while a proximal step is taken on the nonsmooth part. To this end, the error term is denoted as

$$
\mathscr{E}(\boldsymbol{A}, \boldsymbol{X}, \boldsymbol{w}) = ||H(\boldsymbol{X})\boldsymbol{w} - \boldsymbol{z}||_2^2 + \eta ||\Phi(\mathbb{T}) - \Phi(\mathbb{T})\boldsymbol{A}\boldsymbol{X}||_F^2 + \gamma ||\boldsymbol{w}||_2^2
$$

and the original optimization problem is reformulated as

$$
\min_{\boldsymbol{A}, \boldsymbol{X}, \boldsymbol{w}} \mathscr{E}(\boldsymbol{A}, \boldsymbol{X}, \boldsymbol{w}) + \delta_{\mathscr{A}}(\boldsymbol{A}) + \delta_{\mathscr{X}}(\boldsymbol{X}),
\tag{4.15}
$$

where $\delta_{\mathscr{A}}(\boldsymbol{A})$ denotes the indicator function of $\boldsymbol{A}$ which satisfies $\delta_{\mathscr{A}}(\boldsymbol{A}) = 0$ if $\boldsymbol{A} \in \mathscr{A}$ and $+\infty$ otherwise, where

$$
\mathscr{A} = \{\boldsymbol{A} \in \mathbb{R}^{N \times K} : ||\boldsymbol{A}||_{\text{row}-0} \leq P, \ ||\Phi(\mathfrak{T})\boldsymbol{a}_k||_2 = 1, k = 1, 2, \cdots, K\}.
$$

Similarly, the symbol $\delta_{\mathscr{X}}(\boldsymbol{X})$ denotes the indicator function of $\boldsymbol{X}$, where

$$
\mathscr{X} = \{\boldsymbol{X} \in \mathbb{R}^{K \times N} : ||\boldsymbol{x}_i||_0 \leq T \ \text{for} \ i = 1, 2, \cdots, N \ \text{and} \ ||\boldsymbol{X}||_\infty \leq M_c\}.
$$

The value of M_c is simply set to some large number (such as 10^4) which guarantees the boundness of the solution. The boundedness is important for the convergence analysis.

Motivated by the PALM, $\boldsymbol{X}$, $\boldsymbol{A}$, and $\boldsymbol{w}$ need to be alternatively updated. The following subsections will introduce how to solve those unknown matrices. For convenience, the superscript (t) is used to denote the values at the tth iteration.

4.6.1 Calculating the Sparse Coding Vectors

This step tries to get the updated values $X^{(t+1)}$, given the values of $A^{(t)}$, $X^{(t)}$, and $w^{(t)}$. Please note that each column of X can be calculated separately. The partial derivatives of r on x_i is computed as

$$
\begin{aligned}
\nabla_{x_i}\mathscr{E} &= 2(h^T(x_i)w^{(t)} - z_i)\hat{H}w^{(t)} \\
&\quad - 2\eta A^{(t)T}\kappa(\mathbb{T}_i, \mathfrak{T}) + 2\eta A^{(t)T}\kappa(\mathfrak{T}, \mathfrak{T})A^{(t)}x_i,
\end{aligned}
\tag{4.16}
$$

where $\hat{H} \in \mathbb{R}^{K \times L}$ of which (k, l)-th element is calculated as

$$
\hat{H}_{kl} = \frac{\partial h_l(x_i)}{\partial x_{ik}} = h_l(x_i)(1 - h_l(x_i))w_{lk}
$$

and w_{lk} is the kth element of the vector w_l. In addition,

$$
\kappa(\mathbb{T}_i, \mathfrak{T}) = [\kappa(\mathbb{T}_i, \mathbb{T}_1), \cdots, \kappa(\mathbb{T}_i, \mathbb{T}_N)]^T.
$$

The (i, j)th element of $\kappa(\mathfrak{T}, \mathfrak{T})$ is $\kappa(\mathbb{T}_i, \mathbb{T}_j)$. The Lipschitz constant is calculated as

$$
L_{x_i}^{(t+1)} = \eta \|A^{(t)T}\kappa(\mathfrak{T}, \mathfrak{T})A^{(t)}\|_F.
$$

To get the updated values of x_i, the following proximal map is considered:

$$
\begin{aligned}
&\min_{x} <x - x_i^{(t)}, \nabla_{x_i}r> + \frac{\mu_{x_i}^{(t+1)}}{2}\|x - x_i^{(t)}\|_2^2, \\
&\text{s.t. } \|x\|_0 \le S.
\end{aligned}
\tag{4.17}
$$

The step-size $\mu_{x_i}^{(t+1)}$ is set as

$$
\mu_{x_i}^{(t+1)} = \max(\eta L_{x_i}^{(t+1)}, M_\mu),
$$

where $\eta > 1$ is a constant learning rate and M_μ serves as a lower bound of which role will be discussed in the convergence analysis. This problem can be reformulated as

$$
\min_{x} \|x - \tilde{x}_i^{(t)}\|_2^2, \quad \text{s.t. } \|x\|_0 \le S,
\tag{4.18}
$$

where

$$
\tilde{x}_i^{(t)} = x_i^{(t)} - \frac{1}{\mu_{x_i}^{(t+1)})}\nabla_{x_i}r.
$$

The solution to this optimization problem is the vector that keeps the original values in $\tilde{x}_i^{(t)}$ at the positions where absolute values are among the largest S of them. That is to say, one can rank the components in $\tilde{x}_i^{(t)}$ in descending order according to their absolute values, and then select the top S components to maintain their values and set the rest to be 0. Finally, those elements whose absolute values are larger than M_c are changed as M_c.

Using the above procedure for $i = 1, 2, \cdots, N$, the updated values of $X^{(t+1)} = [x_1^{(t+1)}, \cdots, x_N^{(t+1)}]$ can be obtained.

4.6.2 Calculating the Dictionary Atoms

This step tries to update the dictionary coefficient matrix. At the $(t+1)$th iteration, $X^{(t+1)}$ and $A^{(t)}$ are given. Due to the constraints on A, the row or column in A cannot be calculated separately. Thus, the partial derivatives $\nabla_A r$ is computed as

$$\nabla_A \mathscr{E} = -2\eta \kappa(\mathfrak{T}, \mathfrak{T}) X^{(t+1)T} + 2\eta \kappa(\mathfrak{T}, \mathfrak{T}) A X^{(t+1)} X^{(t+1)T}, \qquad (4.19)$$

and the Lipschitz constant is calculated as

$$L_A^{(t+1)} = 2\eta \|\kappa(\mathfrak{T}, \mathfrak{T})\|_F \|X^{(t+1)} X^{(t+1)T}\|_F.$$

To get the updated values of A, the following proximal map is considered:

$$\begin{aligned} \min_A &\ <A - A^{(t)}, \nabla_A r> + \tfrac{\mu_A^{(t+1)}}{2} \|A - A^{(t)}\|_F^2, \\ \text{s.t. } &\|\Phi(\mathfrak{T})a_k\|_2 = 1, \\ &\|A\|_{\text{row}-0} \leq P, \end{aligned} \qquad (4.20)$$

where the step-size $\mu_A^{(t+1)}$ is set as

$$\mu_A^{(t+1)} = \max(\eta L_A^{(t+1)}, M_\mu).$$

This problem can be reformulated as

$$\begin{aligned} \min_A &\ \|A - \tilde{A}^{(t)}\|_F^2, \\ \text{s.t. } &\|\Phi(\mathfrak{T})a_k\|_2 = 1, \quad \|A\|_{\text{row}-0} \leq P, \end{aligned} \qquad (4.21)$$

where

$$\tilde{A}^{(t)} = A^{(t)} - \frac{1}{\mu_A^{(t+1)}} \nabla_A r.$$

To solve this problem, the P rows are preserved in $\tilde{A}^{(t)}$, whose 2-norms are among the largest P of them. Then the column normalization is performed to satisfy the condition $\|\Phi(\mathfrak{T})a_k\|_2 = 1$, which can be transformed as $a_k^T \kappa(\mathfrak{T}, \mathfrak{T}) a_k = 1$.

4.6.3   Calculating the ELM Coefficients

This step tries to update the ELM parameter w. At the $(t+1)$-th iteration, $X^{(t+1)}$ is given. The partial derivatives of $\mathcal{E}$ on w is computed as

$$\nabla_w \mathcal{E} = 2H^T(X^{(t+1)})(H(X^{(t+1)})w - z) + 2\gamma w \qquad (4.22)$$

and the Lipschitz constant is calculated as

$$L_w^{(t+1)} = 2||H^T(X^{(t+1)})(H(X^{(t+1)})||_F + 2\gamma.$$

The ELM coefficient vector is then updated as

$$w^{(t+1)} = w^{(t)} - \frac{1}{\mu_w^{(t+1)}}\nabla_w r, \qquad (4.23)$$

where the step-size $\mu_w^{(t+1)}$ is set as

$$\mu_w^{(t+1)} = \max(\eta L_w^{(t+1)}, M_\mu).$$

With the above updating rules, the proposed algorithm is summarized in Algorithm 1. The convergent condition can be set as $||X^{(t+1)} - X^{(t)}||_F \le \varepsilon$, $||A^{(t+1)} - A^{(t)}||_F \le \varepsilon$, and $||w^{(t+1)} - w^{(t)}||_2 \le \varepsilon$ where ε is the tolerant error, or a prescribed maximum iteration number. In this work, the maximum iteration number is set to 10.

Algorithm 1 Reduced Extreme Kernel Dictionary Learning

Input: Dataset $\{\mathbb{T}_i\}$ for $i = 1, 2, \cdots, N$, the sparsity level S, the size of dictionary K, the number of prototypes P, $\eta = 1.1$, $M_\mu = 10^{-1}$, $M_c = 10^4$.
Output: Solutions $X \in \mathbb{R}^{K \times N}$, $A \in \mathbb{R}^{N \times K}$ and $w \in \mathbb{R}^L$.

1: Set $t = 0$.
2: **while** Not convergent **do**
3:     $\mu_{x_i}^{(t+1)} = \max\{\eta L_{x_i}^{(t+1)}, M_\mu\}$ for $j = 1, 2, \cdots, N$.
4:     Solve Eq. (4.18) to get $x_i^{(t+1)}$ for $j = 1, 2, \cdots, N$.
5:     $\mu_A^{(t+1)} = \max\{\eta L_A^{(t+1)}, M_\mu\}$.
6:     Solve Eq. (4.21) to get $A^{(t+1)}$.
7:     $\mu_w^{(t+1)} = \max\{\eta L_w^{(t+1)}, M_\mu\}$.
8:     Solve Eq. (4.23) to get $w^{(t+1)}$.
9:     Set $t = t + 1$.
10: **end while**

Before closing this section, it is worth noting that the proposed reduced kernel dictionary method, which performs simultaneous prototype selection and discriminative dictionary learning, is easy to be extended for online applications or incremental learning.

4.7 Algorithm Analysis

The developed PLAM has good convergence property, which can be summarized as the following theorem.

Theorem 1 *The sequence $\{X^{(t)}, A^{(t)}, w^{(t)}\}$ generated by the Algorithm 1 converges to a critical point of the optimization problem in Eq. (4.12) and satisfies:*

$$\lim_{t \to +\infty} ||X^{(t+1)} - X^{(t)}||_F = 0,$$
$$\lim_{t \to +\infty} ||A^{(t+1)} - A^{(t)}||_F = 0,$$
$$\lim_{t \to +\infty} ||w^{(t+1)} - w^{(t)}||_2 = 0.$$

Proof The proof is essentially based on the results in [4]. It is obvious that

$$\mathscr{A}_1 = \{A \in \mathbb{R}^{N \times K} : ||A||_{\text{row}-0} \leq P\}$$

and

$$\mathscr{A}_2 = \{A \in \mathbb{R}^{N \times K} : ||\Phi(\mathbb{T})a_k||_2 = 1, k = 1, 2, \cdots, K\}$$

are semi-algebraic sets, and therefore, $\mathscr{A} = \mathscr{A}_1 \bigcap \mathscr{A}_2$ is also a semi-algebraic set. Similarly, the sets

$$\mathscr{X}_1 = \{X \in \mathbb{R}^{K \times N} : ||x_i||_0 \leq T, \text{ for } i = 1, 2, \cdots, N\}$$

and

$$\mathscr{X}_2 = \{X \in \mathbb{R}^{K \times N} : ||X||_\infty \leq M_c\}$$

are semi-algebraic, and therefore, $\mathscr{X} = \mathscr{X}_1 \bigcap \mathscr{X}_2$ is semi-algebraic.

It is noted that the first term $\mathscr{E}(A, X, w)$ in Eq. (4.15) is a semi-algebraic form and the last second terms are indicator functions over semi-algebraic sets and therefore semi-algebraic functions. Thus, the whole objective function is a semi-algebraic function. Further, it is a proper, lower semi-continuous function and hence satisfies the *Kurdyka-Lojasiewicz* property [18]. Finally, the following four observations can be made:

1. The objective function in Eq. (4.15) is nonnegative and therefore is inf-bounded.
2. $\nabla_{x_i} \mathscr{E}, \nabla_A \mathscr{E}$ and $\nabla_w \mathscr{E}$ are Lipschitz continuous with modulis $L_{x_i}^{(t+1)}, L_A^{(t+1)}$, and $L_w^{(t+1)}$ and therefore are Lipschitz continuous with modulis $\mu_{x_i}^{(t+1)}, \mu_A^{(t+1)}$, and $\mu_w^{(t+1)}$.
3. According to the Lines 3, 5, and 7 in Algorithm 1, it is known that $\mu_{x_i}^{(t+1)}, \mu_A^{(t+1)}$, and $\mu_w^{(t+1)}$ are lower bounded by M_μ. On the other hand, the fact $A^{(t+1)} \in \mathscr{A}$ and $X^{(t+1)} \in \mathscr{X}$ implies that both $A^{(t+1)}$ and $X^{(t+1)}$ are bounded from above. According to the definitions of $L_{x_i}^{(t+1)}, L_A^{(t+1)}$, and $L_w^{(t+1)}$, it is known that all of them are bounded from above. Therefore, μ_{x_i}, μ_A, and μ_w are upper bounded.

Fig. 4.5 The convergence
behavior of the proposed
method

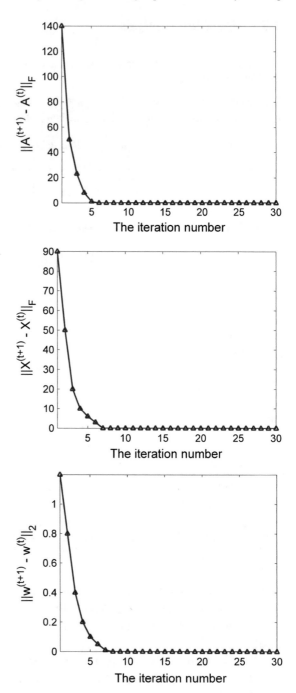

4. Since $\mathscr{E}(\cdot)$ is a continuous and smooth function, $\nabla\mathscr{E}(A, X, w)$ has Lipschitz constant on any bounded set.

Based on the above results, Theorem 3.1 of [4] is directly used to get the conclusion. This completes the proof.

The statement in Theorem 1 discloses that the developed algorithm produces *Cauchy* sequence, which indicates the algorithm achieves whole sequence convergence. Such a property, which is also called global convergence [3], provides an important merit that the number of the iterations does not need to empirically choose to keep the results stable. As a comparison, the K-KSVD method in [26] usually obtains at most subsequence convergence.

Figure 4.5 shows the convergence behavior of the proposed method on one example. It shows that the increment indeed converges to zero after several iterations.

4.8 Experimental Results

4.8.1 Data Description and Experimental Setting

The proposed approach is demonstrated on the Penn Haptic Adjective Corpus 2 (PHAC-2) dataset, which was originally developed in [7].

The PHAC-2 dataset contains tactile signals and images of 60 household objects. In this work, the image information is not used. Each object is explored by a pair of SynTouch biomimetic tactile sensors (BioTacs), which are mounted on the gripper of a Willow Garage Personal Robot2 (PR2). Each object is felt with the following four exploratory procedures: squeeze, hold, slow slide, fast slide, which mimic how humans explore the tactile properties of objects. The BioTac sensor generates five types of signals: low-frequency fluid pressure, high-frequency fluid vibrations, core temperature, core temperature change, and 19 electrode impedance which are spatially distributed across the sensor. Although the image and data on the joint positions and gripper velocity and acceleration are available, this chapter concentrates on classifying the tactile signals using the electrode impedance. Therefore, the electrode impedances data from the two BioTac sensors is concatenated to get $d = 19 \times 2 = 38$-dimensional tactile sequence signal. Ten trials of each exploratory procedure are performed per object, resulting in 600 tactile sequences. The GA kernel is adopted for kernel evaluation.

Each object is described with a set of 24 binary labels, corresponding to the existence or absence of each of the 24 tactile adjectives (e.g., *hard* or *soft*). For the three adjectives *nice*, *sticky* and *unpleasant*, which exhibits only one positive object instance, it is impossible to construct the positive training and testing sets. Therefore, such three ones are simply deleted. As a result, only 21 adjectives are preserved for classification tasks. In Fig. 4.6, the number of objects for each adjective classification task is demonstrated.

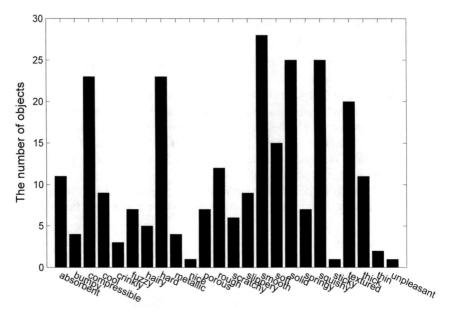

Fig. 4.6 Number of objects for each adjective classification task

Following [7], the 60 objects are partitioned into 21 90/10 train/test splits, one for each adjective (Fig. 4.7). Creating 21 separate train/test splits is necessary because there exists no one split such that each adjective is present in both the train and test split. Note that although a single object has several corresponding measurements, the same object is not allowed to appear in both the train and test split. To this end, the following equation is used to determine the number of objects which are used for training or negative sets.

$$O_{train,p} = [0.9 \times O_p], \; O_{test,p} = O_p - O_{train,p},$$

$$O_{train,n} = 50 - O_{train,p}, \; O_{test,n} = 10 - O_{test,p},$$

where O_p is the number of positive examples for this particular adjective. $O_{train,p}$ and $O_{test,p}$ are the numbers of the positive objects for training and testing, respectively, and $O_{train,n}$ and $O_{test,n}$ are the numbers of the negative objects for testing, respectively.

To give a concrete example of the method for choosing train/test splits, the following method is adopted. Considering the adjective *absorbent*, which has $O_p = 11$ positive object examples and 49 negative object examples, a train set containing $O_{train,p} = 9$ positive *absorbent* object examples and $O_{train,n} = 41$ negative examples are produced. The remaining $O_{test,p} = 2$ positive objects and $O_{test,n} = 8$ negative objects form the test set.

Fig. 4.7 Images of the 60 objects which are used to collect the tactile samples. The images are cited from [7] with slight modification

Further, this chapter aims to create a separate binary classifier for each of the adjectives. Adopting such a strategy guarantees that each task always has 500 samples for training and 100 samples for testing.

To evaluate the performance, the classification accuracy ACC is used as follows:

$$ACC = \frac{1}{21} \sum_{i=1}^{21} \frac{CN_{test}(i)}{N_{test}(i)} \times 100\%,$$

where $CN_{test}(i)$ represents the number of correctly classified test samples for the ith adjective and $N_{test}(i)$ represents the number of test samples for the ith adjective. In our case, $N_{test}(i) = 100$ for all $i = 1, 2, , \cdots, 21$.

4.8.2 Parameter Selection

In the model (4.12), there are six parameters which are summarized in Table 4.1. To comprehensively evaluate their effects is difficult and one feasible solution is to fix some ones and analyze the effects of other parameters. Before the analysis, it is noted that the parameter P is used for reduced dictionary learning and will be discussed later and therefore it is set $P = N$ here.

Firstly, the values of ρ and γ are fixed as the default values and the sparsity level S is set as 5% of K, the values of K are varied from 100 to 400 and the value of L from 100 to 800. The obtained results are shown in Fig. 4.8, from which it is observed that the performance increases with either the number of hidden nodes or the size of the dictionary, and then saturates for $L > 500$. In fact, adopting a larger L shows advantages for the cases when K is rather small.

To analyze the effects of ρ and γ, the values of K and L are fixed as $K = 300$ and $L = 600$, and the values of ρ and γ are varied from 10^{-3} to 10^{3}. The results are shown in Fig. 4.9. Those results show that the proposed algorithm works well when the parameter ρ is about 10. When ρ is too small, the kernel sparse coding is attenuated and the obtained coding vector cannot reflect the characteristics of

Table 4.1 Parameter explanation

Parameter	Meaning	Default value
ρ	The regularization parameter for the reconstruction error	10
γ	The regularization parameter for the ELM coefficients	0.1
S	The sparsity level	$5\% \times K$
P	The number of reduced dictionary	N
K	The size of dictionary	300
L	The number of hidden nodes in ELM	600

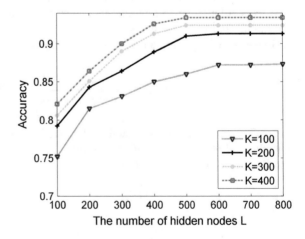

Fig. 4.8 The performance versus the number of the hidden nodes L

Fig. 4.9 The influences of regularization parameters ρ and γ

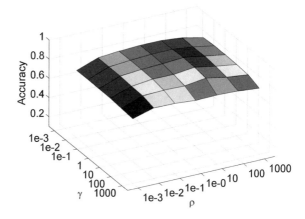

the original tactile sample. On the contrary, when ρ is too large, the role of ELM classifier becomes weak. Therefore, a properly designed sparse coding term indeed plays an important role in tactile dictionary learning. On the other hand, the proposed algorithm is not very sensitive to the parameter γ. This is partially due to the merits of extreme learning.

Unless otherwise mentioned, the default values of the parameters are set as listed in Table 4.1 for the further comparison.

4.8.3 Accuracy Performance Comparison

To show the advantages of the joint learning capability of the proposed method, a fair comparison with other classifiers is made. To this end, Eq. (4.5) is solved to get the kernel dictionary and it is used to obtain the coding vectors for the test samples. Then the Gaussian kernel SVM and ELM classifiers are applied on the obtained coding vectors. The parameters in the SVM and ELM classifiers are determined by the greedy search to obtain the best results. Both of the methods solve the dictionary learning and classification problem separately. By comparison, the proposed EKSL realizes the joint nonlinear learning of dictionary and classifier.

On the other hand, using the GA kernel, the kernel SVM (K-SVM) and Kernel ELM (K-ELM) can also be used to perform the tactile object recognition. Therefore, the K-SVM and K-ELM can be used for comparison. Such methods do not need the coding stage, and therefore, their performance is independent of the dictionary size K.

The averaged accuracy results versus the size of dictionary K are summarized in Fig. 4.10, from which the following observations are concluded:

1. The performance of SVM, ELM, and EKSL improves when the size K is increased. However, EKSL performs consistently better than SVM and ELM. The main reason is that the dictionary and ELM classifier are learned jointly and the obtained results are more adapted to the data structure.

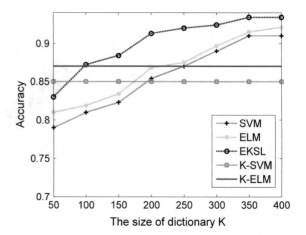

Fig. 4.10 Performance versus the size of the dictionary K

2. K-SVM and K-ELM, which use GA kernel for classification, but do not utilize the dictionary learning and sparse coding, are inferior to the methods which adopt dictionary learning (including SVM, ELM, and EKSL) when K is larger than 250. This shows that dictionary learning indeed introduces more discriminative information as soon as the size of the dictionary is moderately large.
3. When the dictionary size is set to small (such as smaller than 100), all of SVM, ELM, and the proposed EKSL obtain poor results. This is reasonable because too small dictionary cannot represent original samples well.

In addition, the accuracy for each adjective task is listed for clear comparison. Those results show that EKSL obtains the best results for most of the tasks. The main reason is the learned dictionary is rather suitable for the classification task. However, for some adjectives, such as *cool*, the performance is not satisfactory. One possible reason is that the temperature information is not used (Fig. 4.11).

4.8.4   Comparison of Reduced Strategies

As analyzed in Sect. 4.4, the kernel dictionary learning method always utilizes all of the training samples to construct the dictionary atoms. To alleviate this effect, in this section, the reduced strategy for the kernel sparse learning is investigated. Since any strategy can be used to select prototypes before learning, the proposed method is compared with the following techniques throughout the experiments.

1. Rand method, which randomly selects P prototypes from the N training samples.
2. K-Med method, which uses the k-medoids technique to get P prototypes from the N training samples.
3. K-RRSS method, which uses the kernelized robust representation and structured sparsity to select the P representative prototypes [23].

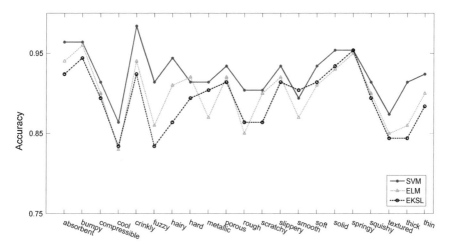

Fig. 4.11 Accuracy for each adjective classification task

Fig. 4.12 Performance versus the number of selected prototypes P

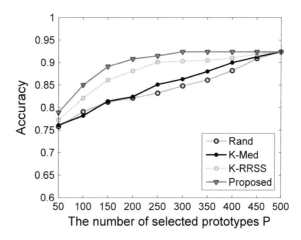

Figure 4.12 shows the classification accuracy versus the number of prototypes P. Note that the upper bound of P is N, but not K. The proposed method consistently outperforms the other prototype selection ones (Rand, K-Med, K-RRSS), sometimes very significantly. This demonstrates its effectiveness in selecting useful training samples for kernel dictionary learning. The reason is that these methods select the prototypes regardless of the kernel dictionary learning task. In addition, the results show that when the number of selected prototypes is small, the proposed method is more effective in selecting the most useful training samples to reconstruct the dictionary in the feature space. This provides practical values of the proposed method. In addition, it should be noticed that if P is set as N, then Rand, K-Med, K-RRSS, and the proposed method obtain the same results because in this case all of the training samples are selected as the prototypes.

4.9 Summary

In this chapter, the tactile object recognition problem is tackled by developing a novel extreme kernel sparse learning methodology. This method simultaneously addresses the dictionary learning problem and the extreme learning machine classifier design problems. Furthermore, a reduced kernel dictionary learning method is developed by introducing row-sparsity constraint. Such a method addresses the intrinsic difficulty which lies in the existing kernel dictionary learning methods and reduces the time cost and storage burdens. A globally convergent algorithm is developed to solve the kernel dictionary learning problem and the theoretical proof is provided. Finally, extensive experimental validations are performed on the public available tactile sequence dataset and show the advantages of the proposed method.

References

1. Anaraki, F.P., Hughes, S.M.: Kernel compressive sensing. In: 20th IEEE International Conference on Image Processing (ICIP), pp. 494–498. IEEE (2013)
2. Bai, Z., Huang, G.B., Wang, D., Wang, H., Westover, M.B.: Sparse extreme learning machine for classification. IEEE Trans. Cybern. **44**(10), 1858–1870 (2014)
3. Bao, C., Ji, H., Quan, Y., Shen, Z.: L0 norm based dictionary learning by proximal methods with global convergence. In: Proceedings of the IEEE Conference on Computer Vision and Pattern Recognition pp. 3858–3865. (2014)
4. Bolte, J., Sabach, S., Teboulle, M.: Proximal alternating linearized minimization for nonconvex and nonsmooth problems. Math. Program. **146**(1–2), 459 (2014)
5. Cao, J., Zhao, Y., Lai, X., Ong, M.E.H., Yin, C., Koh, Z.X., Liu, N.: Landmark recognition with sparse representation classification and extreme learning machine. J. Frankl. Inst. **352**(10), 4528–4545 (2015)
6. Chen, Z., Zuo, W., Hu, Q., Lin, L.: Kernel sparse representation for time series classification. Inf. Sci. **292**, 15–26 (2015)
7. Chu, V., McMahon, I., Riano, L., McDonald, C.G., He, Q., Perez-Tejada, J.M., Arrigo, M., Darrell, T., Kuchenbecker, K.J.: Robotic learning of haptic adjectives through physical interaction. Robot. Auton. Syst. **63**, 279–292 (2015)
8. Decherchi, S., Gastaldo, P., Dahiya, R.S., Valle, M., Zunino, R.: Tactile-data classification of contact materials using computational intelligence. IEEE Trans. Robot. **27**(3), 635–639 (2011)
9. Gao, S., Tsang, I., Chia, L.T.: Kernel sparse representation for image classification and face recognition. Comput. Vis.-ECCV **2010**, 1–14 (2010)
10. Gao, S., Tsang, I.W., Chia, L.T.: Sparse representation with kernels. IEEE Trans. Image Process. **22**(2), 423–434 (2013)
11. Harandi, M., Salzmann, M.: Riemannian coding and dictionary learning: Kernels to the rescue. In: Proceedings of the IEEE Conference on Computer Vision and Pattern Recognition pp. 3926–3935. (2015)
12. Ho, J., Xie, Y., Vemuri, B.: On a nonlinear generalization of sparse coding and dictionary learning. In: International conference on machine learning, pp. 1480–1488. (2013)
13. Huang, G.B.: An insight into extreme learning machines: random neurons, random features and kernels. Cogn. Comput. **6**(3), 376–390 (2014)
14. Huang, G.B., Zhou, H., Ding, X., Zhang, R.: Extreme learning machine for regression and multiclass classification. IEEE Trans. Syst. Man Cybern. Part B (Cybern.) **42**(2), 513–529 (2012)

15. Huang, G.B., Zhu, Q.Y., Siew, C.K.: Extreme learning machine: theory and applications. Neurocomputing **70**(1), 489–501 (2006)
16. Iosifidis, A., Tefas, A., Pitas, I.: On the kernel extreme learning machine classifier. Pattern Recognit. Lett. **54**, 11–17 (2015)
17. Kim, M.: Efficient kernel sparse coding via first-order smooth optimization. IEEE Trans. Neural Netw. Learn. Syst. **25**(8), 1447–1459 (2014)
18. Kurdyka, K.: On gradients of functions definable in o-minimal structures. Annales de l'institut Fourier **48**(3), 769–784 (1998)
19. Li, P., Wang, Q., Zuo, W., Zhang, L.: Log-euclidean kernels for sparse representation and dictionary learning. In: Proceedings of the IEEE International Conference on Computer Vision, pp. 1601–1608. (2013)
20. Li, Y., Ngom, A.: Fast kernel sparse representation approaches for classification. In: 2012 IEEE 12th International Conference on Data Mining (ICDM), pp. 966–971. IEEE (2012)
21. Liu, B.D., Wang, Y.X., Shen, B., Zhang, Y.J., Hebert, M.: Self-explanatory sparse representation for image classification. ECCV **2**, 600–616 (2014)
22. Liu, H., Yu, L., Wang, W., Sun, F.: Extreme learning machine for time sequence classification. Neurocomputing **174**, 322–330 (2016)
23. Nie, F., Wang, H., Huang, H., Ding, C.H.: Early active learning via robust representation and structured sparsity. In: IJCAI pp. 1572–1578. (2013)
24. Shojaeilangari, S., Yau, W.Y., Nandakumar, K., Li, J., Teoh, E.K.: Robust representation and recognition of facial emotions using extreme sparse learning. IEEE Trans. Image Process. **24**(7), 2140–2152 (2015)
25. Tang, J., Deng, C., Huang, G.B.: Extreme learning machine for multilayer perceptron. IEEE Trans. Neural Netw. Learn. Syst. **27**(4), 809–821 (2016)
26. Van Nguyen, H., Patel, V.M., Nasrabadi, N.M., Chellappa, R.: Design of non-linear kernel dictionaries for object recognition. IEEE Trans. Image Process. **22**(12), 5123–5135 (2013)
27. Yang, Y., Wu, Q.J.: Multilayer extreme learning machine with subnetwork nodes for representation learning. IEEE Trans. Cybern. **46**(11), 2570–2583 (2016)
28. Zhang, L., Zhang, D.: Domain adaptation extreme learning machines for drift compensation in e-nose systems. IEEE Trans. Instrum. Meas. **64**(7), 1790–1801 (2015)
29. Zhang, S., Kasiviswanathan, S., Yuen, P.C., Harandi, M.: Online dictionary learning on symmetric positive definite manifolds with vision applications. In: AAAI, pp. 3165–3173. (2015)

Chapter 5
Tactile Adjective Understanding Using Structured Output-Associated Dictionary Learning

Abstract Since many properties perceived by the tactile sensors can be characterized by adjectives, it is reasonable to develop a set of tactile adjectives for the tactile understanding. This formulates the tactile understanding as a multilabel classification problem. This chapter exploits the intrinsic relation between different adjective labels and develops a novel dictionary learning method which is improved by introducing the structured output association information. Such a method makes use of the label correlation information and is more suitable for the multilabel tactile understanding task. In addition, two iterative algorithms are developed to solve the dictionary learning and classifier design problems, respectively. Finally, extensive experimental validations are performed on the publicly available tactile sequence dataset PHAC-2 and show the advantages of the proposed method.

5.1 Introduction

Many physical properties of objects, such as *hard* or *soft*, are very difficult to visually ascertain, particularly without some kind of object manipulation [8, 9, 11]. For example, a cotton sheet and a white paper are difficult to be distinguished by their color, while their softness and elasticity work well. In practice, humans usually glean object properties through active manipulation by hands. Therefore, tactile sensing and feedback play extremely important roles for humans to perceive, understand, and manipulate in the real world. Due to its importance, tactile understanding has now been extensively used for material recognition.

On the other hand, the tactile classification is highly related to the material recognition problem. For example, classifying a surface as *foam* implies the presence of some tactile properties, such as *absorbent*, *bumpy*, *compressible*, and *soft*. However, many exceptions exist. For example, different bottle surfaces have vastly different hardness properties: A glass bottle is *hard*, but an aluminum bottle is *soft*. Consequently, tactile understanding goes beyond simply identifying object materials and exhibits great challenges.

Since many properties perceived by the tactile sensors can be characterized by adjectives such as *hard*, *soft*, *smooth*, it is reasonable to develop a set of tactile

© Springer Nature Singapore Pte Ltd. 2018
H. Liu and F. Sun, *Robotic Tactile Perception and Understanding*,
https://doi.org/10.1007/978-981-10-6171-4_5

adjectives for the tactile understanding. Reference [6] demonstrated that a rich and diverse tactile measurement system that measured temperature, compliance, roughness, and friction was key to accurately discerning between tactile adjectives such as *sticky* and *rough*. Reference [3] detailed the collection of tactile classification datasets and concentrated on classifying objects with binary tactile adjectives. This work relied on handcrafted features for tactile classification. Recently, Ref. [5] proposed a deep learning method of classifying surfaces with tactile adjectives from both visual and physical interaction data. In [13], the authors proposed a framework that conceptualized adjectives and nouns as separate categories that were linked to and interact with each other. They demonstrated how those co-learned concepts might be useful for a cognitive robot.

Objects usually exhibit multiple physical properties. Therefore, the tactile adjective classification can be formulated as a multilabel classification problem. See Fig. 5.1 for some examples. However, existing work such as [3, 5] decomposed the problem into a set of independent binary classification problems. That is to say, each object is described by a set of multiple binary labels corresponding to the existence or absence of each of the tactile adjectives.Such a strategy totally neglected the interdependencies among multiple binary prediction tasks. For example, *absorbent* usually co-occurs with *compressible*; *cool* usually co-occurs with *smooth* and *solid*. On the contrary, *hard* never co-occurs with *soft*. Such relations cannot be exploited by the above simple strategy.

Different from the conventional multiclass problems where each sample should be mapped to a single class label, multilabel classification needs to map each sample to typically a few interdependent class labels in a relatively large output space. The goal of multilabel classification is therefore to discover the underlying label correlation structure to improve the classification performance. However, existing work on multilabel classification is mainly concentrated on the applications of image, video, and text. In [10], an image is typically associated with multiple labels, and its visual representation reflects the combination of the involved labels. It is observed that each label corresponds to certain local patch in the image. Therefore, the entire image representation can be decomposed into a set of local label representations corresponding to the labels associated with an image. However, the tactile signal does not exhibit such properties. That is to say, it is difficult, if impossible, to segment the tactile signal according to different labels.

In this chapter, the intrinsic relation among different adjective labels is exploited and a novel dictionary learning method which is improved by introducing the structured output association information is developed. This method makes use of the label correlation information and is more suitable for the multilabel tactile understanding task. Two iterative algorithms are also developed to solve the dictionary learning and classifier design problems, respectively. Extensive experimental validations on the public available tactile sequence dataset are implemented and show the advantages of the proposed method.

The rest of this chapter is organized as follows: Sect. 5.2 represents the problem formulation and the objective functions of the proposed structured output-associated

Fig. 5.1 Some representative examples which are adopted from PHAC-2 dataset [3]. The red text indicates the name of the object, and the following black texts show the corresponding tactile adjectives. Please note that the images are just used for visualization illustration but not for algorithm development. From such examples, two observations can be made: (1) The adjective recognition is indeed a multilabel classification problem. (2) The *absorbent* usually co-occurs with *compressible*; *cool* usually co-occurs with *smooth* and *solid*. On the contrary, *hard* never co-occurs with *soft*. Such correlation will be further analyzed in this chapter, and such relation will be exploited to improve the tactile understanding performance

dictionary learning method. In Sect. 5.3, the optimization algorithm is introduced. The classifier design is presented in Sect. 5.4, and the experimental results are given in Sect. 5.5.

5.2 Problem Formulation

The measurable space of interested tactile signals is denoted by $\mathcal{T}$. Some representative examples are shown in Fig. 5.2. Given a set of C adjective labels and a set of N training sequences $\{\mathbb{T}_i\}_{i=1}^{N} \subset \mathcal{T}$. The element of the label vector $z_i \in \mathbb{R}^C$ corresponding to the ith sample is defined as

$$z_i(c) = \begin{cases} +1 & \text{If label } c \text{ is associated with sample} \mathbb{T}_i \\ -1 & \text{Othewise} \end{cases} \tag{5.1}$$

for $c = 1, 2, \ldots, C$.

The goal in multilabel tactile adjective classification is to label an unseen tactile sample $\mathbb{T} \in \mathcal{T}$ with the subset of relevant adjective labels from the prespecified adjective set. A tactile sample can be labeled with any of the 2^C possible subsets.

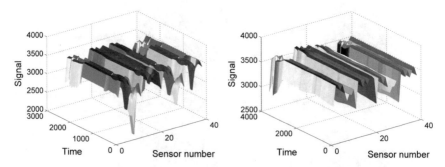

Fig. 5.2 Two representative tactile sequences with different adjective labels. The samples are adopted from PHAC-2 dataset [3]

The main challenge, therefore, lies in optimizing over this exponentially large label space subject to label correlations.

The task of tactile dictionary learning aims to obtain a compact dictionary $\mathfrak{D} = [\boldsymbol{d}_1, ..., \boldsymbol{d}_K]$, where $K < N$ is the size of the dictionary, and $\boldsymbol{d}_k \in \mathcal{H}_T$ for $k = 1, 2, \ldots, K$. Such a dictionary should effectively summarize the whole training set $\{\mathbb{T}_i\}_{i=1}^{N}$ and provides a good basis for sparse coding in the implicit feature space.

By denoting $\Phi(\mathfrak{T}) = [\Phi(\mathbb{T}_1), \ldots, \Phi(\mathbb{T}_N)]$, the following kernel dictionary learning problem is formulated:

$$
\begin{aligned}
\min_{\mathfrak{D}, X} \quad & ||\Phi(\mathfrak{T}) - \mathfrak{D}X||_F^2 + \alpha ||X||_{1,1} \\
\text{s.t.} \quad & ||\boldsymbol{d}_k||_2 = 1 \ \text{ for } \ k = 1, 2, \ldots, K,
\end{aligned}
\tag{5.2}
$$

where $X = [\boldsymbol{x}_1, \boldsymbol{x}_2, \ldots, \boldsymbol{x}_N] \in R^{K \times N}$ is the sparse coding matrix and α is used to control the sparsity. Please note that $||X||_{1,1}$ is the sum of the absolute values of all elements in X. Therefore,

$$
||X||_{1,1} = \sum_{i=1}^{N} ||\boldsymbol{x}_i||_1.
$$

It is well known that the optimization problem in Eq. (5.2) cannot be directly solved since the mapping $\Phi(\cdot)$ is not explicitly represented. Fortunately, the kernel trick provides an effective method to avoid dealing with the mapping $\Phi(\cdot)$ [4, 7]. However, the dictionary learning problem is still nontrivial since the dictionary atoms $\boldsymbol{d}_k$ lie in the implicit feature space. For general cases of kernels, the *Representer Theorem* can be used, which indicates that the dictionary $\mathfrak{D}$ can be represented by

$$
\mathfrak{D} = \Phi(\mathfrak{T})A,
\tag{5.3}
$$

where $A = [\boldsymbol{a}_1, \boldsymbol{a}_2, \ldots, \boldsymbol{a}_K] \in R^{N \times K}$ is the reconstruction matrix. This means that the dictionary atoms can be linearly reconstructed by the training samples in the feature space. Furthermore, the constraint condition on the dictionary atoms $||\boldsymbol{d}_k||_2 = 1$ is in fact $||\Phi(\mathfrak{T})\boldsymbol{a}_k||_2 = 1$, which can be equivalently transformed as

$$\boldsymbol{a}_k^T \kappa(\mathfrak{T}, \mathfrak{T})\boldsymbol{a}_k = 1,$$

where $\kappa(\mathfrak{T}, \mathfrak{T}) \in R^{N \times N}$ is the kernel matrix over all of the training samples. The (i, j)th element of $\kappa(\mathfrak{T}, \mathfrak{T})$ is defined as $\kappa(\mathbb{T}_i, \mathbb{T}_j) = \Phi^T(\mathbb{T}_i)\Phi(\mathbb{T}_j)$. Therefore, the kernel dictionary learning problem can be reformulated as

$$\min_{A,X} \quad ||\Phi(\mathfrak{T}) - \Phi(\mathfrak{T})AX||_F^2 + \alpha||X||_{1,1}$$
$$\text{s.t.} \quad \boldsymbol{a}_k^T \kappa(\mathfrak{T}, \mathfrak{T})\boldsymbol{a}_k = 1. \tag{5.4}$$

It can be observed by this formulation that the original data matrix $\Phi(\mathfrak{T})$ is compressed as a reduced dictionary $\mathfrak{D} = \Phi(\mathfrak{T})A$ and each sample $\mathbb{T}_i \in \mathfrak{T}$ is represented as K-dimensional sparse vector $\boldsymbol{x}_i \in R^K$. The optimization model in (5.4) provides a great advantage since it does not search the dictionary atoms in the feature space, but only calculates the coefficient matrix A. Therefore, this formulation can be used for any type of kernel functions.

After getting the sparse code $\boldsymbol{x}_i$ for the original sample $\mathbb{T}_i$, the conventional classifier can be used for classification. However, such a method exists an obvious disadvantage that the dictionary learning stage and the classifier design stage are independent. This limits the performance of the dictionary. A better solution is to jointly learn the dictionary and the classifier, i.e., introducing the discriminative capability into the dictionary learning.

One straightforward approach for multilabel classification is to decompose the multilabel learning problem into a set of independent binary classification problems. According to this idea, a new label vector $\boldsymbol{l}_c \in \mathbb{R}^N$ is defined for each label $c = 1, 2, \ldots, C$, as

$$l_c(i) = \begin{cases} +1 & z_i(c) = +1 \\ -1 & z_i(c) = -1 \end{cases} \tag{5.5}$$

and the following C independent supervised dictionary learning problems are formulated:

$$\min_{A_c,X_c,\boldsymbol{w}_c} \quad ||\Phi(\mathfrak{T}) - \Phi(\mathfrak{T})A_c X_c||_F^2 + \alpha||X_c||_{1,1}$$
$$+ \beta||\boldsymbol{l}_c^T - \boldsymbol{w}_c^T X_c||_2^2 + \gamma||\boldsymbol{w}_c||_2^2 \tag{5.6}$$

$$\text{s.t.} \quad \boldsymbol{a}_{c,k}^T \kappa(\mathfrak{T}, \mathfrak{T})\boldsymbol{a}_{c,k} = 1,$$

for $c = 1, 2, \ldots, C$. In the above equation, $A_c \in \mathbb{R}^{N \times K}$ and $X_c \in \mathbb{R}^{K \times N}$ are the dictionary coefficient matrix and coding matrix for the cth task, respectively, and $\boldsymbol{w}_c \in \mathbb{R}^K$ is the classifier coefficient vector. The parameters β and γ are used to control the importance of the corresponding regularization terms.

However, the above approach considers each adjective as an independent class task, and the multilabel correlations are neglected. It is well known that the task correlations are helpful for the prediction. Therefore, the shared common dictionary can be used with different designed classifiers for each adjective classification task. This leads to the following optimization problem:

$$\min_{A,X,w_c} ||\Phi(\mathfrak{T}) - \Phi(\mathfrak{T})AX||_F^2 + \alpha||X||_{1,1} + \beta \sum_{c=1}^{C} ||l_c^T - w_c^T X||_2^2 + \gamma \sum_{c=1}^{C} ||w_c||_2^2$$
$$\text{s.t.} \quad a_k^T \kappa(\mathfrak{T}, \mathfrak{T}) a_k = 1,$$

$$(5.7)$$

for $c = 1, 2, \ldots, C$ and $w_c \in \mathbb{R}^K$ is the classifier vector.

Nevertheless, the above formulation does not explicitly incorporate the output association information. In fact, the output components can be considered as auxiliary features and used to complement the more standard input features. It is assumed that the output $z_i(c)$ is related to all the other outputs $z_{i,\neg c}$, which is defined as

$$z_{i,\neg c} = [z_i(1), \ldots, z_i(c-1), z_i(c+1), \ldots, z_i(C)]^T$$

and the discriminative error can be minimized with the linear form

$$z_i(c) - w_c^T x_i - w_c^T z_{i,\neg c}, \tag{5.8}$$

where $w_c \in \mathbb{R}^K$ and $w_c \in \mathbb{R}^{C-1}$ are the classifier coefficient vectors for the cth classification task.

By incorporating the above error term into the original dictionary learning objective function (5.4), the proposed structured output-associated dictionary learning problem is formulated as

$$\min_{A,X,W,W} ||\Phi(\mathfrak{T}) - \Phi(\mathfrak{T})AX||_F^2 + \alpha||X||_{1,1} + \beta \sum_{c=1}^{C} \sum_{i=1}^{N} (z_i(c) - w_c^T x_i - w_c^T z_{i,\neg c})^2$$
$$+ \gamma(||W||_F^2 + ||W||_F^2)$$

$$\text{s.t.} \quad a_k^T \kappa(\mathfrak{T}, \mathfrak{T}) a_k = 1,$$

$$(5.9)$$

where $W = [w_1, w_2, \ldots, w_C] \in \mathbb{R}^{K \times C}$ and $W = [w_1, w_2, \ldots, w_C] \in \mathbb{R}^{(C-1) \times C}$ are classifier parameter matrices which represent the relationship between inputs and outputs.

In Fig. 5.3, a schematic plot is plotted to show the whole procedure of the joint coding and structured output labeling.

Remark 5.1 In Eq. (5.8), only the linear dependence relation is considered between the inputs and outputs. To better characterize the complicated relation between them, the kernel function can employed to design the nonlinear discriminative regularization term

$$z_i(c) - w_c^T \phi(x_i) - w_c^T \psi(z_{i,\neg c}), \tag{5.10}$$

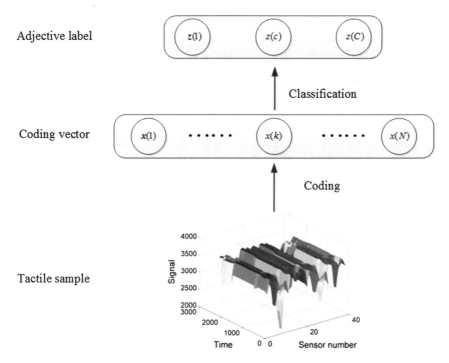

Adjective label

Coding vector

Tactile sample

Classification

Coding

Fig. 5.3 The coding and labeling principle illustration. The tactile sample is coded as a K-dimensional vector, and a classifier could be developed using such a coding vector. The red lines indicate that the structured output association information can be exploited to improve the multilabel classification performance

or even

$$z_i(c) - w_c^T \phi(x_i, z_{i,\neg c}), \tag{5.11}$$

where $\phi(\cdot)$ and $\psi(\cdot)$ are some nonlinear mapping functions which can be explicitly designed by the user or be implicitly represented by the suitably defined kernel functions. Adopting this strategy helps us to obtain better representation of the input–output relation but introduces more tuning parameters and complicates the solving procedure. In this work, it is found that the simple linear dependence relation in Eq. (5.8) can work well in our multilabel tactile understanding tasks.

5.3 Optimization Algorithm

Since the optimization problem in Eq. (5.9) is obviously nonconvex and nonsmooth, the alternative optimization method is adopted to solve it. The algorithm can be divided into the following stages. For conveniences, the superscript t is used to represent the solutions at the tth iteration.

5.3.1 Calculating the Sparse Coding Vectors

This step updates the coding vectors $X^{(t+1)}$, given the values of $A^{(t)}$, $W^{(t)}$, and $U^{(t)}$. Please note that each column of X can be calculated separately and therefore the problem is reduced to

$$\min_{x_i} \; ||\Phi(\mathbb{T}_i) - \Phi(\mathfrak{T})A^{(t)}x_i||_2^2 + \alpha||x_i||_1 + \beta \sum_{c=1}^{C} (\hat{z}_{ci}^{(t)} - w_c^{(t)T}x_i)^2, \qquad (5.12)$$

where $\hat{z}_{ci}^{(t)} = z_i(c) - w_c^{(t)T}z_{i,\neg c}$.
    By denoting

$$\hat{z}_i^{(t)} = [\hat{z}_{1i}^{(t)}, \hat{z}_{2i}^{(t)}, \dots, \hat{z}_{Ci}^{(t)}]^T,$$

the third term in the above equation can be rewritten as $\beta||\hat{z}_i^{(t)} - W^{(t)}x_i||_2^2$.
    Due to the relation

$$||\Phi(\mathbb{T}_i) - \Phi(\mathfrak{T})A^{(t)}x_i||_2^2 = \Phi^T(\mathbb{T}_i)\Phi(\mathbb{T}_i) - 2\kappa(\mathbb{T}_i, \mathfrak{T})A^{(t)}x_i + x_i^T A^{(t)T}\kappa(\mathfrak{T}, \mathfrak{T})A^{(t)}x_i$$

and

$$||\hat{z}_i^{(t)} - W^{(t)}x_i||_2^2 = \hat{z}_i^{(t)T}\hat{z}_i^{(t)} - 2\hat{z}_i^{(t)}W^{(t)}x_i + x_i^T W^{(t)T}W^{(t)T}x_i,$$

Equation (5.12) can be expanded as

$$\min_{x_i} -2(\kappa^T(\mathbb{T}_i, \mathfrak{T})A^{(t)} + \beta\hat{z}_i^{(t)T}W^{(t)})x_i + x_i^T(A^{(t)T}\kappa(\mathfrak{T}, \mathfrak{T})A^{(t)} + \beta W^{(t)}W^{(t)T})x_i$$
$$+ \alpha||x_i||_1.$$

$$(5.13)$$

This problem can be easily solved using any efficient l_1 optimization algorithm such as feature-sign search [4] or alternating direction method of multipliers [2]. Also, popular sparse solver software such as SPAMS [12] can be employed to solve this problem.
    Using the above procedure for $i = 1, 2, \dots, N$, the updated values can be obtained as

$$X^{(t+1)} = [x_1^{(t+1)}, \dots, x_N^{(t+1)}].$$

5.3.2 Calculating the Dictionary Atoms

This step updates the dictionary coefficient matrix. At the $(t + 1)$th iteration, $X^{(t+1)}$, $W^{(t)}$, and $U^{(t)}$ are given. The optimization problem is reduced to

$$\min_{A} \ ||\Phi(\mathfrak{T}) - \Phi(\mathfrak{T})AX^{(t+1)}||_F^2$$
$$\text{s.t. } \ a_k^T \kappa(\mathfrak{T}, \mathfrak{T})a_k = 1, \tag{5.14}$$

By defining $\bar{A} = X^{(t+1)^T}(X^{(t+1)}X^{(t+1)^T})^{-1}$ and

$$a_k^{(t+1)} = \frac{\bar{a}_k}{\sqrt{\bar{a}_k^T \kappa(\mathfrak{T}, \mathfrak{T})\bar{a}_k}},$$

where $\bar{a}_k$ is the kth column of $\bar{A}$, the updated values can be obtained as

$$A^{(t+1)} = [a_1^{(t+1)}, \dots, a_K^{(t+1)}].$$

5.3.3 Calculating the Classifier Parameters

This step updates the classifier parameters W and U. At the $(t+1)$th iteration, $X^{(t+1)}$ and $A^{(t+1)}$ are given. Please note that each column of W and U can be calculated separately and therefore the problem reduces to

$$\min_{w_c, u_c} \ \beta \sum_{i=1}^{N} (z_i(c) - w_c^T x_i^{(t+1)} - u_c^T z_{i,\neg c})^2 \tag{5.15}$$
$$+ \gamma (||w_c||_2^2 + ||u_c||_2^2)$$

By denoting $\bar{w}_c = [w_c^T \ u_c^T]^T$ and $\bar{x}_i^{(t+1)} = [x_i^{(t+1)T} \ z_{i,\neg c}^T]^T$, the above optimization problem can be reformulated as

$$\min_{\bar{w}_c} \ \beta \sum_{i=1}^{N} (z_i(c) - \bar{w}_c^T \bar{x}_i^{(t+1)})^2 + \gamma ||\bar{w}_c||_2^2, \tag{5.16}$$

which admits the following solution

$$\bar{w}_c = \{\beta \bar{X}^{(t+1)} \bar{X}^{(t+1)T} + \gamma I_{K+C-1}\}^{-1}(\beta \bar{X}^{(t+1)}(z^c)^T),$$

where $\bar{X}^{(t+1)} = [\bar{x}_1^{(t+1)}, \bar{x}_2^{(t+1)}, \dots, \bar{x}_N^{(t+1)}]$; $z^c = [z_1(c), \dots, z_N(c)]$; and I_{K+C-1} is the $(K+C-1) \times (K+C-1)$ identity matrix.

Furthermore, the first K rows of $\bar{w}_c$ can easily extracted as $w_c^{(t+1)}$ and other $C-1$ rows of $\bar{w}_c$ as $u_c^{(t+1)}$.

Using the above procedure for $c = 1, 2, \dots, C$, the updated values can be obtained as

$$W^{(t+1)} = [w_1^{(t+1)}, \dots, w_C^{(t+1)}]$$

and

$$U^{(t+1)} = [u_1^{(t+1)}, \ldots, u_c^{(t+1)}].$$

5.3.4 Algorithm Summarization

With the above updating rules, the proposed algorithm is summarized in Algorithm 2. The convergent condition can be triggered when the change of the objective function is smaller than a prescribed tolerant error, or the prescribed maximum iteration number is achieved. In this work, the latter strategy is adopted and the maximum iteration number is set to 30. The initial value of A is set as $[I_K, O_{(N-K) \times K}]^T$. This implies that the first K samples in the training sample set are selected to construct the initial dictionary.

Algorithm 2 Structured Output-Associated Dictionary Learning

Input: Tactile samples set $\{\mathbb{T}_i\}$ for $i = 1, 2, \cdots, N$, the size of dictionary K, the parameters α, β, γ
Output: Solutions $X \in R^{K \times N}$, $A \in R^{N \times K}$, $W \in R^{K \times C}$ and $U \in R^{(C-1) \times C}$.

1: **while** Not convergent **do**
2:   Fix A, W, U and update X according to Section 5.3.1.
3:   Fix X, W, U and update A according to Section 5.3.2.
4:   Fix A, X and update W, U according to Section 5.3.3.
5: **end while**

5.4 Classifier Design

The above learning procedure provides the solutions which are denoted as A^*, W^*, and U^*. Then they are used to design the classifier. Different from previous supervised dictionary learning method which did not consider the output association, an algorithm should be carefully designed for the classifier to preserve the output-associative information.

For a test sample $\mathbb{T} \in \mathfrak{T}$, the label vector is denoted as $l \in \{-1, +1\}^C$ which should be determined. $z \in \mathbb{R}^C$ is used as the relaxed label vector and solve the following joint coding and labeling problem

$$\min_{x, z} \ ||\Phi(\mathbb{T}) - \Phi(\mathfrak{T})A^* x||_F^2 + \alpha ||x||_1 + \beta \sum_{c=1}^{C} (z(c) - u_c^{*T} z_{\neg c} - w_c^{*T} x)^2, \quad (5.17)$$

This problem is also nonconvex, and therefore, the alternative optimization method is resorted. The iterations are divided into the following stages. For convenience, the superscript t is used to indicate the iteration number.

1. Update x as

$$x^{(t+1)} = \underset{x}{\text{argmin}} \ ||\Phi(\mathbb{T}) - \Phi(\mathfrak{T})A^*x||_F^2$$
$$+ \alpha||x||_1 + \beta \sum_{c=1}^{C}(z^{(t)}(c) - u_c^{*T}z_{\neg c}^{(t)} - w_c^{*T}x)^2. \quad (5.18)$$

This problem is similar to the coding problem and can be solved efficiently.
2. Update z as

$$z^{(t+1)} = \underset{z}{\text{argmin}} \ \sum_{c=1}^{C}(\hat{z}_c - w_c^{*T}x^{(t+1)})^2. \quad (5.19)$$

Note $\hat{z}_c$ can be represented as $\bar{u}_c^{*T}z$, where

$$\bar{u}_c^* = [u_c^*(1), \ldots, u_c^*(c-1), 1, u_c^*(c+1), \ldots, u_c^*(C)]^T.$$

Therefore, the objective function in Eq. (5.19) can be represented as

$$||\bar{U}^{*T}z - W^{*T}x^{(t+1)}||_2^2,$$

where $\bar{U}^* = [\bar{u}_1^*, \ldots, \bar{u}_C^*]$ and $\bar{W}^* = [\bar{w}_1^*, \ldots, \bar{w}_C^*]$. The solution can thus be obtained as

$$z^{(t+1)} = (\bar{U}^*\bar{U}^{*T})^{-1}\bar{U}^*W^{*T}x^{(t+1)}.$$

In practice, the developed algorithm follows the suggestions given by [1] to initialize the above optimization problem using prediction given by classifier trained on independent outputs. This strategy significantly improves the convergence speed compared to random initialization. In our experiment, the converged solution z^* can be obtained after at most four iterations.

5.5 Experimental Results

5.5.1 Data Description and Experimental Setting

The approach is demonstrated on the Penn Haptic Adjective Corpus 2 (PHAC-2) dataset, which was originally developed in [3]. The PHAC-2 dataset contains tactile signals of 60 household objects. Each object is explored by a pair of SynTouch biomimetic tactile sensors (BioTacs), which were mounted on the gripper of a Willow Garage Personal Robot2 (PR2). Each object was felt with four exploratory procedures. The BioTac sensor generates five types of signals: low-frequency fluid pressure, high-frequency fluid vibrations, core temperature, core temperature change, and 19 electrode impedance which are spatially distributed across the sensor. Although the joint positions and gripper velocity and acceleration are available, this concentrates on classifying the tactile signals using the electrode impedances. Therefore, the electrode impedance data from the two BioTac sensors are concatenated to get $d = 19 \times 2 = 38$-dimensional tactile sequence signals (see Fig. 5.2 for some representative tactile sequences). For each object, ten trials of each exploratory procedures were performed and 600 tactile sample sequences were obtained. The GA kernel is adopted for kernel evaluation.

Each object is described with a set of 24 binary labels, corresponding to the existence or absence of each of the 24 tactile adjectives (e.g., *hard* or *soft*). The link information is shown in Fig. 5.4, and the calculated correlation information is

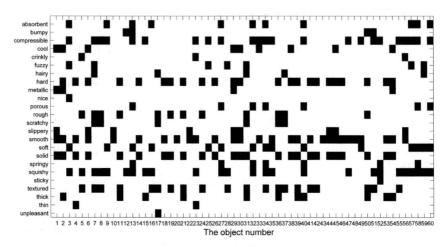

Fig. 5.4 The link information between the adjective and the object number. The occupied box shows that the corresponding object has the exhibited adjective property

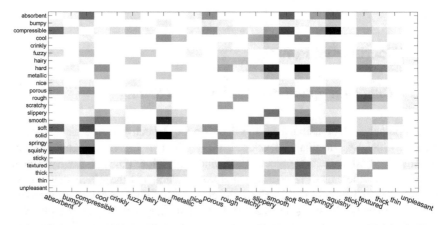

Fig. 5.5 The correlation of multilabel adjectives. This figure shows that *solid* is highly related to *hard*; *compressible* is rather related to *squishy* and *soft*. All of them are consistent to our intuitive knowledge

detailed in Fig. 5.5, which shows that there indeed exists obvious correlation between some adjectives, such as *solid-hard, compressible-squishy, soft-compressible*. For the three adjectives *nice, sticky,* and *unpleasant*, which exhibit only one positive object instance, it is impossible to construct the positive training and testing sets. Therefore, these three ones are deleted. As a result, there are 21 possible adjective labels and the average number of adjective labels for each sample is 4.2. Fig. 5.6 illustrates the label distribution of tactile adjectives. It shows that *smooth, solid,* and *squishy* are the most three popular adjectives.

The performance evaluation of multilabel learning is very different from that of single-label classification, and the popular Hamming loss is used to evaluate the classification score [14]. For the ith testing sample, $\mathcal{G}_i$ is used as the set of ground-truth labels and $\mathcal{R}_i$ as the adjective label set of the algorithm output. Then, the score is calculated as

$$score(i) = 1 - \frac{1}{C}|\mathcal{G}_i \ominus \mathcal{R}_i|,$$

where $\ominus$ stands for the symmetric difference between two sets, and $|\cdot|$ calculates the number of elements in the set. The symmetric difference is the set of elements which are in either of the sets and not in their intersection. For example, if

$$\mathcal{G}_i = \{smooth, rough, cool, squishy\}$$

and

$$\mathcal{R}_i = \{smooth, solid, squishy\},$$

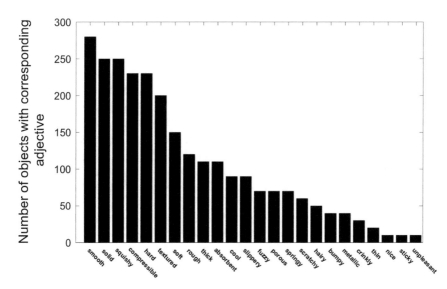

Fig. 5.6 The label distribution of the PHAC-2 dataset. The adjectives *nice, sticky,* and *unpleasant* are not used in the experimental validation

then it can be concluded that

$$\mathcal{G}_i \ominus \mathcal{R}_i = \{rough, cool, solid\}.$$

If $\mathcal{G}_i = \mathcal{R}_i$, then it leads to $\mathcal{G}_i \ominus \mathcal{R}_i = \emptyset$ and therefore the score is 1. Otherwise, only when one of $\mathcal{G}_i$ and $\mathcal{R}_i$ is a full set and the other one is an empty set, the zero score can be obtained. The overall performance is evaluated by averaged score over all of the testing samples.

5.5.2 Performance Comparison

To show the advantages of the proposed method, a fair comparison is made with the following classifiers.

1. Separate k-Nearest Neighborhood (S-kNN) method. It decomposes the original problem into 21 separate binary classification problems (one per adjective) and uses the conventional k-nearest neighborhood method with the GA kernel-induced distance to determine whether the adjective emerges or not. This method does not consider the correlations of labels and serves as a baseline. In this experiment, the value is set as $k = 1$ because increasing the value of k may deteriorate the performance.
2. Multilabel kNN (ML-kNN) method [14]. For each test sample, it firstly identifies its kNNs using the GA kernel-induced distance in the training set. After that, based on statistical information gained from the label sets of these neighboring instances, i.e., the number of neighboring instances belonging to each possible class, maximum a posteriori principle is utilized to determine the label set for the unseen instance. In this chapter, the value is set as $k = 5$ because the experimental results show that larger k does not result in better performance.
3. Separate Dictionary Learning (S-DL) method. This method solves 21 separate optimization problems in Eq. (5.6) to obtain the dictionaries and classifiers. Obviously, the label correlation is not considered in this method.
4. Common Dictionary Learning (C-DL) method. This method solves the optimization problem in Eq. (5.7) which learns a common dictionary and separate classifier for each adjective. Please note this method uses a shared dictionary to construct the connections of all the classification tasks but still does not consider the label correlation.
5. Structured Output-associated Dictionary Learning (SO-DL) method. This method is developed in this work and solves the optimization problem in Eq. (5.9) and explicitly incorporates the effect of label correlations.

In Table 5.1, the information is given to indicate whether some method requires training stage, whether it considers the task correlation, and whether it exploits the label correlation. The task correlation of C-DL and SO-DL is exploited by utilizing

Table 5.1 Method comparison

Method	S-kNN	ML-kNN	S-DL	C-DL	SO-DL
Training	χ	χ	✓	✓	✓
Task correlation	χ	χ	χ	✓	✓
Output correlation	χ	✓	χ	χ	✓

the commonly shared dictionary, and the label correlation of SO-DL is exploited by the introduced output association information.

For S-DL, C-DL, and SO-DL, the dictionary size K is set as the 60% of the number of training samples and other parameters are extensively tuned to get the best results. In the next section, the parameters' effect on the performance will be demonstrated.

The 60 objects are partitioned into five split cases: training/testing = 5/5, 6/4, 7/3, 8/2, and 9/1. For each split case, the objects are randomly split as training set and testing set for ten trials, and the averaged recognition scores are reported. Similar to [3], there is no same object to appear in both the train and test split. This permits us to investigate the capability of the algorithm to deal with new or unseen objects. Figure 5.7 shows the performance of the five cases. The proposed SO-DL method consistently outperforms the other methods. The ML-kNN method, which also incorporates the label correlation information, performs better than S-kNN and is competitive to S-DL and C-DL, but worse than SO-DL. From those results, the following observations are made.

1. S-kNN performs worse than all of the other methods. The reason is obvious: Without considering the correlations of multiple adjectives, it is very difficult for

Fig. 5.7 The performance score for the five train/test splits

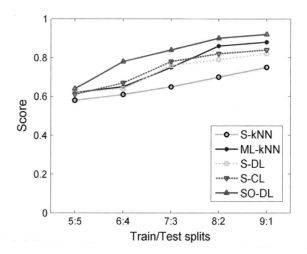

such a method to get satisfactory performance over all of the adjectives. Similarly, S-DL performs better than S-kNN by a very small margin.

2. ML-kNN, which explicitly incorporates the correlation information of adjectives, performs better than S-kNN and S-DL. On the other hand, it is found that C-DL, which just uses the shared common dictionary but does not incorporate the output correlation, obtains similar results with ML-kNN in most cases. The possible reason is that the sparse coding strategy introduces more discriminative information. Please note ML-kNN is just a lazy classifier and does not exploit the discriminative information. From such a comparison, the power of dictionary learning and sparse coding can be observed.

3. The proposed SO-DL method performs better than all of the other methods for all cases. The gained improvement originates from two aspects: (1) the discriminative capability introduced by the dictionary learning and sparse coding; (2) the correlation information of the adjective labels.

4. For the case of 5/5 split, the performance gained by SO-DL is small, while for other cases, the improvement is significant. This is partially due to the fact that the correlation information can be exploited from more training samples.

In Table 5.2, some representative results using different methods are listed. Some explanations are given as follows.

For the sample of *white foam*, the adjective *porous* is difficult to be perceived. However, since *porous* exhibits some correlations with *absorbent*, *compressible*, *soft*, and *squishy*, it is successfully found by the proposed method. ML-kNN, though adopts the multilabel correlation information, fails to find it. The possible reason is that the correlation of *porous* with other adjectives is not strong enough for ML-kNN to work. This example also shows that the proposed method exploits more information than ML-kNN.

For the sample of *toilet paper*, S-kNN and S-DL wrongly find *textured*. Such mistakes do not occur with ML-kNN and SO-DL since the label correlation is fully exploited. However, the adjective *fuzzy*, though can be found by S-DL and S-CL, cannot be found by ML-kNN and SO-DL. The reason is that *fuzzy* exhibits weak correlation with other adjectives and therefore the correlation information in ML-kNN and SO-DL plays very little role.

Both *glass bottle* and *aluminum block* exhibit the property *cool*, which cannot be found by S-kNN, S-DL, and S-CL. Using the proposed method, though no temperature information is used, *cool* can be accurately found. The main reason is that *cool* is related to the adjectives *hard*, *solid*, and *smooth*, and our method can successfully exploit such relations to get correct results.

It is embarrassing to admit that the label correlation does not always play a positive role. One example is that both ML-kNN and SO-DL falsely find *hard* with *aluminum block*. The reason is that *hard* is closely related to *smooth* and *solid*, and therefore, the algorithm would like to assign *hard* adjective to the *aluminum block*, which exhibits the properties of *smooth* and *solid*. It is a pity that *hard* is not included in the ground-truth label set because the annotators feel it is not hard enough.

Table 5.2 Representative results

Method	white foam	toilet paper	glass bottle	aluminum block
Ground-truth	{absorbent, porous, compressible, soft, springy, squishy}	{absorbent, compressible, fuzzy soft, squishy}	{cool, hard, metallic slippery, smooth, solid}	{cool, metallic, slippery smooth, solid}
S-kNN	{compressible, fuzzy soft, scratchy, squishy}	{absorbent, compressible, soft, textured}	{hard, smooth, solid}	{metallic, smooth solid, thick}
ML-kNN	{absorbent, compressible, soft, solid, springy, squishy}	{absorbent, compressible, soft, squishy}	{hard, metallic slippery, smooth, solid}	{cool, hard, metallic, smooth, solid}
S-DL	{compressible, fuzzy, soft, springy, squishy, textured}	{absorbent, compressible, fuzzy soft, squishy, textured}	{hard, slippery, smooth, solid}	{ metallic, slippery smooth, solid}
C-DL	{absorbent, compressible, springy, squishy, thick}	{absorbent, compressible, fuzzy soft}	{hard, slippery smooth, solid, squishy}	{metallic, slippery smooth, solid}
SO-DL	{absorbent, porous, compressible, soft, springy, squishy}	{absorbent, compressible, soft, squishy}	{cool, hard, metallic slippery, smooth, solid}	{cool, hard, metallic, slippery smooth, solid}

5.5.3 Parameter Sensitivity Analysis

In our model (5.9), there are several regularization parameters α, β, and γ. All of them are of physical meanings, and therefore, it is not difficult to tune them for better performance. The results by fixing $\gamma = 10^{-3}$ and varying the values of α and β from 10^{-4} to 10^2 are shown in Fig. 5.8. Those results show that the proposed algorithm works well when the parameter α is in the interval $[10^{-4}, 10^{-3}]$. When β is too large, the reconstruction error term is attenuated and the obtained coding vector cannot reflect the characteristics of the original tactile samples. On the contrary, when β is too small, the role of discriminative classifier becomes weak. Therefore, a properly designed classifier term indeed plays an important role in tactile dictionary learning.

Finally, we fix $\alpha = 0.001$ and $\beta = 0.01$ and vary the ratio K/N for the five split cases, where N is the number of the training samples, and record the scores in Fig. 5.9, which shows that increasing the value of K improves the performance, but the curves almost reach the plateau when the ratio is larger than 0.6. This means that

Fig. 5.8 The sensitivity of α and β

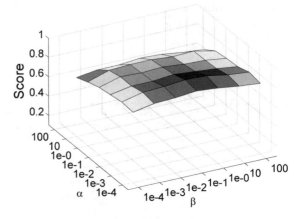

Fig. 5.9 The sensitivity of K for five train/test splits

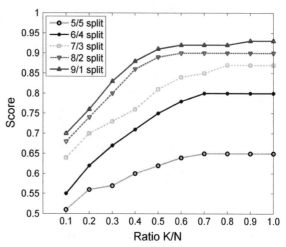

the performance is not sensible to the dictionary size, partially due to the merits of the introduced discriminative learning term.

5.6 Summary

Developing a set of tactile adjectives provides a bridge to understand tactile sense since many properties perceived by the tactile sensors can be characterized by adjectives. However, the adjectives perceived by the tactile sensors exhibit strong and complicated correlations, which provide us challenge and opportunities for cognitive understanding of tactile information. In this chapter, the tactile understanding as a multilabel classification problem is formulated and the intrinsic relation between different adjective labels is exploited by developing a novel dictionary learning method which is improved by introducing the structured output association information. Such a method makes use of the label correlation information and is more suitable for the multilabel tactile understanding task. To solve this problem, two iterative algorithms are developed for dictionary learning and classifier design, respectively. Finally, the adjective correlation on the public available tactile sequence dataset PHAC-2 is analyzed, and extensive experimental validations are performed to show the advantages of the proposed method.

In this chapter, the following findings are concluded:

1. Although tactile sensing is complicated and subtle, it can be well characterized by many adjectives. In practice, tactile adjectives serve as powerful tools to represent the semantic tactile information.
2. By a detailed analysis on the adjectives in the extensive PHAC-2 dataset, it is confirmed that there exists a lot of correlations among the tactile adjectives. This is also consistent with the human's intuition.
3. Exploiting the correlation of tactile adjectives indeed improves the tactile understanding performance. A representative example is that the *cool* property can be found even without the temperature information.

References

1. Bo, L., Sminchisescu, C.: Structured output-associative regression. In: IEEE Conference on Computer Vision and Pattern Recognition, 2009. CVPR 2009, pp. 2403–2410 (2009)
2. Boyd, S., Parikh, N., Chu, E., Peleato, B., Eckstein, J.: Distributed optimization and statistical learning via the alternating direction method of multipliers. Found. Trends®. Mach. Learn. **3**(1), 1–122 (2011)
3. Chu, V., McMahon, I., Riano, L., McDonald, C.G., He, Q., Perez-Tejada, J.M., Arrigo, M., Darrell, T., Kuchenbecker, K.J.: Robotic learning of haptic adjectives through physical interaction. Robot. Auton. Syst. **63**, 279–292 (2015)
4. Gao, S., Tsang, I.W., Chia, L.T.: Sparse representation with kernels. IEEE Trans. Image Process. **22**(2), 423–434 (2013)
5. Gao, Y., Hendricks, L.A., Kuchenbecker, K.J., Darrell, T.: Deep learning for tactile understanding from visual and haptic data. IEEE International Conference on Robotics and Automation (ICRA) **2016**, 536–543 (2016)
6. Griffith, S., Sinapov, J., Sukhoy, V., Stoytchev, A.: A behavior-grounded approach to forming object categories: separating containers from noncontainers. IEEE Trans. Auton. Mental Dev. **4**(1), 54–69 (2012)
7. Harandi, M., Salzmann, M.: Riemannian coding and dictionary learning: kernels to the rescue. In: Proceedings of the IEEE Conference on Computer Vision and Pattern Recognition, pp. 3926–3935 (2015)
8. Hu, X., Zhang, X., Liu, M., Chen, Y., Li, P., Liu, J., Yao, Z., Pei, W., Zhang, C., Chen, H.: High precision intelligent flexible grasping front-end with cmos interface for robots application. Sci. China Inf. Sci. **59**(3), 32,203–1 (2016)
9. Lai, G., Liu, Z., Zhang, Y., Chen, C.P.: Adaptive fuzzy tracking control of nonlinear systems with asymmetric actuator backlash based on a new smooth inverse. IEEE Trans. Cybern. **46**(6), 1250–1262 (2016)
10. Li, T., Mei, T., Yan, S., Kweon, I.S., Lee, C.: Contextual decomposition of multi-label images. In: IEEE Conference on Computer Vision and Pattern Recognition 2009. CVPR 2009, pp. 2270–2277 (2009)

11. Lin, G., Li, Z., Liu, L., Su, H., Ye, W.: Development of multi-fingered dexterous hand for grasping manipulation. Sci. China Inf. Sci. **12**(57), 1–10 (2014)
12. Mairal, J., Bach, F., Ponce, J., Sapiro, G.: Online learning for matrix factorization and sparse coding. J. Mach. Learn. Res. **11**(Jan), 19–60 (2010)
13. Orhan, G., Olgunsoylu, S., Sahin, E., Kalkan, S.: Co-learning nouns and adjectives. IEEE Third Joint International Conference on Development and Learning and Epigenetic Robotics (ICDL) **2013**, 1–6 (2013)
14. Zhang, M.L., Zhou, Z.H.: Ml-knn: a lazy learning approach to multi-label learning. Pattern Recognit. **40**(7), 2038–2048 (2007)

Chapter 6
Tactile Material Identification Using Semantics-Regularized Dictionary Learning

Abstract Perceiving and identifying material properties of surfaces and objects is important for us to interact with the world. Therefore, automatic material identification plays a critical role in the intelligent manufacturing systems. In many scenarios, the tactile samples and the tactile adjective descriptions about some materials can be provided. How to exploit their relation is a challenging problem. In this chapter, a semantics-regularized dictionary learning method is developed to incorporate such advanced semantic information into the training model to improve the material identification performance. A set of optimization algorithms are developed to obtain the solutions of the proposed optimization problem. Finally, extensive experimental evaluations are performed on publicly available datasets to show the effectiveness of the proposed method.

6.1 Introduction

Perceiving and identifying material properties of surfaces and objects is a fundamental aspect which enables us to interact with novel scenes or objects. Therefore, correctly identifying materials is very important for manufacturing industry to realize intelligent manufacturing. For example, understanding materials enables the robot to interact with the real world and influence its decisions, e.g., whether an object is solid enough for a pinch.

Undoubtedly, vision sensors have been extensively used to identify the materials. Reference [5] investigated how 3D geometry could be used with 2D features to improve material classification. Reference [2] argued that even if the precise coefficient of friction could not be predicted from vision before touching a surface, priors and accumulated experience associated with surface material or condition could provide a probability distribution of friction. Reference [8] developed various image pattern recognition methods to classify and assess the condition of silicone rubber insulators. Reference [1] developed deep learning methodology to achieve material recognition and segmentation of images in the wild.

Though visual information plays an important role in material identification, it has some intrinsic limitations, due to the diversity in material appearance. Because instances from a single material category can span a range of object categories, shapes, colors, textures, lighting and imaging conditions. For example, one single material category *Foam* is visually very rich and spans a diverse range of appearances (see, e.g., Fig. 6.1), which may vary due to lighting and viewpoints. Some different material categories, such as *Black Foam* and *Black Eraser*, exhibit very similar visual appearances. All of those observations make the visual material identification very difficult. On the other hand, for humans material identification comes naturally since one can touch and feel the material surface if it is smooth or rough and hard or soft. This motivates the researchers and engineers to adopt the tactile sensors to obtain some complementary properties.

On the other hand, it is well recognized that the tactile adjectives are highly related to material identification. For example, identifying a surface as *Foam* implies the presence of some tactile properties, such as *Squishy*, *Compressible*, *Soft* and *Absorbent*. Reference [4] developed PHAC, a collection of tactile classification datasets, and concentrated on classifying objects with binary tactile adjectives. This work relied on handcrafted features for tactile classification. Recently, Ref. [6] proposed a deep learning method of classifying surfaces with tactile adjectives from both visual and physical interaction data. Please note that the work of [4, 6] concerned the adjective recognition, but did not address the material identification problem.

This chapter focuses on identifying the material category, e.g., *Glass*, *Metal*, *Fabric*, *Plastic*, or *Foam*, from a single tactile sample of surface. The advanced semantic

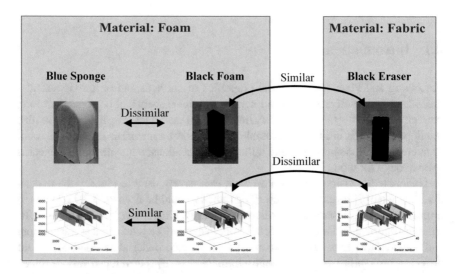

Fig. 6.1 Some examples illustrating the limitations of visual images for differentiating materials. Both *Blue Sponge* and *Black Foam* belong to the category *Foam*. Their visual images are significantly different, but the tactile signals are similar. On the other hand, although *Black Foam* and *Black Eraser* do not belong to the same material category, they exhibit very similar visual appearances but significantly different tactile signals

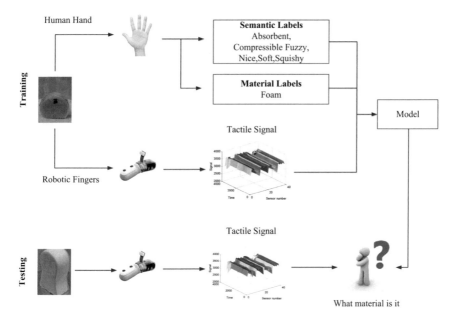

Fig. 6.2 The main framework of the proposed method. The shadow part corresponds to the training stage. In this stage, the investigated material objects are touched by both human hand and the robotic fingers with tactile sensors. The human then provides two kinds of labels: semantic adjective labels and the material label. The robotic fingers can provide the tactile signals only. Then, the obtained data can be used to learn a model. During the testing stage, the material object can only be touched by the robotic fingers to provide the tactile signal, which is used as the input for the trained model to get the material label. Note that the semantic labels are only available for the training stage and therefore it can be used to help learning the model, but cannot be used in the testing stage

information is incorporated into the training model to improve the material identification performance. This is achieved by a joint sparse dictionary learning method. The main flowchart is shown in Fig. 6.2. A semantics-regularized dictionary learning framework is proposed to systematically solve the material identification problem. Then, a set of optimization algorithms are developed to obtain the solutions of the proposed optimization problem. Experimental evaluations on publicly available datasets show the effectiveness of the proposed method.

The rest of this chapter is organized as follows: In Sect. 6.2, a new linearized tactile representation is presented. In Sect. 6.3, the problem and motivation are formulated. Sections 6.4–6.5 present the optimization model and algorithms, respectively. In Sect. 6.6, the identification method is introduced. The experimental results are presented in Sect. 6.7.

6.2 Linearized Tactile Feature Representation

At each time step, the tactile data is obtained from the sensor cells. The ith tactile sample can be represented as multivariable time series $\mathbb{T}_i$. Because the lengths of two tactile samples may not equal, some warping techniques have to be employed to establish their metric. In previous chapters, DTW and GA kernels are investigated, which can be denoted as $\kappa(\mathbb{T}_i, \mathbb{T}_j)$ for the tactile samples $\mathbb{T}_i$ and $\mathbb{T}_j$. Though the kernel function can be used to evaluate the similarity between tactile samples, the resulting optimization problems involve complicated kernel computations. In practice, a coding method which is based on vector feature descriptor of the tactile samples is more preferred. This chapter tries to resort the linearized technique which was proposed in [7]. To this end, the kernel matrix for the training samples is defined as $\kappa(\mathfrak{T}, \mathfrak{T}) \in R^{N \times N}$ whose (i, j)th element is $\kappa(\mathbb{T}_i, \mathbb{T}_j)$. Since $\kappa(\mathfrak{T}, \mathfrak{T})$ is positive-definite, the singular value decomposition can be performed as

$$\kappa(\mathfrak{T}, \mathfrak{T}) = \mathbf{U}\Sigma\mathbf{U}^T,$$

where $\mathbf{U} \in \mathbb{R}^{N \times N}$, $\mathbf{U}\mathbf{U}^T = \mathbf{I}$, and

$$\Sigma = diag\{\sigma_1, \sigma_2, \ldots, \sigma_N\} \in \mathbb{R}^{N \times N},$$

where $\{\sigma_i\}_{i=1,2,\ldots,N}$ are the singular values sorted in descending order.

For linearization approximation, the first d singular values are selected to form the following matrix:

$$\Sigma_{\tilde{d}} = diag\{\sigma_1, \sigma_2, \ldots, \sigma_{\tilde{d}}\}.$$

In addition, the first $\tilde{d}$ columns of $\mathbf{U}$ are extracted to form a new matrix $\mathbf{U}_{\tilde{d}} \in \mathbb{R}^{\tilde{d} \times N}$. Then, the following approximation can be obtained:

$$\kappa(\mathfrak{T}, \mathfrak{T}) \doteq \mathbf{U}_{\tilde{d}}\Sigma_{\tilde{d}}\mathbf{U}_{\tilde{d}}^T,$$

where $\mathbf{U}_{\tilde{d}} \in \mathbb{R}^{N \times \tilde{d}}$, $\Sigma_{\tilde{d}} \in \mathbb{R}^{\tilde{d} \times \tilde{d}}$, and $\mathbf{U}_{\tilde{d}}\mathbf{U}_{\tilde{d}}^T = \mathbf{I}$.

Figure 6.3 shows the top 50 singular values for the tactile samples in PHAC dataset, using GA kernel. It shows how quickly the singular value drops off after the first few values. Therefore, in this work, the value of d can be set as 20. Little information would be lost by dropping the higher values.

Then, the feature vector for $\mathbb{T}_i$ can be defined as

$$t_i = \Sigma_{\tilde{d}}^{-1/2}\mathbf{U}_{\tilde{d}}^T\kappa(\mathbb{T}_i, \mathfrak{T}) \in \mathbb{R}^{\tilde{d}},$$

The feature vector t_i can be regarded as a mapping of the original input samples $\mathbb{T}_i$ to the $\tilde{d}$-dimensional Euclidean space.

Fig. 6.3 Plot of the singular value spectrum

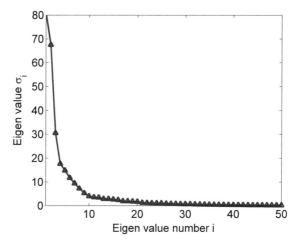

Further, for the testing sample $\mathbb{T}$, the corresponding feature vector representation is given by

$$t = \Sigma_{\tilde{d}}^{-1/2} \mathbf{U}_{\tilde{d}}^T \kappa(\mathbb{T}, \mathfrak{T}) \in \mathbb{R}^{\tilde{d}},$$

6.3 Motivation and Problem Formulation

In practice, the material identification problem is formulated as being able to recognize a given input tactile sample belonging to one of C material categories. To this end, the training sample set is constructed as $\{t_1, t_2, \ldots, t_N\} \subset R^{\tilde{d} \times N}$, where $\tilde{d}$ is the feature dimension and N is the number of the training samples. For each tactile sample t_i, there is one corresponding label vector $l_i \in R^C$. The vector l_i is an elementary vector, where the element 1 indicates the class category. That is to say, the element of the label vector l_i is defined as

$$l_i(c) = \begin{cases} +1 & \text{If } t_i \text{ belongs to the } c - \text{th material} \\ 0 & \text{Othewise} \end{cases} \tag{6.1}$$

for $c = 1, 2, \ldots, C$.

Based on the above settings, the material identification can be regarded as a classical supervised machine learning problem and can be solved using various algorithms. However, in this work, it is noted that there exists some additional information in the tactile material identification problem. As it can be seen, many properties perceived by the tactile sensors can be characterized by adjectives such as *Hard, Soft, Smooth*, and it is reasonable to develop a set of tactile adjectives for the tactile understanding. Therefore, for the training tactile samples, an adjective vector $h_i \in R^H$ can be provided, where H is the number of the concerned adjectives, to indicate its tactile

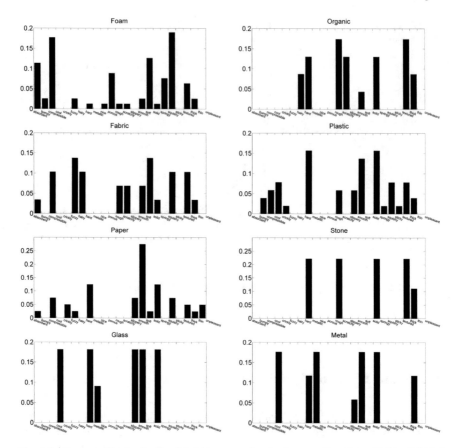

Fig. 6.4 The normalized adjective label histogram for the 8 categories of material in PHAC-2 dataset

attributes. Given a set of H adjective labels, the element of the label vector $\boldsymbol{h}_i \in \mathbb{R}^H$ corresponding to the ith sample is defined as

$$\boldsymbol{h}_i(l) = \begin{cases} +1 & \text{If label } l \text{ is associated with sample } t_i \\ 0 & \text{Othewise} \end{cases} \tag{6.2}$$

for $l = 1, 2, \ldots, H$. Please note that it is permitted multiple elements in $\boldsymbol{h}_i$ are nonzero. Strictly speaking, it is natural to require

$$||\boldsymbol{l}_i||_0 = ||\boldsymbol{l}_i||_1 = 1, \quad ||\boldsymbol{h}_i||_0 = ||\boldsymbol{h}_i||_1 \geq 1.$$

Here is an example to illustrate the power of the adjective labels. It is developed for PHAC-2 tactile dataset which will be introduced later. For the $C(=8)$ categories of materials in PHAC-2 dataset, the normalized histogram over the $H(=24)$ tactile adjectives is calculated according to

$$q_c = \frac{1}{|\mathcal{I}_c|} \sum_{i \in \mathcal{I}_c} h_i$$

where $\mathcal{I}_c$ is the set including the cth material category and $|\mathcal{I}_c|$ denotes the number of the samples in the set. The obtained normalized histogram q_c is listed in Fig. 6.4, which shows that such histograms are very effective to discriminate the materials. For more clear illustration, the most dominative adjectives are selected for each materials and shown in Table 6.1, which also supports the observations.

Although adjective label is so useful for differentiating material, it cannot be served as feature descriptors for material identification task. The core reason is that such labels are only available for the training data. In the testing stage, only the tactile samples can be obtained, but not any annotation data. Figure 6.2 shows a scenario to illustrate this point. In practice, the training material objects are touched by both human hand and the robotic fingers with tactile sensors. The human then provides two kinds of labels: semantic adjective labels and the material label. The robotic fingers can provide the tactile signals only. During the test stage, the material object can only be touched by the robotic fingers to provide the tactile signal, which is used as the input as the trained model to get the material label. Note that the semantic labels are only available for the training stage and therefore it can be used to help learn the model, but cannot be used in the testing stage. Unfortunately, existing work for material identification usually neglects such semantic information.

The task is then formulated as developing an algorithm to identify the material category of a tactile sample $t \in R^{\bar{d}}$, using the information provided by the training set $\{t_1, t_2, \ldots, t_N\}$ and the label set $\{l_1, l_2, \ldots, l_N\}$, with the help of the adjective label set $\{h_1, h_2, \ldots, h_N\}$.

Table 6.1 Dominative adjectives for different materials

Material	Dominative adjectives
Foam	Squishy, Compressible, Soft, Absorbent
Organic	Rough, Textured, Hard, Scratch, Solid
Fabric	Soft, Fuzzy, Compressible, Hairy, Squishy, Textured
Plastic	Hard, Solid, Smooth, Cool, Squishy, Textured
Paper	Smooth, Hard, Solid
Stone	Hard, Rough, Solid, Textured
Glass	Cool, Hard, Slippery, Smooth, Solid
Metal	Cool, Metallic, Smooth, Solid

6.4 Proposed Model

To exploit the intrinsic relation among the tactile samples, material labels, and adjective labels, the popular dictionary leaning methodology [9] is employed. The conventional dictionary learning problem can be formulated as

$$
\min_{D, x_i} \sum_{i=1}^{N} ||t_i - Dx_i||_2^2 + \lambda ||x_i||_1
$$
$$
\text{s.t.}\quad ||d_k||_2 \leq 1, \quad \text{for } k \in \{1, 2, \ldots, K\}
$$
(6.3)

where $D = [d_1 \, d_2 \, \ldots \, d_K] \in R^{\tilde{d} \times K}$ is called as dictionary. This model transforms the tactile sample t_i into a sparse coding vector $x_i \in R^K$, and λ is used to penalty the role of the sparsity. The obtained coding vector has discriminant capability and can be used as the feature descriptor for subsequent classifier design. However, a more effective method is to incorporate the classification error into the optimization and jointly learn the dictionary and the classifier. This leads to the following optimization problem:

$$
\min_{D, W, x_i} \sum_{i=1}^{N} \left\{ ||t_i - Dx_i||_2^2 + \alpha ||l_i - Wx_i||_2^2 + \lambda ||x_i||_1 \right\}
$$
$$
\text{s.t.}\quad ||d_k||_2 \leq 1, \quad \text{for } k \in \{1, 2, \ldots, K\}
$$
(6.4)

where $W \in R^{C \times K}$ is the classifier parameter, and α is used to penalty the role of the classification error.

The above model utilizes a linear coding and a linear classifier, and therefore, the discriminative capability is limited. In addition, the calculated coding vector lacks semantic meaning. On the other hand, based on previous analysis, the adjective label $h_i \in R^H$ is a semantic annotation label and is discriminative for classification. Therefore, it is highly expected to establish the connection between the calculated coding x_i and the adjective label vector h_i. To this end, two properties are recalled:

1. For tactile sample t_i, its adjective label vector $h_i \in R^H$ is sparse, especially when H is large. The reason is that usually only very few adjectives are associated with one single material.
2. For tactile sample t_i, its coding vector $x_i \in R^K$ is also sparse, due to deliberatively designed optimization objective function.

Based the above analysis, a natural idea by setting $K = L$ and enforcing $x_i = h_i$ can be obtained. Such a setting is too rigid and does not exploit the intrinsic sparsity of the vectors. Alternatively, we set $K = L$ and enforce x_i and h_i can enable to share the same sparsity pattern, but do not require their corresponding elements to be equal. In Fig. 6.5, the difference among those coding strategies is simply illustrated.

The symbol $Sp(x_i)$ is used to denote the sparse pattern vector whose jth element is 1 when the jth element of x_i is nonzero, and 0 otherwise. Obviously, this vector hides the information of the values in x_i, but preserves the structure information of x_i.

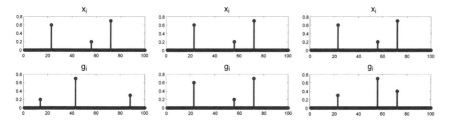

Fig. 6.5 Illustration of different coding strategies. LEFT: No constraints on x_i and g_i; MIDDLE: $x_i = g_i$; RIGHT: $Sp(x_i) = Sp(g_i)$

Then, the optimization problem (6.4) is reduced to

$$\min_{D,W,x_i} \sum_{i=1}^{N} \left\{ ||t_i - Dx_i||_2^2 + \alpha ||l_i - Wx_i||_2^2 \right\}$$
$$\text{s.t.} \quad ||d_k||_2 \leq 1, \quad \text{for } k \in \{1, 2, \dots, K\} \tag{6.5}$$
$$Sp(x_i) = Sp(h_i)$$

This problem is very easy to solve because the sparsity pattern has been determined and the sparse optimization procedure is avoided. However, it exhibits two demerits: (1) It requires the size of dictionary K to be equal to the number of material categories, and therefore, the flexibilities are reduced. (2) For test sample, since the adjective label vector is unavailable, the coding vector cannot be solved.

To formulate a more practical and general model, a relaxed coding vector $g_i \in R^K$ and transformation matrix $M \in R^{L \times K}$ are introduced and they are enforced to satisfy the requirement

$$h_i = Mg_i.$$

In addition, g_i and x_i share the common sparsity pattern. This leads to the following optimization problem:

$$\min_{D,W,M,x_i,g_i} \sum_{i=1}^{N} ||t_i - Dx_i||_2^2 + \alpha ||l_i - Wx_i||_2^2 + \beta ||h_i - Mg_i||_2^2 + \lambda ||[x_i \ g_i]||_{2,1}$$
$$\text{s.t.} \quad ||d_k||_2 \leq 1, \quad \text{for } k \in \{1, 2, \dots, K\}$$
$$||m_k||_2 \leq 1, \quad \text{for } k \in \{1, 2, \dots, K\} \tag{6.6}$$

where m_k is the kth column of M and α, β, and γ are the corresponding penalty parameters. Compared with general supervised dictionary learning methods such as (6.4), this formulation exhibits two supervised terms. The term $||l_i - Wx_i||_2^2$ plays the same role with linear classifier. That is to say, once the coding vector is got for some tactile sample, W can be used to calculate the material label of this sample. The term $||h_i - Mg_i||_2^2$ is used as a regularizer which is special for this task, because h_i contains the adjective label information. In fact, this term plays the roles of a multilabel classification task, which encourages the coding vector to reconstruct the multilabel adjective label h_i. In this sense, this term helps the coding vector to achieve semantic interpretation.

This optimization model is a little like the multitask learning, where the term $||h_i - Mg_i||_2^2$ encourages the model to learn the adjective label and $||l_i - Wx_i||_2^2$ encourages the model to learn the material label. The two tasks are bridged with the joint sparsity. Since there exists a strong connection between the two tasks, the joint learning will be beneficial.

6.5 Optimization Algorithm

The optimization problem in Eq. (6.6) is obviously nonconvex and nonsmooth. The alternative optimization method is adopted to solve it. The algorithm can be divided into the following stages. For conveniences, the superscript t is used to represent the solutions at the tth iteration.

6.5.1 Calculating the Sparse Coding Vectors

This step updates the coding vectors $x_i^{(t+1)}$ and $g_i^{(t+1)}$, given the values of $D^{(t)}$, $W^{(t)}$, and $M^{(t)}$. In this case, the optimization problem (6.6) is reduced to

$$\min_{x_i, g_i} \; ||t_i - D^{(t)}x_i||_2^2 + \alpha||l_i - W^{(t)}x_i||_2^2$$
$$+ \beta||h_i - M^{(t)}g_i||_2^2 + \lambda||[x_i \; g_i]||_{2,1} \qquad (6.7)$$

This problem is convex and can be easily solved using any efficient l_1 optimization algorithm. In this work, the popular sparse solver software SPAMS [9] is used to solve this problem.

6.5.2 Calculating the Dictionary Atoms

This step updates the dictionary D and the coefficient matrices W and M. At the $(t + 1)$th iteration, $x_i^{(t+1)}$ and $g_i^{(t+1)}$ are given. The optimization problem is reduced to

$$\min_{D,W,M} \sum_{i=1}^{N} ||t_i - Dx_i||_2^2 + \alpha||l_i - Wx_i||_2^2 + \beta||h_i - Mg_i||_2^2$$
$$\text{s.t.} \quad ||d_k||_2 \le 1, \quad \text{for } k \in \{1, 2, \ldots, K\}$$
$$||m_k||_2 \le 1, \quad \text{for } k \in \{1, 2, \ldots, K\} \qquad (6.8)$$

In this regard, the optimizations of D, W, and M can be performed separately as the following two dictionary learning problems.

$$\begin{cases} \min_{\hat{D}} \sum_{i=1}^{N} ||\hat{t}_i - \hat{D}x_i^{(t+1)}||_2^2, \quad \text{s.t. } ||d_k||_2 \leq 1 \\ \min_{M} \sum_{i=1}^{N} ||h_i - Mg_i^{(t+1)}||_2^2, \quad \text{s.t. } ||m_k||_2 \leq 1 \end{cases} \quad (6.9)$$

where $\hat{t}_i$ and the kth column of $\hat{D}$ are designed as

$$\hat{t}_i = \begin{bmatrix} t_i \\ \sqrt{\alpha}l_i \end{bmatrix}, \quad \hat{d}_k = \begin{bmatrix} d_k \\ \sqrt{\alpha}w_k \end{bmatrix},$$

where w_k is the kth column of W. The dictionary learning problems in (6.9) are typically quadratically constrained quadratic programs which can be efficiently solved.

6.5.3 Algorithm Summarization

With the above updating rules, the proposed algorithm is summarized in Algorithm 3. The convergent condition can be triggered when the change of the objective function is smaller than a prescribed tolerant error, or the prescribed maximum iteration number is achieved. In this work, the latter strategy is adopted and the maximum iteration number is set to 30.

Algorithm 3

Input: Tactile sample set $\{t_i\}$, $\{l_i\}$ and $\{h_i\}$ for $i = 1, 2, \ldots, N$, the size of dictionary K, the parameters α, β, λ
Output: Solutions $x_i \in R^K$, $g_i \in R^K$, $D \in R^{d \times K}$, $W \in R^{C \times K}$, and $M \in R^{L \times K}$.
1: **while** Not convergent **do**
2:    Fix D, W, M and update x_i and g_i according to (6.7).
3:    Fix x_i, g_i and update D, W and M according to (6.9).
4: **end while**

6.6 Classifier Design

The above learning procedure provides us the solutions which are denoted as D^*, W^*, and M^*. Then, they are used to design the classifier. For a test sample $t \in R^d$, its label vector is denoted as $l \in \mathscr{E}_C$, where $\mathscr{E}_C$ is the set of the elementary C-dimensional vectors.

$g \in \mathbb{R}^C$ is used as the relaxed label vector, and the following joint coding and labeling problem are solved.

$$\min_{x,g,h,l} \ ||t - D^*x||_2^2 + \alpha||l - W^*x||_2^2 + \beta||h - M^*g||_2^2 + \lambda||[x \quad g]||_{2,1} \quad (6.10)$$

This problem is also nonconvex, and therefore, the alternative optimization method is employed. The iterations are divided into the following stages. For convenience, the superscript t is used to indicate the iteration number.

First, the solutions of x are initialized as

$$x^{(0)} = \underset{x}{\mathrm{argmin}} \ ||t - D^*x||_2^2 + \lambda||x||_1 \qquad (6.11)$$

and $g^{(0)} = x^{(0)}$.

Given $x^{(t)}$ and $g^{(t)}$, l and h can be updated as

$$\{l^{(t+1)}, h^{(t+1)}\} = \underset{l,h}{\mathrm{argmin}} \ \alpha||l - W^*x^{(t)}||_2^2 + \beta||h - M^*g^{(t)}||_2^2 \qquad (6.12)$$

which exhibits the explicit solution

$$h^{(t+1)} = M^*g^{(t)}.$$

$l^{(t+1)}$ can be obtained as

$$l^{(t+1)} = \underset{l \in \mathscr{E}_C}{\mathrm{argmin}} \ ||l - W^*x^{(t)}||$$

Given $l^{(t)}$ and $h^{(t)}$, x and g are updated by solving the following optimization problem:

$$\min_{x,g} \ ||t - D^*x||_2^2 + \alpha||l^{(t)} - W^*x||_2^2 + \beta||h^{(t)} - M^*g||_2^2 + \lambda||[x \quad g]||_{2,1}$$
$$(6.13)$$

In our experiment, the converged solution l^* can be achieved after at most eight iterations. Note the constraint $l \in \mathscr{E}_C$ guarantees that only one atom in l is 1 and others are zeros. Therefore, the class label can be naturally determined.

6.7 Experimental Results

6.7.1 Experimental Setting

PHAC-2 is very suitable for the task because it provides two types of labels. The first one is the material label. According to the primary material property, the objects in PHAC-2 could be divided into eight categories: *Foam*, *Organic*, *Fabric*, *Plastic*, *Paper*, *Stone*, *Glasses*, and *Metal*. The second one is the semantic adjective label.

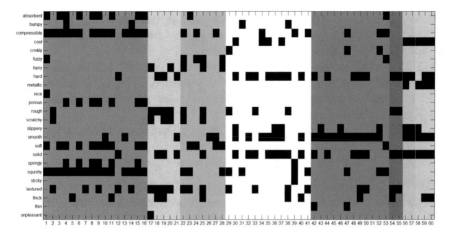

Fig. 6.6 The link information between the material label and the adjective label. The horizontal axis indicates the material object number, and the vertical axis indicates the adjective label. The solid small black block indicates that the corresponding adjective is associated to the material object. Different colors are used to differentiate the materials. The corresponding relation is Yellow-*Foam*, Pink-*Organic*, Blue-*Fabric*, White-*Plastic*, Tender Green-*Paper*, Brown-*Stone*, Lilac-*Glass*, Yellowish-*Metal*

Each object is described with a set of 24 binary labels, corresponding to the existence or absence of each of the 24 tactile adjectives (e.g., *Solid* or *Hard*).

Figure 6.6 shows the link information between the material label and the adjective label, which verifies that there exists a significant correlation between the two labels. For example, Soft frequently occurs in the *Form*, but never occurs in *Metal*. *Fuzzy* frequently occurs in *Faric* but never occurs in *Glass*. Such examples also indicate the utilization of adjective label information may help classifier design.

For each material category, half of the objects are randomly selected for training and the rest for testing evaluation. Such a setting ensures that the training set and testing set do not contain the instances from the same objects. Ten trials are performed, and the averaged results are reported.

6.7.2   Performance Comparison

For the performance comparisons, the same feature vectors are adopted and the following algorithms are considered:

1. k-NN: This is the most classical pattern recognition method which does not require training stages. The method searches the k- nearest neighborhoods in the training set and uses majority voting to get the category label. In practice, it is found one single nearest neighborhood achieves the best results and the value is fixed as $k = 1$ in the comparison.

2. SVM: This is one of the most popular classification methods. It adopts the support vector machine as the classifier. The details can be referred to [3]. LIBSVM provided by [3] is used for implementation.
3. DL: This method performs the dictionary learning and the classifier design independently. That is to say, the optimization problem (6.3) is first solved to get the dictionary and coding vectors, and then, the classifier parameter W is trained using the obtained coding vectors.
4. S-DL: This method tackles the optimization problem (6.4) and solves the dictionary and the classifier parameters jointly.
5. SR-DL: This method solves (6.6) to get the semantics-regularized coding vectors.

For the above methods, the parameters are tuned to obtain the best results. k-NN serves as the baseline. SVM serves as representative discriminative learning method. DL, S-DL, and SR-DL are all based on dictionary learning, and therefore, their comparison serves as the ablation study.

In Fig. 6.7, it shows the identification accuracy versus the size of the dictionary. The identification error is defined as

$$\frac{\text{The number of correctly identified testing samples}}{\text{The number of testing samples}}$$

From the results shown in Fig. 6.7, the following observations are made:

1. The methods k-NN and SVM are not related to dictionary learning and therefore are independent of the size of dictionary. It shows that when the size of dictionary is small, the performance of SVM is comparable to the dictionary learning methods. However, when increasing the value of K, the advantages of dictionary learning become more significant.

Fig. 6.7 The identification accuracy versus the size of dictionary

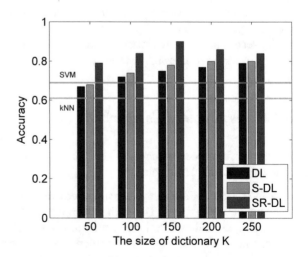

2. It is not surprising that the performance of S-DL is always better than DL, and the performance of SR-DL is always better than S-DL and DL. The reason is that S-DL performs joint learning of dictionary and classifier, while DL learns them separately. In addition, the results show that the semantic adjectives play important roles in improving the performance.

3. It is interesting to find that the performances of DL and S-DL are monotonically increasing with the increase of K, while SR-DL achieves the best performance at $K = 150$. When $K > 150$, its performance decreases slightly, though it is still better than DL and S-DL. The reason is that the explicit semantical regularization term is introduced into SR-DL. When the value of K is too large, the role of semantical regularization term becomes weak. The relation between the semantic labels and the size of the dictionary is still an open problem which is worth of further study.

4. Compared to DL and S-DL, the performance of SR-DL is more insensitive to the size of dictionary. This is also due to the reason that the introduced semantic regularization term helps guiding the coding vectors to approach the better direction and therefore the role of the size of dictionary becomes weak.

Before closing this section, the confusion matrix in Fig. 6.8 which shows the identification error for each material category should be illustrated. The results exhibit three-cluster characteristics: {*Foam, Organic, Fabric*}, {*Plastic, Paper*}, {*Stone, Glass, Metal*}. For example, some object instance of the material *Foam* may be identified as *Fabric*, but never be classified as *Metal*. The reasons for the poor performance of {*Stone, Glass, Metal*} are twofolds: (1) The sense of touch about such materials is indeed little similar; (2) the number of training samples for such material objects is fewer.

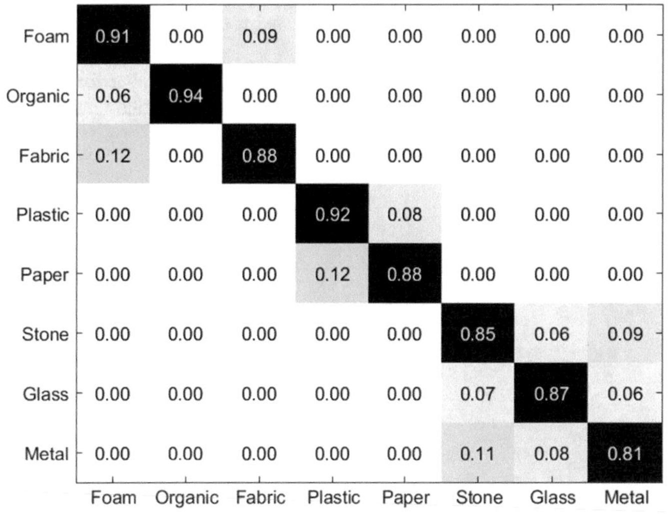

	Foam	Organic	Fabric	Plastic	Paper	Stone	Glass	Metal
Foam	0.91	0.00	0.09	0.00	0.00	0.00	0.00	0.00
Organic	0.06	0.94	0.00	0.00	0.00	0.00	0.00	0.00
Fabric	0.12	0.00	0.88	0.00	0.00	0.00	0.00	0.00
Plastic	0.00	0.00	0.00	0.92	0.08	0.00	0.00	0.00
Paper	0.00	0.00	0.00	0.12	0.88	0.00	0.00	0.00
Stone	0.00	0.00	0.00	0.00	0.00	0.85	0.06	0.09
Glass	0.00	0.00	0.00	0.00	0.00	0.07	0.87	0.06
Metal	0.00	0.00	0.00	0.00	0.00	0.11	0.08	0.81

Fig. 6.8 The confusion matrix

6.8   Summary

In this chapter, a semantics-regularized dictionary learning method is developed to incorporate the advanced semantic information into the training model. It can improve the material identification performance. The experimental evaluations on PHAC-2 dataset show the effectiveness of the proposed method.

References

1. Bell, S., Upchurch, P., Snavely, N., Bala, K.: Material recognition in the wild with the materials in context database. In: Proceedings of the IEEE Conference on Computer Vision and Pattern Recognition, pp. 3479–3487 (2015)
2. Brandao, M., Shiguematsu, Y.M., Hashimoto, K., Takanishi, A.: Material recognition CNNs and hierarchical planning for biped robot locomotion on slippery terrain. In: 2016 IEEE-RAS 16th International Conference on Humanoid Robots (Humanoids), pp. 81–88 (2016)
3. Chang, C.C., Lin, C.J.: Libsvm: a library for support vector machines. ACM Trans. Intell. Syst. Technol. (TIST) **2**(3), 27 (2011)
4. Chu, V., McMahon, I., Riano, L., McDonald, C.G., He, Q., Perez-Tejada, J.M., Arrigo, M., Darrell, T., Kuchenbecker, K.J.: Robotic learning of haptic adjectives through physical interaction. Robot. Auton. Syst. **63**, 279–292 (2015)
5. DeGol, J., Golparvar-Fard, M., Hoiem, D.: Geometry-informed material recognition. In: Proceedings of the IEEE Conference on Computer Vision and Pattern Recognition, pp. 1554–1562 (2016)
6. Gao, Y., Hendricks, L.A., Kuchenbecker, K.J., Darrell, T.: Deep learning for tactile understanding from visual and haptic data. 2016 IEEE International Conference on Robotics and Automation (ICRA), pp. 536–543 (2016)
7. Golts, A., Elad, M.: Linearized kernel dictionary learning. IEEE J. Sel. Top. Signal Process. **10**(4), 726–739 (2016)
8. Jarrar, I., Assaleh, K., El-Hag, A.H.: Using a pattern recognition-based technique to assess the hydrophobicity class of silicone rubber materials. IEEE Trans. Dielectr. Electr. Insul. **21**(6), 2611–2618 (2014)
9. Mairal, J., Bach, F., Ponce, J., Sapiro, G.: Online dictionary learning for sparse coding. In: Proceedings of the 26th Annual International Conference on Machine Learning, pp. 689–696 (2009)

Part III
Visual–Tactile Fusion Perception

This part of the book extends the structured sparse coding and dictionary learning methods to solve the visual–tactile fusion perception and understanding problems. It comprises three chapters. In Chap. 7, a basic visual–tactile fusion framework is formulated and the joint group sparse coding method is developed. This chapter can be regarded as the nontrivial extension of Chap. 3, which solves the multifingered tactile object recognition problem. In Chap. 8, the complicated dictionary learning technology is developed to tackle more general weakly paired multimodal fusion problem. Finally, the visual–tactile cross-modal retrieve problem is solved in Chap. 9. This part therefore presents a new perceptive to connect the sense of vision and touch.

Chapter 7
Visual–Tactile Fusion Object Recognition Using Joint Sparse Coding

Abstract Visual and tactile measurements offer complementary properties that make them particularly suitable for fusion. It is helpful for the robust and accurate recognition of objects, which is a necessity in many automation systems. In this chapter, a visual–tactile fusion framework is developed for object recognition tasks. This work uses the multivariate time series model to represent the tactile sequence, and the covariance descriptor to characterize the image. Further, a joint group kernel sparse coding method is designed to tackle the intrinsically weak-pairing problem in visual–tactile data samples. Finally, a visual–tactile dataset is developed, which is composed of 18 household objects for validation. The experimental results show that considering both visual and tactile input is beneficial and the proposed method indeed provides an effective strategy for fusion.

7.1 Introduction

In spite of the significant progress made in object recognition using visual or tactile information alone, the issue of how to combine visual and tactile information to improve the perception capability is more attractive, since the two sensing modalities offer complementary characteristics that make them the ideal choice for robust perception. The motivation for this work comes from human cognition capabilities. In practice, humans make extensive use of input from several sensor modalities when executing grasps. When recognizing materials and objects, humans often combine touch with vision, and even hearing [8]. Several studies have shown that the human brain employs multisensory models of objects [8]. By using such a shared model, humans can transfer knowledge about an object from one sensory modality to another. This sharing of information is especially useful. For example, experiments examining both vision and touch have shown that humans rely more on touch when the texture has small details that are difficult to see [9].

Visual and tactile modalities are vastly different. Firstly, the format, frequency, and range of object information are different. The tactile modality can only obtain information about objects it can touch, while the visual modality can simultaneously obtain information for multiple salient features of an object from a distance.

© Springer Nature Singapore Pte Ltd. 2018
H. Liu and F. Sun, *Robotic Tactile Perception and Understanding*,
https://doi.org/10.1007/978-981-10-6171-4_7

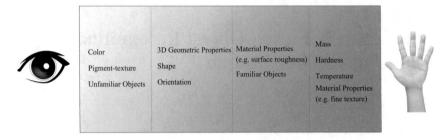

Color	3D Geometric Properties	Material Properties (e.g. surface roughness)	Mass
Pigment-texture	Shape	Familiar Objects	Hardness
Unfamiliar Objects	Orientation		Temperature
			Material Properties (e.g. fine texture)

Fig. 7.1 Difference between visual and tactile modalities. The ones presented in the left are more suitable for identified by visual modality while the ones presented in the right are more suitable for identification by tactile modality. This figure is adopted from [19] with slight modification

Furthermore, some salient features can only be obtained by one perceptual modality. For example, the color of an object can only be obtained visually, while the texture, hardness, and temperature of a surface can only be obtained through the tactile modality. In Fig. 7.1, it shows the difference, which was originally summarized by [19]. Asynchronous information obtained from two modalities and from different perception ranges brings a great challenge to multimodal fusion.

Currently, there is significant work in the fields of cognition and psychology. One important mechanism of the brain is to integrate visual and tactile information to achieve a consistent representation of stimuli. Reference [6] studied the use of vision and touch in humans. In this work, vision monitored hand movement, while the tactile sense collected surface texture information. It was later pointed out that visual and tactile information are mutually complemented in object shape recognition [14]. Reference [19] demonstrated the role of visual and tactile modalities in cross-modal object recognition, and Ref. [4] analyzed the optimal fusion method for humans. Additionally, Ref. [12] preliminarily verified the unified representation of visual and tactile information in the brain, and Ref. [2] showed that an area in the posterior thalamus processes cross-pattern information. Study of the human posterior thalamus also found cross-modal information processing areas: STS, LO, and MT. STS responds to meaningful visual and auditory stimuli, LO responds to visual and tactile object shape information, and MT is important for visual processing and shows weak response to tactile or auditory stimulation. This provides a basis for further study of visual–tactile fusion. Meanwhile, it is very important problem to assess how humans utilize these multimodal cognitive mechanisms for visual–tactile fusion. Although there are many differences between visual and tactile modalities, together, they can be used to describe objects more completely. When cross-modal information is consistent in time and space, the fusion of visual and tactile information is easy. To illustrate this, Ref. [18] studied collaborative localization based on visual and tactile perception modalities. Lastly, Ref. [1] combined tactile and stereo vision information so that they complemented each other, and built a 3D object model containing rich hierarchical information and capable of recognizing curvature and depression in objects. Visual–tactile fusion obtained more comprehensive information about objects, and further study of this technology can promote our understanding of the interactions between human visual and tactile perception.

In this chapter, the widely applicable industrial manipulation scenarios in structured environments are taken into consideration. When identifying an object, the manipulator may see it using a camera and touch it using fingers. This allows us to obtain a pair of test samples made up of one image sample and one tactile sample. The manipulator should then use this pair of samples to identify the object using a classifier that was constructed using offline collected training samples. However, when preparing training samples, the image samples and the tactile samples may be collected independently. In effect, the training samples may not paired, while the test samples are paired.

To tackle such a problem, a novel method for visual–tactile fusion in object recognition tasks is carefully developed. A novel visual–tactile fusion framework for object recognition is developed. Under this framework, the training samples for visual modality and tactile modality can be separately collected. During the test phase, the manipulator captures one image of the object and grasps it to obtain a tactile sequence. The test pair, which includes the image and tactile sequences, is then used to recognize the object. Obviously, the problem description is close to the application of the practical manipulator. A joint group kernel sparse coding method is developed for classification. An important merit of this method is that it does not require the visual data and the tactile data to be fully paired. A visual–tactile dataset that includes 18 household objects are established for verification. The experimental results show that the performance of visual–tactile fusion is significantly better than that of single modality methods.

The rest of this chapter is organized as follows: In Sect. 7.2, the problem formulation is presented. Section 7.3 presents the proposed visual–tactile fusion framework. Section 7.4 gives the data collection procedure and the experimental evaluation results.

7.2 Problem Formulation

The goal of this chapter is to have a manipulator accurately discriminate between different objects by *seeing and touching* them. It is initially allowed the manipulator to learn about objects by both touching and visually inspecting them separately. *Seeing* allows the robot to obtain some images about an object, and by *touching* the robot obtains the tactile sequences about the object. The robot should subsequently combine both modalities to improve its knowledge of fusion sensing.

Formally, it is assumed that there are C distinct objects. During the training phase, an image set can be captured

$$\mathfrak{V} = \{\mathbb{V}_1, \mathbb{V}_2, \ldots, \mathbb{V}_M\} \subset \mathcal{V},$$

where $\mathcal{V}$ represents the manifold in which the image descriptors lie and M is the number of the captured images. The images in this set are captured under different conditions (such as viewpoint, scale, and illumination). On the other hand, the manipulator can use its hand to grasp this object to obtain the tactile sequences. The collected tactile sequences are denoted as

$$\mathfrak{T} = \{\mathbb{T}_1, \mathbb{T}_2, \ldots, \mathbb{T}_N\} \subset \mathcal{T},$$

where $\mathcal{T}$ represents the manifold in which the tactile sequences lie and N is the number of the collected tactile sequences.

Unfortunately, since the visual modality data and tactile modality data are usually collected separately, a full pairing does not exist, which implies a one-to-one correspondence between the image and the tactile sequence. Instead, a group of samples from the visual modality is paired to a group of samples in the tactile modality, where the class label determines the group. Such a case is called weakly paired multimodal data [7]. In the case of weak pairings, subsets of observations of one modality are paired with those of another modality. The intrinsic difference between full pairings and weak pairings is that the former requires samples to be obtained from the same source, while the latter only requires samples be acquired from similar sources. Unfortunately, acquiring perfectly paired samples across modalities is often problematic in practice, especially in our case. The main reasons are listed as follows:

1. Visual modality is represented by a single image, which is captured for a moment; the tactile modality is represented by a tactile sequence, which should be captured during the grasp period.
2. Any inaccuracies in moving the object or the camera's visual inspection will result in incorrect pairings.
3. When using different types of sensors, it is common to obtain different numbers of samples from them. For example, vision sensors can easily obtain information regarding an object's appearance, while tactile sensors are limited to the regions they make contact with. In addition, the tactile sequence is more difficult to collect than the visual modality. Thus, there will usually be many visual samples weakly paired to a few tactile samples.

Given the above reasons, it is assumed that there is weakly paired visual–tactile data. Ultimately, the condition of weakly paired data is a relaxation of the standard fully paired requirement and is, therefore, easier for industrial manipulators to fulfill. A clear comparison between different pairing cases is illustrated in Fig. 7.2.

During the test phase, the manipulator explores the object and obtains a pair data $\{\mathbb{V}, \mathbb{T}\}$, where $\mathbb{V}$ represents the test image and $\mathbb{T}$ represents the tactile sequence. In this work, it is assumed that the manipulator has obtained one image and one tactile sequence. This is straightforward and easy to implement. The objective here is to design a classifier to recognize the object using the obtained testing paired data.

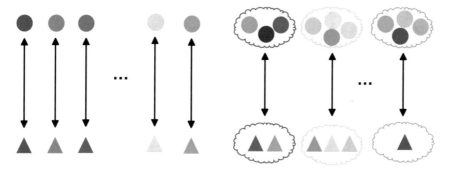

Fig. 7.2 Illustration of the full pairing and weak pairing. The left panel shows the full pairing, which exhibits one-to-one correspondence between the samples in different modalities. The right panel shows the weak pairing, which exhibits group-to-group correspondence between the samples in the different modalities

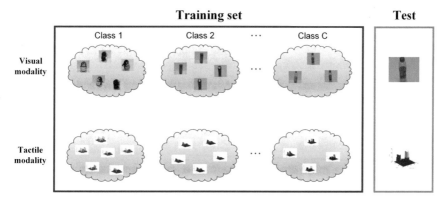

Fig. 7.3 Illustration of visual–tactile pair. The red box is used to surround the training samples and the green box is used to surround the test sample pair. The training samples of images and tactile sequences are weakly paired, while the testing samples are paired

Such a task, however, exhibits a great challenge on how to design an effective fusion method for the weakly paired visual–tactile data. In Fig. 7.3, it shows the illustration of the typical visual–tactile fusion recognition problem.

7.3 Kernel Sparse Coding for Visual–Tactile Fusion

7.3.1 Kernel Sparse Coding

In this section, the kernel sparse coding method is adopted under the multimodal fusion framework. The general goal of kernel sparse coding is to perform sparse coding in a high-dimensional feature space instead of the original space in order to capture the nonlinear structure of signals more efficiently [5].

For the visual modality, the symbol $\Psi(\cdot) : \mathcal{V} \to \mathcal{H}_V$ is used as the implicit nonlinear mappings from $\mathcal{V}$ into higher-dimensional (possibly infinite dimensional) dot product space $\mathcal{H}_V$. Then, the given M training samples can be arranged as a matrix

$$\Psi(\mathfrak{V}) = [\Psi(\mathbb{V}_1) \ \Psi(\mathbb{V}_2) \ \cdots \ \Psi(\mathbb{V}_M)]. \tag{7.1}$$

Similarly, for the tactile modality, the symbol $\Phi(\cdot) : \mathcal{T} \to \mathcal{H}_T$ is used as the implicit nonlinear mappings from $\mathcal{T}$ into higher-dimensional (possibly infinite dimensional) dot product space $\mathcal{H}_T$. Then, the given N training samples can be arranged as a matrix

$$\Phi(\mathfrak{T}) = [\Phi(\mathbb{T}_1) \ \Phi(\mathbb{T}_2) \ \cdots \ \Phi(\mathbb{T}_N)]. \tag{7.2}$$

In the context of classification using the visual and tactile modality information, $\Psi(\mathfrak{V})$ and $\Phi(\mathfrak{T})$ are called as the visual and tactile dictionaries in the higher-dimensional space. Given sufficient training samples, any new (test) sample pair $\{\mathbb{V}, \mathbb{T}\}$ would lie approximately in the corresponding linear span of the few training samples associated with that class [5]. Therefore, the following combined kernel sparse coding problem is reformulated:

$$\min_{x,y} ||\Phi(\mathbb{T}) - \Phi(\mathfrak{T})x||_2^2 + ||\Psi(\mathbb{V}) - \Psi(\mathfrak{V})y||_2^2 + \lambda||x||_1 + \lambda||y||_1, \tag{7.3}$$

where $x \in \mathbb{R}^N$ and $y \in \mathbb{R}^N$ are the coefficient vectors. The 1-norms $||x||_1$ and $||y||_1$, which calculate the sum of the absolute values of elements in x and y, are used to encourage the sparsity [5]. The parameter λ is the corresponding penalty parameter.

Then, the visual–tactile pair $\{\mathbb{T}, \mathbb{V}\}$ can be classified based on these approximations by assigning it to the object class that minimizes the residue

$$r^{(c)} = ||\Phi(\mathbb{T}) - \Phi(\mathscr{T})\delta^{(c)}(x^*)||_2^2 + ||\Psi(\mathbb{V}) - \Psi(\mathscr{V})\delta^{(c)}(y^*)||_2^2. \tag{7.4}$$

where x^* and y^* are the solutions of (7.3).

Finally, the combined residue can be used to get the final label of the test samples:

$$c^* = \operatorname*{arg\,min}_{c \in \{1,...,C\}} r^{(c)}. \tag{7.5}$$

Since the mapping function $\Phi(\cdot)$ and $\Psi(\cdot)$ are associated with the kernels, the utilization of the kernel avoids the requirement of the explicit forms of the complicated feature mapping.

7.3.2 Joint Kernel Group Sparse Coding

The above-mentioned kernel sparse coding method uses different kernels to realize the coding of the tactile sequence and image descriptor. The two coding vectors are obtained separately. In practice, the visual modality and tactile modality provide complementary information and a method by which the intrinsic relation between them can be exploited is important for object recognition. Unfortunately, the optimization problem in Eq. (7.3) can be separated into two independent sub-problems over x and y, and it is impossible to find any constraint on the relationships across x and y. That is to say, the intrinsic relations between multimodal sources are neglected. In this section, this problem is addressed by resorting to a more complicated kernel sparse coding method, which jointly solves the two optimization problems with some constraints which characterize the intrinsic relation between different modalities.

By the sparsity terms $||x||_1$ and $||y||_1$ in the objective function (7.3), it is encouraged that only a few elements in x and y are nonzero which means only a few atoms in the dictionary $\Phi(\mathcal{T})$ and $\Phi(\mathcal{V})$ are activated. In Fig. 7.4, an illustration of this case is demonstrated, in which two modalities, visual and tactile are considered. Considering $C = 5$, different colored lines are used to represent the atoms corresponding to different classes. A typical results show that using visual modality, the atoms corresponding to the 2nd, 3th, and 5th classes are activated, while using tactile modality, the atoms corresponding to the 2nd and 3th classes are activated.

As mentioned, the visual–tactile data are weakly paired. In Fig. 7.2, it shows a clear difference between the full pairing and the weak pairing. The canonical way to construct multimodal fusion algorithms is to use the dependencies between paired samples. An effective coding strategy to deal with multimodal fusion is the joint sparse coding [15]. This coding strategy encourages the similarity of the sparsity pattern of x and y and therefore requires their lengths to be equal. This leads to $N = M$. In addition, this requires strict sample-to-sample correspondence between the dictionaries $\Phi(\mathcal{T})$ and $\Psi(\mathcal{V})$. The classical joint sparse coding method cannot be used in our scenario because the training samples are weakly paired. Also, the multiple kernel sparse learning [16] is an effective multimodal fusion method. It is,

Fig. 7.4 An illustration of the sparse coding methods (different color blocks on the horizontal axis represent different groups). The sparsity patterns of the two vectors are totally different. This can be achieved by the solving the optimization problem (7.3). However, this approach neglects the intrinsic common group structure of the dictionaries

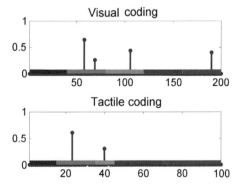

however, still dependent on the fully paired data. In the following, it demonstrates how to overcome this limitation and make use of weakly paired data.

Regardless of whether the multimodal data are fully paired or weakly paired, they are collected from C classes of objects. Therefore, the labels of the objects provide an effective link between the multimodal data. Our method assumes that each of the C groups represents a series of observations of the same object. The observations with the same label are paired in group level. In this way, the label information is integrated to boost the recognition performance.

During the test phase, a set of data samples $\{\mathbb{T}, \mathbb{V}\}$ is obtained, which could be captured independently. It is required that different modality feature form one test sample share the same sparsity pattern at the higher group level, but not necessarily at the lower (inside the group) level. This means that they share the same active groups, but not necessarily the same active set. This is a relaxed version of joint sparse coding, which strictly requires the sparsity patterns of different sparse vectors to be equal. Obviously, the requirement of joint sparse coding is too rigid and even impossible for our practical applications.

In Fig. 7.5, it shows an expected coding result. In this case, the only requirement is that both visual modality and tactile modality activate the atoms corresponding to the same group (class). Such an effect is referred as *Same Group, but Different Atoms*. Since this coding method requires samples belonging to the same class that reconstruct the test sample, the result will be more robust.

Obviously, the sparsity penalty terms $||\mathbf{x}||_1$ and $||\mathbf{y}||_1$ in (7.3) can only encourage *Different Atoms*. To further encourage the effect of the *Same Group*, a new matrix $\mathbf{Z} \in \mathbb{R}^{C \times 2}$ is constructed which can be represented as

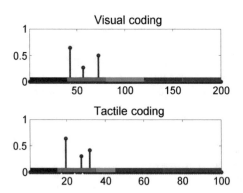

Fig. 7.5 An illustration of the joint group sparse coding methods (different color blocks on the horizontal axis represent different groups). The two coding vectors share the same sparsity pattern at the higher group level, but not necessarily at the lower (inside the group) level. This can be achieved by solving the optimization problem (7.6). Please note that in this example, the joint sparse coding cannot be applicable due to the reason that the atoms in different dictionaries are not paired

$$\mathbf{Z} = \begin{bmatrix} ||\delta^{(1)}(\boldsymbol{x})||_2 & ||\delta^{(1)}(\boldsymbol{y})||_2 \\ ||\delta^{(2)}(\boldsymbol{x})||_2 & ||\delta^{(2)}(\boldsymbol{y})||_2 \\ \vdots & \vdots \\ ||\delta^{(C)}(\boldsymbol{x})||_2 & ||\delta^{(C)}(\boldsymbol{y})||_2 \end{bmatrix}.$$

From the definition of $\mathbf{Z}$, it can be known that $\mathbf{Z}$ provides a joint representation of the weakly paired visual–tactile data at the group level. To encourage the joint group sparsity, the matrix $\mathbf{Z}$ is required to be row-sparse. This can be realized by using the $L_{2,1}$-norm, which calculates the sum of the 2-norm of each row. Therefore, the optimization model is improved in (7.3) as

$$\min_{x,y} ||\Phi(\mathbb{T}) - \Phi(\mathcal{T})\boldsymbol{x}||_2^2 + ||\Psi(\mathbb{V}) - \Psi(\mathcal{V})\boldsymbol{y}||_2^2 + \lambda(||\boldsymbol{x}||_1 + ||\boldsymbol{y}||_1) + \alpha||\mathbf{Z}||_{2,1}, \quad (7.6)$$

where α is the parameter to control the importance of the row-sparsity of $\mathbf{Z}$. The independent sparse coding solutions for each modality can be obtained by setting $\alpha = 0$. In fact, this model encourages all the signals to share the same groups, while the active set inside each group is signal dependent. This model is particularly well suitable for our case where the data are not sample-paired, but group-paired.

The optimization problem (7.6) can be reformulated to a convex optimization problem and can be easily solved by using a conventional software package such as CVX. Also, specific solving algorithms can be developed to achieve better efficiency [17].

7.4 Experimental Results

In this section, the collected dataset and the experimental validation results are introduced.

7.4.1 Data Collection

7.4.1.1 Objects

In order to understand how the method proposed in this chapter would work on their intended subject, household real-world objects, a collection of 18 common objects are gathered, shown in Fig. 7.6. The common requirement for these objects is that they all have to be within the manipulator's perception and manipulation capabilities (not too large to grasp, etc.). The objects included in the collection are as follows: Green Portable Cup(GPC), Blue Portable Cup(BPC), Empty Beer Can(EBC), Full Beer Can(FBC), Empty Tea Can(ETC), Full Tea Can(FTC), Coffee Disposable Cup(CDC), Soft Disposable Cup(SDC), Hard Disposable Cup(HDC), PLastic

Fig. 7.6 18 objects used in our experimental validation. These objects have a wide range of properties including; hard/soft, full/empty, paper/plastic, green/blue. [2017] IEEE. Reprinted, with permission, from Ref. [11]

Cup(PLC), Empty Mizone Bottle(EMB),[1] Full Mizone Bottle(FMB), Empty Pocari Bottle(EPB), Full Pocari Bottle(FPB), Toy PEnguin(TPE), Toy DRagon(TDR), Toy DOll(TDO), Toy PAnda(TPA). These objects were divided into five categories and the classification difficulty within each category was analyzed. Please note the category information is just used for illustration but is not used for classifier design. In Table 7.1, it provides the details about the dataset. The last two columns list the difficulty using either visual or tactile modality only. Generally speaking, the appearance information makes the visual modality useful and the material information makes the tactile modality useful. In Figs. 7.7 and 7.8, some representative examples are demonstrated. From those figures, it can be seen that EPB and FPB are visually similar but distinguishable by touch. Otherwise, the TDO and TPA are visually dissimilar but indistinguishable by touch. However, for some objects, such as the ones in the categories *Can* (EBC, FBC, ETC, and FTC), it is difficult to classify them using a single modality.

---

[1]Mizone and Pocari are just two trademarks.

Table 7.1 Description of the 18 objects

Category	Name	Abbr.	Difficulty	
			Visual	Tactile
Portable Cup	Green Portable Cup	GPC	✓	✗
	Blue Portable Cup	BPC		
Can	Empty Beer Can	EBC	✗	✗
	Full Beer Can	FBC		
	Empty Tea Can	ETC		
	Full Tea Can	FTC		
Cup	Coffee Disposable Cup	CDC	✓	✓
	Soft Disposable Cup	SDC		
	Hard Disposable Cup	HDC		
	PLastic Cup	PLC		
Bottle	Empty Mizone Bottle	EMB	✗	✓
	Full Mizone Bottle	FMB		
	Empty Pocari Bottle	EPB		
	Full Pocari Bottle	FPB		
Toy	Toy PEnguin	TPE	✓	✗
	Toy DRagon	TDR		
	Toy DOll	TDO		
	Toy PAnda	TPA		

7.4.1.2 Visual Modality Collection

To validate the power of the proposed method on weakly paired visual–tactile data, the visual modality data and tactile modality data are deliberately collected separately. This is also practical for the manipulator since the relative spatial relationship between the camera and the manipulator is potentially unknown or otherwise changing.

The visual modality data collection procedure is similar to the work in [13]. Each object was placed in a stable configuration at the approximate center of a clear table and an image was then acquired with a camera. To get different poses, an electrical dial was used to rotate the object through 360° and 10 images were taken per objects one at every about 36° of rotation. Furthermore, the height of the camera was changed and repeated this procedure. Thus, 20 images corresponding to different poses for each object were obtained. Finally, the object was clipped out using a fixed rectangular bounding box and was resized to 80 × 100. In Fig. 7.9, some representative images of certain objects are listed. It can be clear to analyze the roles of visual modality by constructing such a dataset.

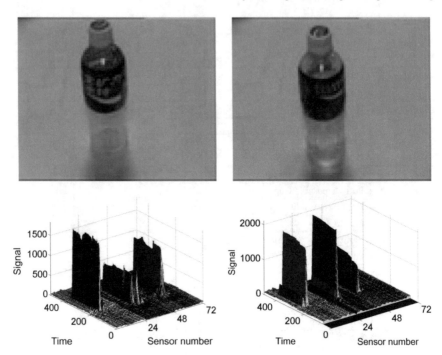

Fig. 7.7 Representative examples of EPB and FPB: The first row shows the samples of the visual modality and the second row shows the samples of tactile modality

7.4.1.3   Tactile Modality Collection

As mentioned, the tool used for gathering the tactile data is a Schunk manipulator equipped with a BarrettHand that includes tactile sensors. The experimental setup is shown in Fig. 7.10.

The objects were placed in a fixed graspable position on a table and the trajectory planning of the manipulator was performed offline. The data collection procedure is similar to the active perception workflow in [3], as a static reading of tactile information is insufficient to classify the object under inspection. To this end, a grasp controller is devised that executed a palpation procedure: first, it fixed the hand position and orientation and then fully opened the hand fingers, yielding the pre-shape. After the manipulator's effector reached the graspable position, the hand closed the fingers with constant velocity along a pre-defined trajectory. Because the tactile sensor outputs zero when the sensor is not touching an object, the start of a palpation event is determined when the tactile sensor input was above a specified small threshold. Furthermore, the hand pressed on the object by moving each finger along the same trajectory. This continued until the motion was blocked or the trajectory motion was finished. Motion blocks were detected by checking that motor encoder values remained unchanged for 0.5 s. During this activity, the tactile sensors were stimu-

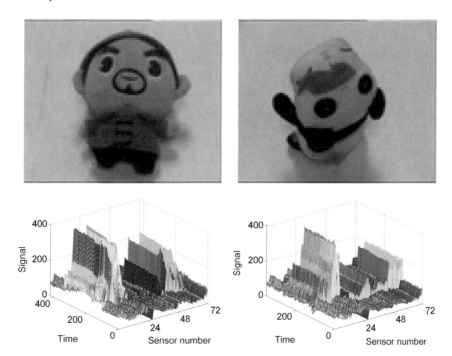

Fig. 7.8 Representative examples of TDO and TPA: The first row shows the samples of the visual modality and the second row shows the samples of tactile modality

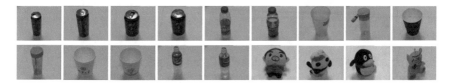

Fig. 7.9 Representative images of the objects. [2017] IEEE. Reprinted, with permission, from Ref. [11]

lated with a sequence of tactile measurements. As the execution time varied with each operation, the length of each tactile sequence likewise varied. Finally, all measurements were normalized to the sensor's maximum response. Figure 7.10 shows some details regarding the grasp procedure.

During the tactile data collection, each object was randomly placed on the table and grasped 10 times using the three fingers of the dexterous hands. Each grasp action lasted 8.2–18 s. The sampling period was 0.04 s, and therefore, the length of the obtained sequence was 205–450. For each of these classes, a dataset of 10 samples is created using our grasp controller and recorded the data for the pressing portion of the grasp, yielding a total of $18 \times 10 = 180$ tactile sequence samples.

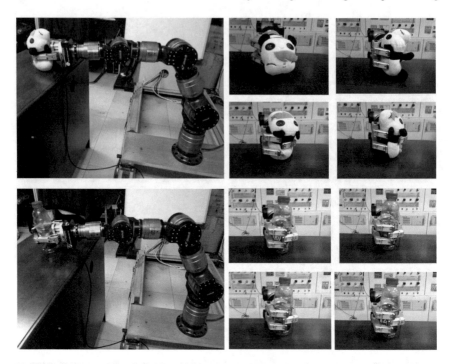

Fig. 7.10 Grasp procedure. The left columns show the grasp action for two objects: Toy and Bottle. The right-top and right-bottom panels show four trials of the grasp for the two objects, respectively. Since the object is randomly placed on the table, the grasp points are different for each trial. [2017] IEEE. Reprinted, with permission, from Ref. [11]

Please note that the object was randomly placed to ensure some variability in the dataset. Figure 7.11 shows the representative tactile sequences for each object.

7.4.2   Methods

Throughout the experiments, the following methods are compared:

1. The k-Nearest Neighborhood (k-NN) methods: Those methods search the k nearest neighborhoods in the training set and use majority voting to get the class label. If only using the visual modality, the distance d_{COV} would be used and the method is referred to k-NN-V. If only using the tactile modality, the distance d_{CTW} would be used and the method is referred to k-NN-T. Note that since there is no explicit correspondence between samples for visual modality and tactile modality, there is no clear formulation for fusion under this framework.

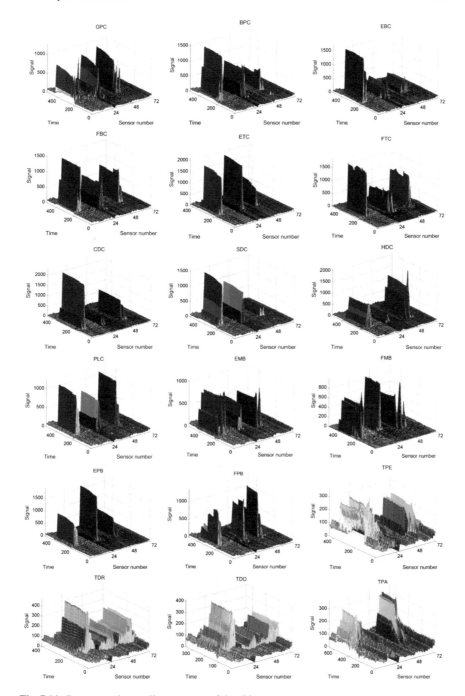

Fig. 7.11 Representative tactile sequences of the objects

2. Kernel Sparse Coding with Visual modality (KSC-V) [5]: This method uses the visual modality only and solves the kernel sparse coding optimization problem to perform the classification.
3. Kernel Sparse Coding with Tactile modality (KSC-T) [5]: This method uses the tactile modality only and solves the kernel sparse coding optimization problem to perform the classification.
4. Joint Group Kernel Sparse Coding (JGKSC): This is the proposed method that fuses the visual and tactile modalities under the joint group kernel sparse coding framework.

By comparison with k-NN methods, the roles of kernel sparse coding can be shown. In addition, by comparing the proposed method with KSC-V and KSC-T, the role of the multimodal fusion can be clearly observed.

Regarding the k-NN-V and k-NN-T methods, it can be observed that the classification performance decreases during increases in the values of k. This is consistent with the results presented in [3]. Therefore, the value is fixed as $k = 1$. As to KSC-V, KSC-T, and JKSC methods, it is empirically to set the parameters $\lambda = \alpha = 0.001$, where λ corresponds to the sparsity penalty terms for the visual modality and the tactile modality; α is the penalty parameter to control the joint group sparsity term. The parameter sensitivity will be analyzed later.

7.4.3 Result Analysis

To fairly compare the different methods, a test protocol for the constructed multi-modal dataset which includes 360 image samples and 180 tactile sequence samples is firstly devised. For each class, 10 images and 5 tactile sequences are randomly selected to form 50 testing pairs. The remaining 10 images and 5 tactile sequences for this class are regarded as training samples. Therefore, for this test $10 \times 18 = 180$ training images and $5 \times 18 = 90$ training tactile sequences can be obtained. The total number of the testing pairs is $50 \times 17 = 900$.

In Fig. 7.12, the classification accuracy is listed, which shows that the sparse coding methods including KSC-V, KSC-T, and JGKSC always outperform k-NN methods. In fact, KSC-V achieves 11% improvements compared with k-NN-V, while KSC-T achieves 16% improvements compared with k-NN-T. This verifies that the sparse coding method can improve performance even using single modality. On the other hand, the proposed method, JGKSC, obtains significant improvements compared with KSC-V and KSC-T. The experimental results show that considering both visual and tactile input is beneficial and the proposed method indeed provides an effective method for fusion.

For a detailed analysis, three cases are considered for which test pairs are shown in Fig. 7.13. The test pairs come from the objects EMB, TPE, and EBC. All of the sparse coding results are shown in Figs. 7.14, 7.15, and 7.16. In all of the figures, the left panel shows the results of separate sparse coding and the right panel shows the

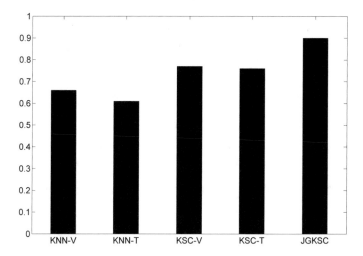

Fig. 7.12 Accuracy of different methods on the dataset

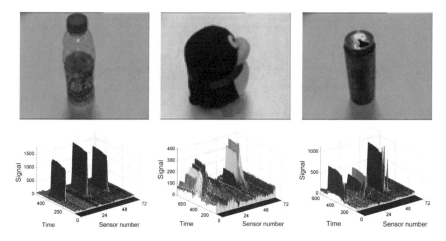

Fig. 7.13 Three test pairs: EMB, TPE, EBC. [2017] IEEE. Reprinted, with permission, from Ref. [11]

joint group sparse coding. In addition, a red solid line is imposed on the x-axis to indicate the correct class.

The sparse coding results of the EMB test pair are shown in Fig. 7.14, in which it can be seen that this object looks similar to FMB and the sparse coding using visual modality admits a significant bias. In the bottom-left panel, it can be seen that most of the coding coefficients are clustered around the true class, with the exception of a few coding coefficients corresponding to the wrong object. In fact, in this example, the touch sense of EMB is a little like that of EPB. This explains why certain isolated elements do not lie in the correct position. However, the results from the proposed

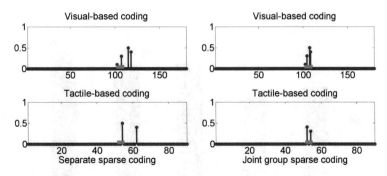

Fig. 7.14 Sparse coding results for the test pair EMB

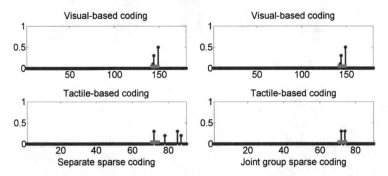

Fig. 7.15 Sparse coding results for the test pair TPE

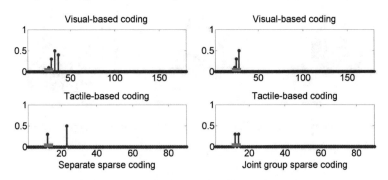

Fig. 7.16 Sparse coding results for the test pair EBC

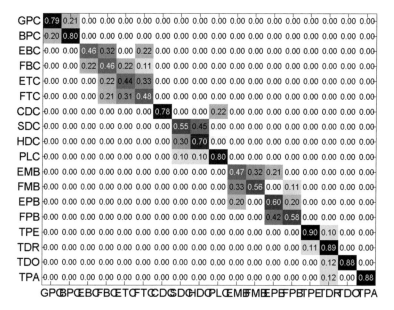

Fig. 7.17 Confusion matrices for k-NN-V method

JGKSC are very robust. According to the right panel of Fig. 7.14, it can be observed that both results cluster around the true class.

Figure 7.15 shows the results of TPE object. The visual modality gives good results since this object is visually distinguished. The tactile results are a little diversified and do not cluster around the true class. This is reasonable since the four toys are made of similar materials, which makes it difficult to differentiate them using tactile modality. Nevertheless, the proposed JGKSC model obtains correct results since it exploits the intrinsic relationship between visual and tactile modalities.

According to the analysis in Table 7.1, the EBC object is difficult to correctly classify using single modality. Figure 7.16 illustrates such a point. In fact, the sparse coding vectors obtained using single modality lack interpretation capability since the results are too cluttered. The results obtained by the proposed JGKSC method, however, still show satisfactory performance.

In Figs. 7.17, 7.18, 7.19, 7.20, and 7.21, the confusion matrices are listed. By comparing the confusion matrices of the five classifiers, it is evident that the results are consistent with both the difficulty analysis in Table 7.1 and our intuition. For example, visual modality is good at recognizing *Toy*, while tactile modality is good at recognizing *Bottle*. The results are significantly improved by using the visual–tactile fusion method, which leads to 100% accuracy for 8 objects. Additionally, in our dataset, there are also some bottles or cans, in which the empty one and the full one appear almost completely similar, visually speaking. In the experiments, it is observed that these two objects could be successfully differentiated from each other.

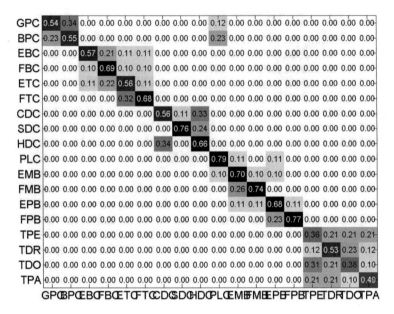

Fig. 7.18 Confusion matrices for *k*-NN-T method

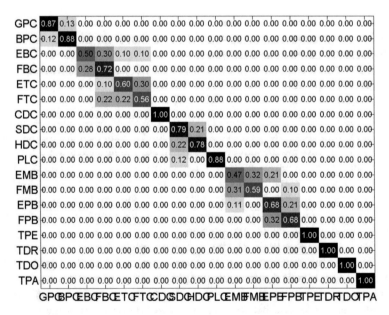

Fig. 7.19 Confusion matrices for KSC-V method

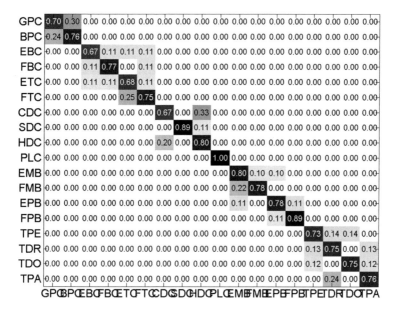

Fig. 7.20 Confusion matrices for KSC-T method

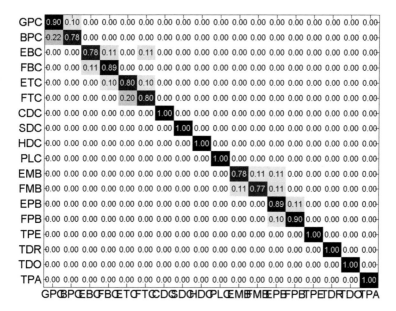

Fig. 7.21 Confusion matrices for JGKSC method

Fig. 7.22 Classification accuracy versus the varying values of the parameters λ and α. The results show that the accuracy does not vary monotonically with λ and α. This illustrates the different roles of the reconstruction errors, sparsity and the joint sparsity

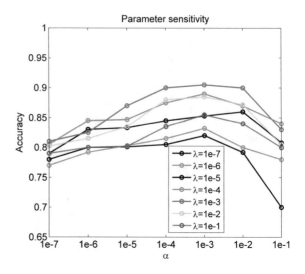

7.4.4   Parameter Sensitivity

In this section, the result demonstrating parameter sensitivity is represented. For facilitation, λ and α are varied from 10^{-7} to 10^{-1}. The classification accuracies are illustrated in Fig. 7.22, from which it can tell that as α increases, the classification performance does not monotonically increase. The satisfactory performance can be obtained when the values of λ are selected from the interval $[10^{-4}, 10^{-2}]$. This means that all of the kernel reconstruction error term, the sparse term, and the joint group sparse term play important roles in finding good solutions.

7.4.5   Time Cost

The developed joint group kernel sparse coding method does not require a training phase, and therefore, only the time cost of the test phase is concerned. Using an un-optimized MATLAB program on a PC platform (3.4 GHz CPU, 16 G Memory), it is found that the calculation of kernels between the test sample pair and the dictionary atoms needs about 1.5 s and the coding stage needs about 0.9 s. Therefore, the whole test time for one test sample pair is about 2.4 s. An un-optimized C program is also developed to evaluate the efficiency and it is found that only 0.22 s are needed for one test pair. The recognition calculation time is rather lower than the grasping time for the manipulator. Therefore, it does satisfy the requirements of most of the practical visual–tactile fusion object recognition tasks. Additionally, the time efficiency can be improved by resorting the kernel dictionary learning [10] to reduce the size of dictionary.

7.5 Summary

In this chapter, a novel object recognition method is proposed using visual–tactile fusion information. Due to the weak-pairing intrinsic characteristics, a joint group kernel sparse coding method is developed to effectively represent visual–tactile information. The experimental results show that the utilization of visual–tactile multimodal information significantly improves the classification accuracy.

Although our focus is on combining visual and tactile information, the described problem framework is quite common in the automation community. The algorithms described in this paper were, therefore, designed to work with weak pairings between a variety of sensors. The next chapter will extend this method to other more general application scenarios.

References

1. Allen, P.K.: Integrating vision and touch for object recognition tasks. Int. J. Robot. Res. **7**(6), 15–33 (1988)
2. Beauchamp, M.S.: See me, hear me, touch me: multisensory integration in lateral occipital-temporal cortex. Curr. Opin. Neurobiol. **15**(2), 145–153 (2005)
3. Drimus, A., Kootstra, G., Bilberg, A., Kragic, D.: Design of a flexible tactile sensor for classification of rigid and deformable objects. Robot. Auton. Syst. **62**(1), 3–15 (2014)
4. Ernst, M.O., Banks, M.S.: Humans integrate visual and haptic information in a statistically optimal fashion. Nature **415**(6870), 429–433 (2002)
5. Gao, S., Tsang, I.W., Chia, L.T.: Sparse representation with kernels. IEEE Trans. Image Process. **22**(2), 423–434 (2013)
6. Heller, M.A.: Visual and tactual texture perception: intersensory cooperation. Atten. Percept. Psychophys. **31**(4), 339–344 (1982)
7. Kroemer, O., Lampert, C.H., Peters, J.: Learning dynamic tactile sensing with robust vision-based training. IEEE Trans. Robot. **27**(3), 545–557 (2011)
8. Lacey, S., Campbell, C., Sathian, K.: Vision and touch: multiple or multisensory representations of objects? Perception **36**(10), 1513–1521 (2007)
9. Lederman, S.J., Klatzky, R.L.: Multisensory texture perception. Handb. Multisens. Process., 107–122 (2004)
10. Liu, H., Qin, J., Cheng, H., Sun, F.: Robust kernel dictionary learning using a whole sequence convergent algorithm. IJCAI **1**(2), 5 (2015)
11. Liu, H., Yu, Y., Sun, F., Gu, J.: Visual-tactile fusion for object recognition. IEEE Trans. Autom. Sci. Eng. **14**(2), 996–1008 (2017)
12. Natale, L., Metta, G., Sandini, G.: Learning haptic representation of objects. In: International Conference on Intelligent Manipulation and Grasping (2004)
13. Nene, S.A., Nayar, S.K., Murase, H., et al.: Columbia Object Image Library (coil-20) (1996)
14. Norman, J.F., Norman, H.F., Clayton, A.M., Lianekhammy, J., Zielke, G.: The visual and haptic perception of natural object shape. Atten. Percept. Psychophys. **66**(2), 342–351 (2004)
15. Shekhar, S., Patel, V.M., Nasrabadi, N.M., Chellappa, R.: Joint sparse representation for robust multimodal biometrics recognition. IEEE Trans. Pattern Anal. Mach. Intell. **36**(1), 113–126 (2014)
16. Shrivastava, A., Patel, V.M., Chellappa, R.: Multiple kernel learning for sparse representation-based classification. IEEE Trans. Image Process. **23**(7), 3013–3024 (2014)
17. Sprechmann, P., Ramirez, I., Sapiro, G., Eldar, Y.C.: C-hilasso: a collaborative hierarchical sparse modeling framework. IEEE Trans. Signal Process. **59**(9), 4183–4198 (2011)

18. Wang, D., Zhang, Y., Zhou, W., Zhao, H., Chen, Z.: Collocation accuracy of visuo-haptic system: metrics and calibration. IEEE Trans. Haptics **4**(4), 321–326 (2011)
19. Woods, A.T., Newell, F.N.: Visual, haptic and cross-modal recognition of objects and scenes. J. Physiol. Paris **98**(1), 147–159 (2004)

Chapter 8
Visual–Tactile Fusion Material Identification Using Dictionary Learning

Abstract It is highly expected to develop methodologies capable of integrating information from visual and tactile modality in order to improve the performance of perception. However, real multimodal data often suffers from significant weak-pairing characteristics; i.e., the full pairing between data samples may not be known, while a group of samples from one modality is paired to a group of samples in another modality is known. In this chapter, a novel projective dictionary learning framework is established for weakly paired multimodal data fusion. By introducing a latent-pairing matrix, the simultaneous dictionary learning and pairing matrix estimation are realized, which improves the fusion effect. In addition, the kernelized version and the optimization algorithms are also addressed. Extensive experimental validations on some existing datasets are performed to show the advantages of the proposed method.

8.1 Introduction

The ever-growing development of sensor technology has led to the use of multiple modalities to develop robotic and automation systems. So it is highly expected to develop methodologies capable of integrating information from multiple sensors with the goal of improving the performance of surveillance, diagnosis, prediction, and so on. Reference [11] presented a decision rule to optimally fuse binary sensor decisions in a surveillance sensor system. Reference [25] developed a data fusion model to construct a composite health index via fusion of multiple degradation-based sensor data. Recently, multimodal learning has attracted a lot of research interests. The reason is that there exists more useful information for recognition in multiple modalities than that in a single modality. Some advanced machine learning methods have been developed for sensor fusion. Reference [5] presented novel Gaussian process decentralized data fusion and active sensing algorithms for real-time, fine-grained traffic modeling and prediction with a fleet of vehicles. Reference [4] developed a Bayesian nonparametric Dirichlet Process decision-making approach for real-time monitoring using the data gathered from multiple, heterogeneous sensors. Besides, multimodality has been extensively used in the tasks of classification and clustering [2, 17, 55].

© Springer Nature Singapore Pte Ltd. 2018   159
H. Liu and F. Sun, *Robotic Tactile Perception and Understanding*,
https://doi.org/10.1007/978-981-10-6171-4_8

In many industrial environments, multiple heterogeneous sensors which provide multimodal information are usually used. For example, in surveillance systems, the color and depth images are frequently used to detect and track the targets. The visual and auditory information can be integrated to perform fault diagnosis. In the case of manipulation and grasp, the visual and haptic information are combined to get more accurate object properties. In the unmanned systems, the visual-inertial combination has become a very popular navigation method [32]. In such cases, multimodal data exhibits many challenges.

The first challenge originates from *Different Signal Patterns*. Generally speaking, data collected from multiple sensors may contain different forms of signals. For example, optical camera provides color images; depth camera provides distance images; acoustic sensor provides sound waves; haptic sensor provides tactile sequences. All of these signals exhibit different spatial and temporal resolutions. It is unreasonable, if not impossible, to concatenate them in the original data-level space. Feature coding, such as joint sparse coding method [2, 24], provides feasible solutions to this problem, because it utilizes the dictionary to project the signals into some shared space. To get the coding vectors for the sensor, an optimization problem including costly sparsity computation should be solved and this complicates the engineering system design. A straightforward coding method which provides joint representation for the multimodal data fusion is highly expected in practical development.

The second challenge originates from *Weakly Paired Data*. Most existing multimodal fusion algorithms require that the data is fully paired; i.e., every object has representations in all the modalities, representations from different modalities representing a same object are exactly known, and the representations of the same object have the same index in different modalities. However, this requirement may not be satisfied in many practical settings. Since data from different modalities are usually collected and processed independently, it is hard to ensure the full pairing. A representative example occurs in the task of robotic recognition using both the visual and tactile information [19, 21]. In practice, while cameras can quickly acquire data from large surface areas, haptic sensors obtain information from their relatively small contact region with the surface. Therefore, it is assumed that there is only weakly paired data, which is defined as a group of samples from one modality is paired to a group of samples in another modality [21].

How to relax the full-pairing requirement of the multimodal learning has been an active research topic. Reference [48] proposed an approach to establish the correspondences between misaligned two-resolution metrology data that differ by a nearly rigid body transformation. References [19, 21, 30] developed unsupervised joint dimension reduction method for weakly paired data. Reference [27] addressed the cross-modal matching problems. References [52, 53] investigated the partial multiview clustering problem, which focused on the case that every view suffered from some missing information. Reference [39] developed similar model for learning to Hash on partial multimodal data. Reference [41] tackled the partially paired multimodal sparse dictionary learning by preserving the intermodality and intramodality similarities between the sparse coding coefficients. Reference [50] investigated the problem of multiview clustering for unpaired data. Reference [9] tackled the problem of missing modality in transfer learning using low-rank subspace learning techniques. Reference [36] learned a projection that mapped data instances (from two different spaces) to a lower-dimensional space simultaneously matching the local geometry and preserving the neighborhood relationship within each set. However, the above work focused on solving the partial-pairing or unpairing problem.

To tackle the above challenges, the Projective Dictionary pair Learning (PDL) [12] is employed, which learns a synthesis dictionary and an analysis dictionary jointly to achieve the goal of signal representation and discrimination. Since PDL removes the costly sparsity regularization [15], it is significantly faster in both training and testing, while achieving competitive accuracy. Compared with the above work, this work systematically provides a unified method to deal with full-pairing, partial-pairing, unpairing, and weak-pairing problem. The problem is solved by joint learning of the latent-pairing information and the projective dictionary pair, which has not been addressed.

Before proceeding, here is a brief review about PDL. Since the original PDL formulation was proposed in [12], many successful extensions and applications have been recently reported. This technology has now become an important feature learning technique that owns state-of-the-art recognition performance. It has been extensively utilized for skeletal action recognition [42], door knob recognition [29], illicit drug abuse face classification [43], plastic surgery for face verification [18], and EEG signal classification [1].

Besides the unsupervised feature selection [54], most of the existing work focuses on improving the discriminative capability of PDL by exploiting the structure of the dictionaries and coding vectors. Reference [13] integrated structure preserving and discriminative characters into the basic analysis model to improve the discriminant capability. Reference [47] incorporated the block-diagonal structure of coding coefficient matrix and a block-diagonal structure of analysis dictionary was enforced. In [46], the discrimination of universality and particularity representation was jointly exploited by simultaneously learning a pair of analysis dictionary and synthesis dictionary. Reference [28] presented a correntropy-induced dictionary pair learning framework. The adopted maximum correntropy criterion was much more insensitive to outliers. Reference [14] proposed a triplet-constraint-based topology preserving loss function to capture the underlying local topological structures of data in a supervised manner.

For supervised learning, incorporating label information into the objective functions of PDL also attracted a lot of attentions [33]. In [45], a discriminative analysis–synthesis dictionary was combined with a linear classifier and they could be jointly learned to get better recognition performance. Reference [37] argued that discrimination of paired dictionary can be also achieved through learning from pairs of classes. Reference [31] extended PDL to the partially labeled data. In [26], a nonnegative projection and dictionary with discriminative graph constraints was developed. In [51], a joint label consistent embedding and dictionary learning approach was proposed for delivering a linear sparse codes auto-extractor and a multiclass classifier by simultaneously minimizing the sparse reconstruction, discriminative sparse code,

code approximation and classification errors. Very recently, Ref. [38] incorporated a dictionary pair classifier layer into the deep architecture and developed an end-to-end learning algorithm for optimizing the dictionary pairs and the neural networks simultaneously.

The above work dealt with single modality only. The application of PDL in multimodal data is still rare. Reference [44] proposed unsupervised domain adaptive dictionary pair learning to deal with transfer learning. Reference [8] proposed fast and efficient multimodal eye biometrics using projective dictionary pair learning. Reference [22] proposed a cross-view projective dictionary learning method to tackle the misalignment of the image patches. The core idea of this work was the assumption that the patches in different views could share a similar dictionary. This requires that the data in different views share the same dimension size and therefore this model cannot be used in general heterogeneous cases.

In this chapter, a unified formulation for multimodal fusion problem is systematically developed under the nonlinear projective dictionary pair learning framework. A kernelized projective dictionary pair learning framework is established to deal with samples which do not lie in Euclidean space. It is used to tackle the weakly paired visual–tactile samples. Extensive experimental validations including the weakly paired visual-haptic fusion recognition problem on the PHAC-2 are performed to show the effectiveness of the proposed method.

The rest of this chapter is organized as follows: In Sect. 8.2, the problem formulation is presented. Section 8.3 gives the optimization model and Sect. 8.4 is about the experimental results. In Sect. 8.5, some extensive applications are presented.

8.2 Problem Formulation

The samples for the visual and tactile modalities are denoted as

$$\mathfrak{T} = \{\mathfrak{T}_1, \mathfrak{T}_2, \ldots, \mathfrak{T}_C\}, \quad \mathfrak{V} = \{\mathfrak{V}_1, \mathfrak{V}_2, \ldots, \mathfrak{V}_C\},$$

where $\mathfrak{T}_c$ represents a set of training samples from the tactile modality labeled with the cth class, and $\mathfrak{V}_c$ represents a set of training samples from the visual modality labeled with the cth class. The feature space representation is given by $\Phi(\mathfrak{T}_c)$ and $\Psi(\mathfrak{V}_c)$, respectively.

Although different modalities of data have different feature sets, they share the same semantics if they represent the same content or topic. To preserve such inter-modality similarity, it is assumed that $\mathfrak{T}_c$ can be divided into G_c disjoint subsets $\mathfrak{T}_{c,g}$ for $g = 1, 2, \ldots, G_c$, and $\mathfrak{V}_c$ can be divided into H_c disjoint subsets $\mathfrak{V}_{c,h}$ for $h = 1, 2, \ldots, H_c$. That is to say,

$$\mathfrak{T}_c = \cup_{g=1,2,\ldots,G_c} \mathfrak{T}_{c,g}, \quad \mathfrak{V}_c = \cup_{h=1,2,\ldots,H_c} \mathfrak{V}_{c,h}$$

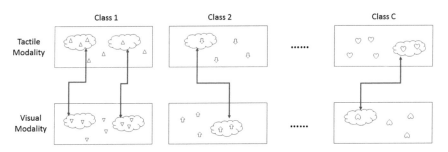

Fig. 8.1 An illustration of the weakly paired two-modality case. The rectangles represent the classes and the clouds represent the groups. The paired groups between modalities are connected with the arrowed red lines. For example, a *Class* is a set of images of bananas and *Groups* are the same banana but different viewpoints. Note that the numbers of samples in paired groups are permitted to be different

where $\mathfrak{T}_{c,g_1} \cap \mathfrak{T}_{c,g_2} = \varnothing$ for $g_1 \neq g_2$, and $\mathfrak{V}_{c,h_1} \cap \mathfrak{V}_{c,h_2} = \varnothing$ for $h_1 \neq h_2$. Figure 8.1 illustrates the weakly paired cases.

Then the pairing set between the visual and tactile modalities can be defined as

$$\mathcal{M}_c = \{(g, h) | \mathfrak{T}_{c,g} \text{ is paired with } \mathfrak{V}_{c,h}\} \tag{8.1}$$

Without loss of generalization, it is assumed that for any element pairs $(g_1, h_1) \in \mathcal{M}_c$ and $(g_2, h_2) \in \mathcal{M}_c$, neither the relation $g_1 \neq g_1$ nor $h_1 \neq h_1$ holds. The representation in Eq. (8.1) is very general because it produces the following well-known special cases:

1. Full pairing:
$$N_c = M_c = G_c = H_c = |\mathcal{M}_c| > 0.$$

2. Partial pairing:
$$N_c = M_c = G_c = H_c > |\mathcal{M}_c| > 0.$$

3. Unpairing:
$$\mathcal{M}_c = \emptyset.$$

In fact, in this framework, the requirements of $N_c = M_c$ or $G_c = H_c$ are not imposed at all, which are common in the above cases. Figure 8.2 shows an illustration of such cases.

This work develops a classification method using the multimodal dataset $\mathfrak{T}$ and $\mathfrak{V}$ and the available weak-pairing sets in Eq. (8.1). Its goal is to give a label for the multimodal test sample set $\{\mathbb{T}, \mathbb{V}\}$.

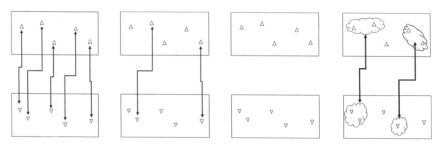

Fig. 8.2 An illustration of different pairing forms. The paired samples are connected with the thin red lines and the paired groups (represented by clouds) are connected with the thick red lines. From LEFT to RIGHT: Full pairing, partial pairing, unpairing, and weak pairing

8.3 Proposed Model

In real-world data, the mappings between different modalities can be complex. In addition, the original samples may contain noisy or redundancy components. There-fore, the PDL method is resorted to obtain the coding vectors which bridge the dif-ferent modalities. Therefore, the single modal PDL problem [12] can be formulated as

$$
\begin{cases}
\min\limits_{\mathfrak{D}_c, \mathfrak{P}_c, X_c} \sum\limits_{c=1}^{C} \|\Phi(\mathfrak{T}_c) - \mathfrak{D}_c X_c\|_F^2 + \|X_c - \mathfrak{P}_c\Phi(\mathfrak{T}_c)\|_F^2 + \lambda\|\mathfrak{P}_c\Phi(\mathfrak{T}_{\bar{c}})\|_F^2 \\
\min\limits_{\mathfrak{F}_c, \mathfrak{P}_c, Y_c} \sum\limits_{c=1}^{C} \|\Psi(\mathfrak{V}_c) - \mathfrak{F}_c Y_c\|_F^2 + \|Y_c - \mathfrak{Q}_c\Psi(\mathfrak{V}_c)\|_F^2 + \lambda\|\mathfrak{Q}_c\Psi(\mathfrak{V}_{\bar{c}})\|_F^2
\end{cases}
$$

(8.2)

where $\mathfrak{D}_c$ and $\mathfrak{P}_c$ are the synthesis dictionaries; $X_c \in R^{K \times N_c}$ and $Y_c \in R^{K \times M_c}$ are the coding matrices; $\mathfrak{P}_c$ and $\mathfrak{Q}_c$ are the analysis dictionaries. The number of K is the size of the dictionaries which should be prescribed by the designer. $\mathfrak{T}_{\bar{c}}$ and $\mathfrak{V}_{\bar{c}}$ denote the complementary set of $\mathfrak{T}_c$ and $\mathfrak{V}_c$ in the whole training set $\mathfrak{T}$ and $\mathfrak{V}$. The parameter λ is used to penalize the third term, which encourages the sub-dictionaries $\mathfrak{P}_c$ and $\mathfrak{Q}_c$ to project the samples which are not from the cth class to a null space, and therefore enhance the discriminative capability.

Since the mapping $\Phi(\cdot)$ and $\Psi(\cdot)$ are just implicitly described, the above opti-mization problems can not be solved. Using the generalized *Representer Theorem* [16, 34], it can be induced that the dictionaries can be reconstructed by the samples in the feature space. That is to say, they admit the following forms:

$$
\begin{cases}
\mathfrak{D}_c = \Phi(\mathfrak{T}_c) A_c \\
\mathfrak{P}_c = C_c \Phi^T(\mathfrak{T}_c)
\end{cases}
\qquad
\begin{cases}
\mathfrak{F}_c = \Psi(\mathfrak{V}_c) E_c, \\
\mathfrak{Q}_c = B_c \Psi^T(\mathfrak{V}_c)
\end{cases}
$$

(8.3)

For some reconstruction matrices, $A_c \in R^{N_c \times K}$, $E_c \in R^{M_c \times K}$, $C_c \in R^{K \times N_c}$, and $B_c \in R^{K \times M_c}$. Using the above relation, the optimization problem can be formulated as

$$
\begin{cases}
\min\limits_{A_c, C_c, X_c} \sum\limits_{c=1}^{C} \|\Phi(\mathbb{T}_c) - \Phi(\mathbb{T}_c) A_c X_c\|_F^2 + \|X_c - C_c K_c\|_F^2 + \lambda \|C_c K_{\bar{c}}\|_F^2 \\
\min\limits_{E_c, B_c, Y_c} \sum\limits_{c=1}^{C} \|\Psi(\mathbb{V}_c) - \Psi(\mathbb{V}_c) E_c Y_c\|_F^2 + \|Y_c - E_c R_c\|_F^2 + \lambda \|B_c R_{\bar{c}}\|_F^2
\end{cases}
\tag{8.4}
$$

where $K_c = \Phi^T(\mathbb{T}_c)\Phi(\mathbb{T}_c)$ and $K_{\bar{c}} = \Phi^T(\mathbb{T}_c)\Phi(\mathbb{T}_{\bar{c}})$, $R_c = \Psi^T(\mathbb{V}_c)\Psi(\mathbb{V}_c)$ and $R_{\bar{c}} = \Psi^T(\mathbb{V}_c)\Psi(\mathbb{V}_{\bar{c}})$.

The above formulation is in fact the kernelized version of the work in [12] for the multimodal cases and is quite general to deal with any kernels. However, it totally neglects the intrinsic relation among the different modalities.

The canonical way to construct multimodal algorithms is to use the dependencies between paired groups. If $\mathbb{T}_{c,g}$ and $\mathbb{V}_{c,h}$ are paired, it is intuitive to require their coding vector sets

$$
\{\mathfrak{P}_c \Phi(\mathbb{T}_{c,i})\}_{i \in \mathscr{T}_{c,g}} \quad \text{and} \quad \{\mathfrak{Q}_c \Psi(\mathbb{V}_{c,i})\}_{i \in \mathscr{V}_{c,h}}
$$

to share similar centers. This leads to the following regularization term

$$
\hat{\mathscr{L}}_c = \sum_{\{g,h\} \in \mathscr{M}_c} \|C_c k_{c,g} - B_c r_{c,h}\|_2^2
\tag{8.5}
$$

where

$$
k_{c,g} = \frac{1}{|\mathscr{T}_{c,g}|} K_{c,g} \mathbf{1}, \quad r_{c,h} = \frac{1}{|\mathscr{V}_{c,h}|} R_{c,h} \mathbf{1},
$$

and

$$
K_{c,g} = \Phi^T(\mathbb{T}_c)\Phi(\mathbb{T}_{c,g}), \quad R_{c,h} = \Psi^T(\mathbb{V}_c)\Psi(\mathbb{V}_{c,h}).
$$

This setting is flexible and can be incorporated into existing work [40, 55] which requires full pairing.

However, the above setting is too coarse to capture the possible sample-to-sample relation. Since this relation is unknown, it is reasonable to develop a permutation matrix

$$
\Pi_{c,\{g,h\}} \in \mathfrak{I}^{|\mathscr{V}_{c,h}| \times |\mathscr{T}_{c,g}|}
$$

to encourage the coding matrix $\mathfrak{P}_c \Phi(\mathbb{T}_{c,g})$ to be similar with the coding matrix $\mathfrak{Q}_c \Psi(\mathbb{V}_{c,h}) \Pi_{c,\{g,h\}}$. Note that the set $\mathfrak{I}$ is defined as

$$\mathfrak{I}^{N \times M} \doteq \{\boldsymbol{\Pi} = [\pi_{ij}] \in R^{N \times M} | \pi_{ij} \in \{0, 1\}, \sum_{i=1}^{N} \pi_{ij} \leq 1 \text{ for } j = 1, 2, \ldots, M,$$

$$\sum_{j=1}^{M} \pi_{ij} \leq 1, \text{ for } i = 1, 2, \ldots, N.\}.$$

(8.6)

This means to transform the orders of some columns in Ψ ($\mathbb{V}_{c,h}$) to be matched to Φ ($\mathbb{T}_{c,g}$). Recall the representations in Eq. (8.3), the following can be constructed

$$\mathscr{L}_c = \sum_{\{g,h\} \in \mathscr{M}_c} ||\boldsymbol{C}_c \boldsymbol{K}_{c,g} - \boldsymbol{B}_c \boldsymbol{R}_{c,h} \boldsymbol{\Pi}_{c,\{g,h\}}||_F^2 \qquad (8.7)$$

to model the intermodality relationship. This method assumes the coding coefficients from one modality to be similar to those obtained by the other modality via a permutation matrix which characterizes the pairing relations between samples. The multimodal PDL problem can then be formulated as

$$\min_{A_c, C_c, X_c, E_c, B_c, Y_c, \Pi_{c,g,h}} \sum_{c=1}^{C} \mathscr{L}_c^T + \mathscr{L}_c^V + \gamma \mathscr{L}_c$$

$$\text{s.t.} \quad ||\boldsymbol{a}_{c,k}||_2 = 1 \text{ for } k = 1, 2, \ldots, K.$$

$$||\boldsymbol{e}_{c,k}||_2 = 1 \text{ for } k = 1, 2, \ldots, K.$$

(8.8)

where

$$\mathscr{L}_c^T = ||\Phi(\mathbb{T}_c) - \Phi(\mathbb{T}_c) A_c X_c||_F^2 + ||X_c - C_c K_c||_F^2 + \lambda||C_c K_{\bar{c}}||_F^2 \qquad (8.9)$$

and

$$\mathscr{L}_c^V = ||\Psi(\mathbb{V}_c) - \Psi(\mathbb{V}_c) E_c Y_c||_F^2 + ||Y_c - E_c R_c||_F^2 + \lambda||B_c R_{\bar{c}}||_F^2 \qquad (8.10)$$

Note that here $\boldsymbol{a}_{c,k}$ and $\boldsymbol{e}_{c,k}$ are used to denote the kth column of A_c and E_c, respectively. The constraints on $\boldsymbol{a}_{c,k}$ and $\boldsymbol{e}_{c,k}$ are imposed to avoid the trivial solutions. In the above optimization problem, the pairing term $\mathscr{L}_c$ is used to model the intermodality relationship. The parameter γ is introduced to penalize the role of the intermodality term. In Fig. 8.3, different pairing strategies are illustrated.

Although there are many variables in Eq. (8.8), they can be alternatively optimized as follows.

8.3.1   Updating the Coding Vectors

This step tries to update X_c and Y_c. By fixing other variables, Eq. (8.8) is reduced to $2C$ separate problems:

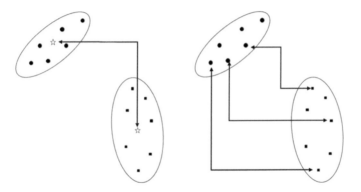

Fig. 8.3 Pairing strategy. The clouds represent the paired groups in different modalities and the lines represent the adopted pairing strategy. LEFT: The virtual mean samples (represented by the pentagrams) are constructed and the similarity constraints on them are imposed. RIGHT: The partial-pairing information between samples are automatically detected and the similarity constraints are imposed on them

$$
\begin{cases}
\min_{X_c} \| \Phi(\mathbb{T}_c) - \Phi(\mathbb{T}_c) A_c X_c \|_F^2 + \| X_c - C_c K_c \|_F^2 \\
\min_{Y_c} \| \Psi(\mathbb{V}_c) - \Psi(\mathbb{V}_c) E_c Y_c \|_F^2 + \| Y_c - E_c R_c \|_F^2
\end{cases}
\tag{8.11}
$$

for $c = 1, 2, \ldots, C$. It can be transformed as:

$$
\begin{cases}
\min_{X_c} Tr\{-2(K_c^T(A_c + C_c^T) X_c) + X_c^T(A_c^T K_c A_c + I) X_c\} \\
\min_{Y_c} Tr\{-2(R_c^T(E_c + B_c^T) Y_c) + Y_c^T(E_c^T R_c E_c + I) Y_c\}
\end{cases}
\tag{8.12}
$$

and the analytic solution is obtained

$$
\begin{cases}
X_c = (A_c^T K_c A_c + I)^{-1}(A_c^T + C_c) K_c. \\
Y_c = (E_c^T R_c E_c + I)^{-1}(E_c^T + B_c) R_c.
\end{cases}
\tag{8.13}
$$

8.3.2 Updating the Dictionary Coefficients

This step tries to update A_c and C_c, E_c and B_c. By fixing other variables, they can be solved independently. For each class $c = 1, 2, \ldots, C$,

$$
\min_{C_c, B_c} \{ \| X_c - C_c K_c \|_F^2 + \| Y_c - B_c R_c \|_F^2 + \lambda \| C_c K_{\bar{c}} \|_F^2 + \lambda \| B_c R_{\bar{c}} \|_F^2
$$
$$
+ \gamma \sum_{\{g,h\} \in \mathcal{M}_c} \| C_c K_{c,g} - B_c R_{c,h} \Pi_{c,\{g,h\}} \|_F^2 \}.
\tag{8.14}
$$

This problem can be easily solved using the block-coordinate descent method [55].

On the other hand, for each class $c = 1, 2, \ldots, C$ and $k = 1, 2, \ldots, K$,

$$\min_{A_c} \| \Phi(\mathfrak{T}_c) - \Phi(\mathfrak{T}_c) A_c X_c \|_F^2$$
$$\text{s.t. } \| a_{c,k} \|_2 = 1. \tag{8.15}$$

and

$$\min_{E_c} \| \Psi(\mathfrak{V}_c) - \Psi(\mathfrak{V}_c) E_c Y_c \|_F^2$$
$$\text{s.t. } \| e_{c,k} \|_2 = 1. \tag{8.16}$$

Those problems can be efficiently solved using ADMM algorithm as introduced in [12].

8.3.3   Updating the Pairing Matrix

This step tries to update the pairing matrix $\boldsymbol{\Pi}_{c,g,h}$. Before developing the algorithm, a theorem which is useful for the derivations is presented:

Theorem 8.1   *Given any matrix* $V \in R^{N_1 \times N_2}$ *and* $\boldsymbol{\Pi} \in \mathfrak{I}^{N_2 \times N_1}$, *there is*

$$Tr(\boldsymbol{\Pi}^T V^T V \boldsymbol{\Pi}) = Tr(V \boldsymbol{\Lambda}_V \boldsymbol{\Pi}),$$

where **V** *is an all-one matrix with compatible dimensions, and* $\boldsymbol{\Lambda}_V = \text{diag}(V^T V)$.

Proof From the property of matrix trace it is easy to get

$$Tr(\boldsymbol{\Pi}^T V^T V \boldsymbol{\Pi}) = Tr(V^T V \boldsymbol{\Pi} \boldsymbol{\Pi}^T).$$

Denote the (i, j)th element of Π as π_{ij}, then the (i, j)th element of $\boldsymbol{\Pi\Pi}^T$ is $\sum_{k=1}^{N_2} \pi_{ik} \pi_{jk}$. According to the property of $\boldsymbol{\Pi}$, it is known that either π_{ik} or π_{jk} should be zero when $i \neq j$. Therefore, $\boldsymbol{\Pi\Pi}^T$ is a diagonal matrix of which (i, i)th element is $\sum_{k=1}^{N_2} \pi_{ik}^2$. Since π_{ik} takes values in the set $\{0, 1\}$, it is easy to get $\pi_{ik}^2 = \pi_{ik}$. Thus, the (i, i)th element of $\boldsymbol{\Pi\Pi}^T$ is $\sum_{k=1}^{N_2} \pi_{ik}$. Finally, the following relation can be achieved.

$$Tr(V^T V \boldsymbol{\Pi} \boldsymbol{\Pi}^T) = Tr(\boldsymbol{\Lambda}_V \boldsymbol{\Pi} V) = Tr(V \boldsymbol{\Lambda}_V \boldsymbol{\Pi}).$$

This completes the proof.   □

The updating of $\boldsymbol{\Pi}_{c,\{g,h\}}$ requires solving the optimization problems:

$$\min_{\boldsymbol{\varPi}_{c,\{g,h\}}} \sum_{\{g,h\}\in\mathcal{M}_c} ||\boldsymbol{C}_c\boldsymbol{K}_{c,g} - \boldsymbol{B}_c\boldsymbol{R}_{c,h}\boldsymbol{\varPi}_{c,\{g,h\}}||_F^2$$

By using the Lemma, it can be separated into $\sum_{c=1}^{C} |\mathcal{M}_c^{m,n}|$ problems

$$\min_{\boldsymbol{\varPi}_{c,\{g,h\}}} Tr((-2\boldsymbol{K}_{c,g}^T\boldsymbol{C}_c^T\boldsymbol{C}_c\boldsymbol{R}_{c,h} + \boldsymbol{V}\boldsymbol{\Lambda}_c)\boldsymbol{\varPi}_{c,\{g,h\}}) \tag{8.17}$$

where $\boldsymbol{\Lambda}_c = \text{diag}(\boldsymbol{K}_{c,h}^T\boldsymbol{C}_c^T\boldsymbol{C}_c\boldsymbol{K}_{c,h})$. This is a typical linear assignment problem which can be efficiently solved using Hungarian algorithm [19].

8.3.4 Algorithm Summarization

The above procedures are repeated until convergence. The whole algorithm is summarized in Algorithm 4.

Algorithm 4 Multimodal Projective Dictionary Learning

Input: Dataset $\mathfrak{T}$ and $\mathfrak{V}$.
Output: Solutions $\boldsymbol{A}_c$, $\boldsymbol{C}_c$, $\boldsymbol{E}_c$ and $\boldsymbol{B}_c$.
1: Initialize $\boldsymbol{A}_c$, $\boldsymbol{C}_c$, $\boldsymbol{E}_c$, $\boldsymbol{B}_c$. and $\boldsymbol{\varPi}_{c,\{g,h\}}$.
2: **while** Not convergent **do**
3:      Fix $\boldsymbol{A}_c$, $\boldsymbol{C}_c$, $\boldsymbol{E}_c$, $\boldsymbol{B}_c$, update $\boldsymbol{X}_c$ by Eq. (8.13).
4:      Fix $\boldsymbol{X}_c$, $\boldsymbol{Y}_c$ and $\boldsymbol{\varPi}_{c,\{g,h\}}$, update $\boldsymbol{C}_c$, $\boldsymbol{A}_c$, $\boldsymbol{E}_c$ and $\boldsymbol{B}_c$ by Eqs. (8.14) and (8.15), respectively.
5:      Fix $\boldsymbol{C}_c$, update $\boldsymbol{\varPi}_{c,\{g,h\}}$ by Eq. (8.17).
6: **end while**

In practice, $\boldsymbol{A}_c$, $\boldsymbol{C}_c$, $\boldsymbol{E}_c$, $\boldsymbol{B}_c$ are initialized to be random matrix. All of the elements in the matrix $\boldsymbol{\varPi}_{c,\{g,h\}}$ are initialized to be

$$1/(|\mathcal{V}_{c,h}| \times |\mathcal{T}_{c,g}|).$$

This implies that all data samples have equal influences. The constraint on $\boldsymbol{\varPi}_{c,\{g,h\}} \in \mathfrak{Z}^{|\mathcal{V}_{c,g}|\times|\mathcal{V}_{c,h}|}$ will be satisfied during the first iteration of Eq. (8.17).

The algorithm is empirically shown good convergent property because the objective function is minimized in each step. The termination is declared when the difference between subsequence objective function values is smaller than 10^{-4}.

For the multimodal test sample pair $\{\mathbb{T}, \mathbb{V}\}$, their coding vectors for the cth class are firstly obtained as

$$\hat{\boldsymbol{x}}_c = \mathfrak{P}_c\boldsymbol{\Phi}(\mathbb{T}) = \boldsymbol{C}_c\boldsymbol{\Phi}^T(\mathfrak{T}_c)\boldsymbol{\Phi}(\mathbb{T}) \tag{8.18}$$

and

$$\hat{\boldsymbol{y}}_c = \mathfrak{Q}_c\boldsymbol{\Psi}(\mathbb{V}) = \boldsymbol{B}_c\boldsymbol{\Psi}^T(\mathfrak{V}_c)\boldsymbol{\Psi}(\mathbb{V}) \tag{8.19}$$

for $c = 1, 2, \ldots, C$ and then use the reconstruction error to estimate its label as

$$c^* = \operatorname{argmin}_c ||\Phi(\mathbb{T}) - \mathfrak{D}_c \hat{\mathbf{x}}_c||_2^2 + ||\Psi(\mathbb{V}) - \mathfrak{F}_c \hat{\mathbf{y}}_c||_2^2. \qquad (8.20)$$

From Eq. (8.18), it can be found that one important advantage of PDL, i.e., the coding vectors for the testing sample, can be obtained explicitly, without any other optimization procedure such as [2, 24].

8.4 Experimental Results

This chapter demonstrates weakly paired multimodal fusion on the Penn Haptic Adjective Corpus 2 (PHAC-2) dataset [6], which is shown in Fig. 8.4. PHAC-2 contains 53 household objects exhibiting both the visual and haptic data [10]. For each object, there are 10 haptic sequences and 8 image samples, both of which are collected independently. For the haptic sequences, the Global Alignment kernel [7] is used to construct the kernel functions. The setting in [10] is followed to extract a central crop including the object. And then, the RCovDs for RGB image and the kernel functions are extracted based on the above subsection.

According to the primary material property, the objects in PHAC-2 could be divided into 8 categories: Foam(14), Organic(4), Fabric(7), Plastic(13), Paper(10), Stone(2), Glasses(1), and Metal(2), where the number in the parentheses indicates the number of instances belonging to the corresponding category. The latter three categories are removed due to the limited numbers. Since the images and haptic

Fig. 8.4 Sample images of PHAC datasets. The original images are adopted from [6], with slight modification

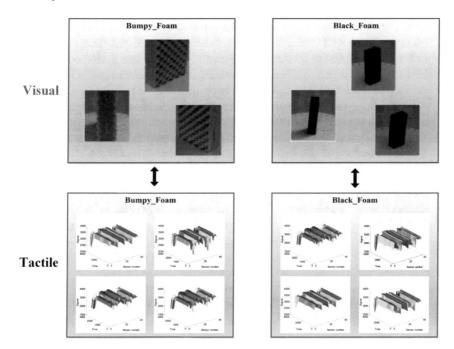

Fig. 8.5 An illustration of the weakly paired visual-haptic case. For each instance, the numbers of visual and haptic samples are not equal and the samples are not paired

signals are unpaired for each instance, a natural weakly paired visual-haptic fusion category recognition problem is formulated. In Fig. 8.5, an illustration about this case is demonstrated.

For each object category, one instance is randomly selected for testing and the rest for training. For each trial, there are 5 object instances, which produce $5 \times 8 \times 10 = 400$ visual-haptic testing pairs for testing. Ten trials are performed and the averaged results are reported.

For the comparisons, the following algorithms are considered:

1. PDL-X: This corresponds single modal method which is based on the optimization problem presented in Eq. (8.2). The symbol X will be replaced by the name of adopted modality or feature and will be introduced later.

2. SliM^2 [55] is adopted for each class. The group structure in [55] is determined by the class label, while in our implementation, the intraclass group structure is used. Using the *Representer Theorem*, the kernel extension is straightforward. Further, it is noticed that SliM^2 requires the fully paired data between modalities. Therefore, the mean coding term in Eq. (8.5) is used to replace the full-pairing term to ensure SliM^2 could be used for the weakly paired data.

3. CDL [40]: The difference between SCDL and SliM^2 is SCDL does not utilize the group structure information. Here the similar kernel trick and mean coding term in Eq. (8.5) are used to perform SCDL on the weakly paired multimodal data.
4. M^{2}PDL is developed in this work. Equation (8.5) is used to replace Eq. (8.7) to develop the method M^{2}PDL-Mean. In addition, the atoms are randomly selected in the pairing group and it is assumed that they are sample-to-sample paired. Such a method is denoted as M^{2}PDL-Rand.
5. WMCA [21]: This method adopts the maximum covariance analysis to perform the joint learning of the latent pairing and subspace. The classifier is designed based on the procedure of [21].

By comparing the M^{2}PDL-related methods with SliM^2, the roles of the projective dictionary learning can be demonstrated. By comparing M^{2}PDL with other pairing methods, the roles of the proposed weak-pairing method can be demonstrated.

Since this dataset is unbalanced across the categories, and the sample numbers in different modalities are not equal, the influences of r are investigated, which is defined as the ratio between the size of the dictionary (K) and the size of the corresponding class (N_c^m). The ratio is varied from 0.1 to 0.9. The results are shown in Fig. 8.6, where PDL-V and PDL-H are the single modal methods which use visual information and the haptic information, respectively. The following observations are obtained:

1. The visual information performs worse than haptic information in most cases. The reason is that sometimes there exists small between-class difference in visual modality, while the haptic characteristics are more useful for classification.

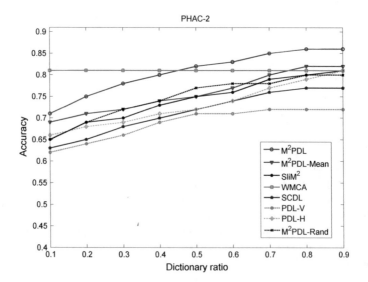

Fig. 8.6 Accuracy versus the dictionary size ratio r

2. M^2PDL exhibits excellent performance for most cases. The mean coding strategy, which is adopted by SliM^2, SCDL, and M^2PDL-Mean, performs similar effects and is inferior to M^2PDL.

3. An interesting result can be found that the random-pairing strategy, which is adopted by M^2PDL-Rand, performs even better than the mean coding strategies in some cases. A possible reason is that all of the combinations of visual and haptic samples are enumerated in the testing stage, and it is difficult for the mean coding strategy to capture such complicated pairing relations.

4. In some times, the M^2PDL-H performs better than some multimodal fusion methods. That is to say, using combination of both visual and haptic signals does not always lead to better results. The reason is that the naive combination methods such as SliM^2, SCDL, and M^2PDL-Mean just use the group-pairing information but do not consider the latent-pairing relation. Such coarse fusion methods may deteriorate the recognition performance. The proposed M^2PDL method obtains the fine-grained-pairing information and therefore achieves better recognition results.

It should be noted that [6] considered the haptic signals only and [10] investigated how to utilize the visual information to help the haptic sensing. This work differs with them in two aspects: (1) This work focuses on weakly paired object material recognition, which was not investigated by [6, 10], and it shows that such a problem indeed exhibits significant weakly paired multimodal characteristics. (2) Though [10] also utilized the visual information, their focus was still haptic classification and the visual information was just used to enhance the haptic understanding. This idea is a little similar with [19], which learned dynamic tactile sensing with robust vision-based training. However, this work focuses on how to fuse the visual and haptic information for object material category recognition.

8.5 Extensive Applications

Though the proposed weakly paired dictionary learning method works well for the visual–tactile fusion material recognition task, it can be also used for other multisensor fusion problem. In this section, some case studies are presented, which illustrate the application of the proposed approach using both synthetic data as well as practical samples.

8.5.1 Weakly Paired Multiple Feature Fusion

Firstly, two datasets which are artificially set to be weakly paired multimodal cases are considered. Such artificial examples can help us to get more insights about the methods.

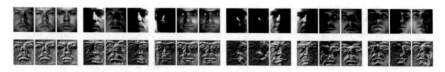

Fig. 8.7 Sample images of Extended YaleB dataset. A natural group structure in the face recognition. The first row is the gray-level samples and the second row is the corresponding LBP images. The samples belong to the same class form a group. [2011] IEEE. Reprinted, with permission, from Ref. [23]

1. Extended YaleB dataset consists of 2,414 frontal-face images for 38 subjects (about 64 images per person). Some sample images are shown in Fig. 8.7. The images are cropped and resized to the dimension of 24×21 pixels and projected to a vector of dimension 504. Thirty-two images are randomly selected for training and the other ones for testing in each class. The dictionary size is set to $K = 10$. For each image, two modalities, Grayscale pixels values and Linear Binary Pattern (LBP) which were used in [49], are adopted. To make a comparison between different modalities, the single modal methods PDL-Gray and PDL-LBP are investigated, which use Gray pixels and LBP, respectively.
2. UCI handwritten digit consists 0–9 handwritten digits data from UCI repository. It includes 2000 samples, with one modality being the 76 Fourier coefficients and the other modality being the 240-pixel averages in 2×3 windows. About 128 samples of each class are randomly selected for training and the rest for testing. The dictionary size is set to $K = 20$. Similarly, PDL-F and PDL-A are used to represent the single modal methods which use the Fourier feature and pixel averages, respectively.

For both datasets, the polynomial kernel with degree 2 is used. It is worth noting that the original YaleB and UCI datasets are sample-to-sample fully paired. Similar to some work [50, 52, 53] which manually established the partial pairing, the group-level weak pairing is simulated by uniformly dividing the sample set in each class and each modality into G groups and randomly establish the group-to-group pairing. For YaleB and UCI, the cases of $G \in \{1, 2, 4, 8, 16, 32\}$ and $G \in \{1, 2, 4, 8, 16, 32, 64, 128\}$ are investigated, respectively.

The parameter sensitivity experiment on λ and γ is firstly performed by tuning only one parameter while fixing the other one. The results when the number of groups is 4 are shown in Fig. 8.8. It shows that the performance is rather stable with respect to $\lambda \in [10^{-4}, 10^{-3}]$ and $\gamma \in [10^{-3}, 10^{-2}]$. In all of the rest experimental validation, the values of λ and γ are fixed as $\lambda = 10^{-3}$ and $\gamma = 10^{-2}$.

Figure 8.9 shows the classification performances with increasing number of groups. From the results, the following observations are obtained:

1. When the number of groups is small, neither SliM^2 nor SCDL gives satisfactory performance. The reason is that they use very coarse group-level relation information and do not fully exploit the intermodality relation. On the contrary, the proposed M^{2}PDL is rather robust to the number of the groups.

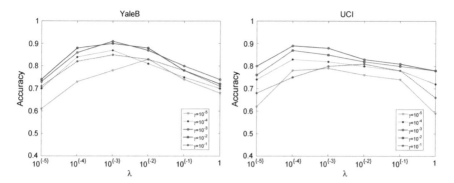

Fig. 8.8 Parameter sensitivity. It shows that the performance is rather stable with respect to $\lambda \in [10^{-4}, 10^{-3}]$ and $\gamma \in [10^{-3}, 10^{-2}]$

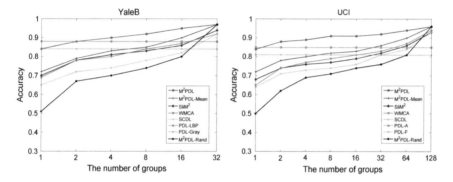

Fig. 8.9 Accuracy versus the number of groups

2. M^2PDL-Mean, being worse than M^2PDL, is still superior to SliM^2 and SCDL in almost all the setting. Such results disclose the advantages of the dictionary pair learning because all of the three methods use the same intermodality relation.
3. Though the performance of M^2PDL is promising, its random version, M^2PDL-Rand, performs very poor. This shows that the performance is strongly dependent of the estimation of the pairing matrix.

The convergence curves with different sizes of the dictionary are empirically demonstrated in Fig. 8.10. It shows that the objective function value monotonically decreases as the iteration number increases. In practice, about 10–15 iterations are sufficient to achieve satisfactory results. The training time depends on the number of atoms and the training data. Using an unoptimized MATLAB program on PC platform (3.4-GHz CPU, 16-GB memory), the averaged training time on those two datasets for 10 iterations is about 38.4 s.

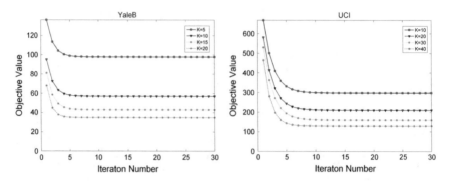

Fig. 8.10 Objective function value convergence curve versus the iteration number

Fig. 8.11 Sample images of RGB-D 300 dataset. This figure is adopted from the Web site https://sites.google.com/site/kevinlai726/datasets

8.5.2   RGB-D Fusion for Object Category Recognition

The RGB-D object dataset contains visual and depth images of 300 physically distinct objects [20]. Each of the 300 objects in the dataset belongs to one of the 51 categories. The number of instances is between 3 to 14 in each category. The experiments focus on the category recognition task, which is defined as determining if a previously unseen object belongs to the same category of objects that have previously been seen. The same setup is adopted as [20, 35] by randomly leaving one object out from each category for testing and train on all samples of the remaining objects. The averaged accuracy across 10 random splits are reported. For each split, there were about 34000 samples for training and 6900 samples for testing (Fig. 8.11).

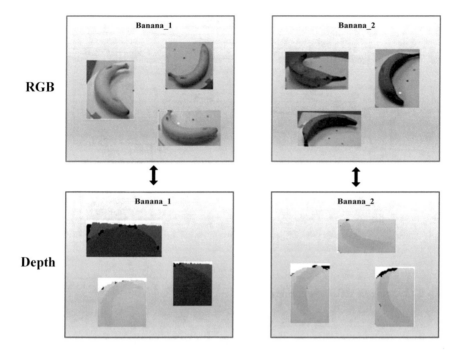

Fig. 8.12 An illustration of the weakly paired RGB-D case. For each instance such as Banana_1 or Banana_2, the RGB and depth samples are captured from different viewpoints and are not fully paired

Although the original RGB-D dataset is sample-to-sample fully paired, a weakly paired setting can be naturally constructed by regarding the category as the class and the instance as the group, and removing the sample-to-sample correspondence relation, but preserving the instance-to-instance correspondence relation only. In Fig. 8.12, an illustration about this setting is given.

Reference [3] has demonstrated that Region Covariance Descriptors (RCovDs) achieved state-of-the-art performance on the RGB-D dataset. Thus, RCovDs are used to represent the images. However, the feature vectors provided in [3] cannot be used here because any of their feature vectors include both RGB and depth information, and therefore, the sample-to-sample correspondence is required to be known. Here the feature vector

$$\boldsymbol{f}_{RGB} = [x, y, r, g, b, I_x, I_y, I_{xx}, I_{yy}, I_{xy}, \sqrt{I_x^2 + I_y^2}]^T$$

is developed for RGB image and

$$\boldsymbol{f}_D = [x, y, z, n_x, n_y, n_z, k_1, k_2, k_1 k_2]^T$$

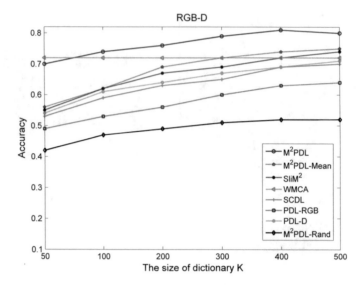

Fig. 8.13 Accuracy versus the dictionary size K

for depth image, where x, y, z represent the coordinates, and r, g, b represent the color information provided by the different color channels. I_x and I_y correspond to an approximation of the gradient by the Sobel operator applied to the grayscale image along x and y, respectively. Applying the operator a second time on the image patch results in I_{xx} and I_{yy}. n_x, n_y, and n_z are the coordinates of the surface normal. k_1 and k_2 are the principal curvatures. Using f_{RGB} and f_D, the covariance descriptors for RGB image and depth image can be constructed.

Since RCovDs do not lie in Euclidean space, the Log-Euclidean kernel which is presented in Chap. 2 is used.

At testing stage, an RGB and depth image pair containing an object is assigned a category label. The dictionary size K is varied from 100 to 500 to report the results of SliM^2, SCDL, M^{2}PDL-Mean, M^{2}PDL-Rand, and M^{2}PDL in Fig. 8.13. In addition, the single modal methods PDL-RGB and PDL-D are investigated, which use RGB and depth information, respectively. The results show that M^{2}PDL consistently performs better than other methods and it is observed that when K is small, the merits of M^{2}PDL is more obvious.

8.5.3 Discussions

In this subsection, some consistent results across the different datasets YaleB, UCI, RGB-D, and PHAC-2 are summarized.

From the experimental protocol of the datasets, it can be seen that the difficulty of YaleB and UCI is relatively low, but PHAC-2 is high. The reason is that there exists explicit sample-to-sample correspondence in YaleB and UCI, while PHAC-2 is intrinsically a weakly paired dataset. In fact, the numbers of visual samples and the haptic samples are not equal. From the above experimental results, the following results are summarized:

1. M^2PDL-Mean, though just uses the group-pairing information, may obtain relatively good performance, especially for the YaleB and UCI. However, when more difficult dataset is concerned, the merit of M^2PDL-Mean tends to diminish. For example, for RGB-D dataset, M^2PDL-Mean shows significant performance margins only when the size of dictionary is large. For PHAC-2, M^2PDL-Mean does not show significant advantages. Therefore, it is believed that M^2PDL-Mean is more suitable for some simple cases such as homogeneous feature fusion. When there exists complicated mapping between modalities, such a strategy is not good enough.
2. M^2PDL-Rand, which adopts the random-pairing strategy, is just used for baseline. In fact, It achieves poor performance on YaleB, UCI, and RGB-D. Note that when $G = 32$ for YaleB and $G = 128$ for UCI, M^2PDL-Rand is equivalent to M^2PDL-Mean because Group reduces to Sample. Therefore, the good performance of M^2PDL-Rand at those points is of no sense. On the other hand, as indicated, it may occasionally obtain better results than other methods on PHAC-2. Therefore, it is guessed that such a strategy may be effective when the mapping relation between modalities is more complicated. But the theoretical justification is still open and remains the future work. Even though, due to the random nature, M^2PDL-Rand is difficult to be used in practical scenarios and it is still recommended to use M^2PDL-Mean with higher priority.
3. WMCA also learns the latent-pairing information from the weakly paired multimodality data. The main difference between WMCA and the proposed M^2PDL is that WMCA constructs the mapping between the reduced feature space, while the M^2PDL learns the mapping between coding vectors. Since the dictionary learning technology is introduced, the coding vectors can be more flexible to capture the relation between modalities. Therefore, M^2PDL consistently performs better than WMCA. However, WMCA provides an elegant theoretic basis for joint dimension reduction for weakly paired dataset.

8.6 Summary

In many industrial environments, multiple heterogeneous sensors are usually used, which provide multimodal information. Such multimodal data usually leads to two technical challenges. First, different sensors may provide different patterns of data. Second, the full-pairing information between modalities may not be known. In this chapter, a unified model to tackle such problems are developed. This model is based on a projective dictionary learning method, which efficiently produces the representation vector for the original data by an explicit form. In addition, the latent-pairing relation between samples can be learned automatically and be used to improve the classification performance. Such a method can be flexibly used for multimodal fusion with full-pairing, partial-pairing, and weak-pairing cases.

References

1. Ameri, R., Pouyan, A., Abolghasemi, V.: Projective dictionary pair learning for eeg signal classification in brain computer interface applications. Neurocomputing **218**, 382–389 (2016)
2. Bahrampour, S., Nasrabadi, N.M., Ray, A., Jenkins, W.K.: Multimodal task-driven dictionary learning for image classification. IEEE Trans. Image Process. **25**(1), 24–38 (2016)
3. Beksi, W.J., Papanikolopoulos, N.: Object classification using dictionary learning and rgb-d covariance descriptors. In: 2015 IEEE International Conference on Robotics and Automation (ICRA), pp. 1880–1885 (2015)
4. Beyca, O.F., Rao, P.K., Kong, Z., Bukkapatnam, S.T., Komanduri, R.: Heterogeneous sensor data fusion approach for real-time monitoring in ultraprecision machining (upm) process using non-parametric bayesian clustering and evidence theory. IEEE Trans. Autom. Sci. Eng. **13**(2), 1033–1044 (2016)
5. Chen, J., Low, K.H., Yao, Y., Jaillet, P.: Gaussian process decentralized data fusion and active sensing for spatiotemporal traffic modeling and prediction in mobility-on-demand systems. IEEE Trans. Autom. Sci. Eng. **12**(3), 901–921 (2015)
6. Chu, V., McMahon, I., Riano, L., McDonald, C.G., He, Q., Perez-Tejada, J.M., Arrigo, M., Darrell, T., Kuchenbecker, K.J.: Robotic learning of haptic adjectives through physical interaction. Robot. Auton. Syst. **63**, 279–292 (2015)
7. Cuturi, M.: Fast global alignment kernels. In: Proceedings of the 28th International Conference on Machine Learning (ICML-11), pp. 929–936 (2011)
8. Das, A., Mondal, P., Pal, U., Ferrer, M.A., Blumenstein, M.: Fast and efficient multimodal eye biometrics using projective dictionary pair learning. IEEE Congr. Evol. Comput., 1402–1408 (2016)
9. Ding, Z., Shao, M., Fu, Y.: Latent low-rank transfer subspace learning for missing modality recognition. In: AAAI, pp. 1192–1198 (2014)
10. Gao, Y., Hendricks, L.A., Kuchenbecker, K.J., Darrell, T.: Deep learning for tactile understanding from visual and haptic data. In: 2016 IEEE International Conference on Robotics and Automation (ICRA), pp. 536–543 (2016)
11. Gokce, E.I., Shrivastava, A.K., Cho, J.J., Ding, Y.: Decision fusion from heterogeneous sensors in surveillance sensor systems. IEEE Trans. Autom. Sci. Eng. **8**(1), 228–233 (2011)
12. Gu, S., Zhang, L., Zuo, W., Feng, X.: Projective dictionary pair learning for pattern classification. Adv. Neural Inf. Process. Syst., 793–801 (2014)
13. Guo, J., Guo, Y., Kong, X., Zhang, M., He, R.: Discriminative analysis dictionary learning. In: AAAI, pp. 1617–1623 (2016)
14. Guo, J., Guo, Y., Wang, B., Kong, X., He, R.: Topology preserving dictionary learning for pattern classification. In: International Joint Conference on Neural Networks, pp. 1709–1715 (2016)
15. Haddad, B.M., Yang, S., Karam, L.J., Ye, J., Patel, N.S., Braun, M.W.: Multifeature, sparse-based approach for defects detection and classification in semiconductor units. IEEE Trans. Autom. Sci. Eng., 1–15 (2016)
16. Harandi, M., Salzmann, M.: Riemannian coding and dictionary learning: Kernels to the rescue. In: Proceedings of the IEEE Conference on Computer Vision and Pattern Recognition, pp. 3926–3935 (2015)
17. Jing, X.Y., Hu, R., Wu, F., Chen, X.L., Liu, Q., Yao, Y.F.: Uncorrelated multi-view discrimination dictionary learning for recognition. In: AAAI, pp. 2787–2795 (2014)

18. Kohli, N., Yadav, D., Noor, A.: Multiple projective dictionary learning to detect plastic surgery for face verification. IEEE Access **3**, 2572–2580 (2015)
19. Kroemer, O., Lampert, C.H., Peters, J.: Learning dynamic tactile sensing with robust vision-based training. IEEE Trans. Robot. **27**(3), 545–557 (2011)
20. Lai, K., Bo, L., Ren, X., Fox, D.: A large-scale hierarchical multi-view rgb-d object dataset. In: 2011 IEEE International Conference on Robotics and Automation (ICRA), pp. 1817–1824 (2011)
21. Lampert, C., Krömer, O.: Weakly-paired maximum covariance analysis for multimodal dimensionality reduction and transfer learning. Comput. Vis.-ECCV **2010**, 566–579 (2010)
22. Li, S., Shao, M., Fu, Y.: Cross-view projective dictionary learning for person re-identification. In: IJCAI, pp. 2155–2161 (2015)
23. Liu, H., Sun, F.: Hierarchical orthogonal matching pursuit for face recognition. In: 2011 First Asian Conference on Pattern Recognition (ACPR), pp. 278–282. IEEE (2011)
24. Liu, H., Yu, Y., Sun, F., Gu, J.: Visual-tactile fusion for object recognition. IEEE Trans. Autom. Sci. Eng. **14**(2), 996–1008 (2017)
25. Liu, K., Huang, S.: Integration of data fusion methodology and degradation modeling process to improve prognostics. IEEE Trans. Autom. Sci. Eng. **13**(1), 344–354 (2016)
26. Liu, W., Yu, Z., Wen, Y., Lin, R., Yang, M.: Jointly learning non-negative projection and dictionary with discriminative graph constraints for classification (2015). arXiv preprint arXiv:1511.04601
27. Mandal, D., Biswas, S.: Generalized coupled dictionary learning approach with applications to cross-modal matching. IEEE Trans. Image Process. **25**(8), 3826–3837 (2016)
28. Mathews, S.M., Kambhamettu, C., Barner, K.E.: Maximum correntropy based dictionary learning framework for physical activity recognition using wearable sensors. In: International Symposium on Visual Computing, pp. 123–132 (2016)
29. Qu, X., Zhang, D., Lu, G., Guo, Z.: Door knob hand recognition system. IEEE Trans. Syst. Man Cybern. Syst., 1–12 (2016)
30. Rasiwasia, N., Mahajan, D., Mahadevan, V., Aggarwal, G.: Cluster canonical correlation analysis. In: Proceedings of the International Conference on Artificial Intelligence and Statistics, pp. 823–831 (2014)
31. Rong, Y., Xiong, S., Gao, Y.: Discriminative dictionary pair learning from partially labeled data. In: International Conference on Image Processing, pp. 719–723 (2016)
32. Santoso, F., Garratt, M.A., Anavatti, S.G.: Visual-inertial navigation systems for aerial robotics: sensor fusion and technology. IEEE Trans. Autom. Sci. Eng., 260–275 (2017)
33. Son, D.D., Sang, D.V., Binh, H.T.T., Thuy, N.T.: Label associated dictionary pair learning for face recognition. In: Proceedings of the Seventh Symposium on Information and Communication Technology, pp. 302–307 (2016)
34. Van Nguyen, H., Patel, V.M., Nasrabadi, N.M., Chellappa, R.: Design of non-linear kernel dictionaries for object recognition. IEEE Trans. Image Process. **22**(12), 5123–5135 (2013)
35. Wang, A., Lu, J., Cai, J., Cham, T.J., Wang, G.: Large-margin multi-modal deep learning for rgb-d object recognition. IEEE Trans. Multimed. **17**(11), 1887–1898 (2015)
36. Wang, C., Mahadevan, S.: Manifold alignment without correspondence. In: IJCAI **2**, 3 (2009)
37. Wang, H.H., Chen, Y.L., Chiang, C.K.: Discriminative paired dictionary learning for visual recognition. In: Proceedings of the 2016 ACM Conference on Multimedia, pp. 67–71 (2016)
38. Wang, K., Lin, L., Zuo, W., Gu, S., Zhang, L.: Dictionary pair classifier driven convolutional neural networks for object detection. In: Proceedings of IEEE Conference on Computer Vision and Pattern Recognition, pp. 2138–2146 (2016)
39. Wang, Q., Si, L., Shen, B.: Learning to hash on partial multi-modal data. In: IJCAI, pp. 3904–3910 (2015)
40. Wang, S., Zhang, L., Liang, Y., Pan, Q.: Semi-coupled dictionary learning with applications to image super-resolution and photo-sketch synthesis. In: 2012 IEEE Conference on Computer Vision and Pattern Recognition (CVPR), pp. 2216–2223 (2012)
41. Wu, F., Yu, Z., Yang, Y., Tang, S., Zhang, Y., Zhuang, Y.: Sparse multi-modal hashing. IEEE Trans. Multimed. **16**(2), 427–439 (2014)

42. Xiang, Y., Xu, J.: Discriminative dictionary learning for skeletal action recognition. In: International Conference on Neural Information Processing, pp. 531–539 (2015)
43. Yadav, D., Kohli, N., Pandey, P., Singh, R., Vatsa, M., Noore, A.: Effect of illicit drug abuse on face recognition. In: IEEE Winter Conference on Applications of Computer Vision, pp. 1–7 (2016)
44. Yan, K., Zheng, W., Cui, Z., Zong, Y.: Cross-database facial expression recognition via unsupervised domain adaptive dictionary learning. In: International Conference on Neural Information Processing, pp. 427–434 (2016)
45. Yang, M., Chang, H., Luo, W.: Discriminative analysis-synthesis dictionary learning for image classification. Neurocomputing **219**, 404–411 (2017)
46. Yang, M., Liu, W., Luo, W., Shen, L.: Analysis-synthesis dictionary learning for universality-particularity representation based classification. In: Association for the Advancement of Artificial Intelligence, pp. 2251–2257 (2016)
47. Yang, M., Luo, W., Shen, L.: Dictionary pair learning with block-diagonal structure for image classification. In: International Conference on Intelligent Science and Big Data Engineering, pp. 288–299 (2015)
48. Wang, Y., Moreno-Centeno, E., Ding, Y.: Matching misaligned two-resolution metrology data. IEEE Trans. Autom. Sci. Eng., 222–237 (2017)
49. Yuan, X.T., Liu, X., Yan, S.: Visual classification with multitask joint sparse representation. IEEE Trans. Image Process. **21**(10), 4349–4360 (2012)
50. Zhang, X., Zong, L., Liu, X., Yu, H.: Constrained nmf-based multi-view clustering on unmapped data. In: AAAI, pp. 3174–3180 (2015)
51. Zhang, Z., Li, F., Chow, T.W., Zhang, L., Yan, S.: Sparse codes auto-extractor for classification: a joint embedding and dictionary learning framework for representation. IEEE Trans. Signal Process. **64**(14), 3790–3805 (2016)
52. Zhao, H., Liu, H., Fu, Y.: Incomplete multi-modal visual data grouping. In: IJCAI, pp. 2392–2398 (2016)
53. Zhi, S.Y., Zhou, H.: Partial multi-view clustering. In: AAAI Conference on artificial intelligence (2014)
54. Zhu, P., Hu, Q., Zhang, C., Zuo, W.: Coupled dictionary learning for unsupervised feature selection. In: AAAI, pp. 2422–2428 (2016)
55. Zhuang, Y., Wang, Y., Wu, F., Zhang, Y., Lu, W.: Supervised coupled dictionary learning with group structures for multi-modal retrieval. In: AAAI, pp. 1070–1076 (2013)

Chapter 9
Visual–Tactile Cross-Modal Matching Using Common Dictionary Learning

Abstract Tactile and visual measurements are two classes of sensing modalities which frequently occur in manufacturing industry and robotics. Their matching problem is highly interesting in many practical scenarios since they provide different properties about objects. This chapter investigates the visual–tactile cross-modal matching problem which is formulated as retrieving the relevant sample in an unlabeled gallery visual dataset in response to the tactile query sample. Such a problem exhibits nontrivial challenges that there does not exist sample-to-sample-pairing relation between tactile and visual modalities, which exhibit significantly different characteristics. To this end, a dictionary learning model is designed, which can simultaneously learn the projection subspace and the latent common dictionary for the visual and tactile measurements. In addition, an optimization algorithm is developed to effectively solve the common dictionary learning problem. Based on the obtained solution, the visual–tactile cross-modal matching algorithm can be easily developed. Finally, experimental validations are performed on the PHAC-2 datasets to show the effectiveness of the proposed visual–tactile cross-modal matching framework and method.

9.1 Introduction

Despite of the significant achievements of the tactile sensors, there still exists a great gap between the true tactile properties and the measured tactile characteristics. This tactile information exchange problem is more significant in the case of Internet shopping, which is more risky than traditional shopping due to the lack of opportunity to physically examine the product and the lack of personal contact [6]. In the clothing and textile category, touch is very relevant as it plays a dual role in evaluating the physical attributes of the product such as texture. Reference [3] pointed out that one of the five most important reasons for not purchasing online was an inability to touch the merchandise.

The most straightforward method to solve this problem is to develop the tactile display technology, which can provide diverse tactile feeling to people. However, displaying real tactile feeling is difficult because tactile display requires the actuator

© Springer Nature Singapore Pte Ltd. 2018
H. Liu and F. Sun, *Robotic Tactile Perception and Understanding*,
https://doi.org/10.1007/978-981-10-6171-4_9

which can drive with high frequency, large displacement, and high density due to the characteristics of human tactile receptors.

Many scholars have made great efforts to solve this problem using different methods. Reference [13] developed the *Need For Touch* scale to measure consumer preference for obtaining and using information acquired through the haptic sensory system. The authors in [2] proposed to address this issue by providing consumers with scores from industry experts who have rated these objects using metrics, which attempt to quantify the tactile properties that people prefer. These metrics are designed for internal product reviews and are not as useful for the average consumer as a detailed and unbiased verbal description of the product's feel. Such a system would allow consumers to search directly for the haptic adjectives they would like a product to have, such as soft, smooth, and nice. They also provided a publicly available visual–tactile dataset, of which collection procedure is illustrated in Fig. 9.1. In addition, SynTouch explored the texture-gallery to understand standard unique 15-dimensional representations of the sense of touch, which helps to gain understanding of the subtle differences in various textures [1].

Inspired by some finding from cognitive psychology, this work tries to make a step toward answering the questions *Is there any mechanism which compensates for the inability to touch in an online context*. When encoding properties of familiar objects, vision may be sufficient because visual recognition of an object may rapidly trigger the retrieval of information about its properties stored in memory, eliminating the need for direct perceptual encoding by tactile exploration [7]. For example, when a person sees an apple, he can easily recall its senses of touch, taste, smell, and so on. However, when he sees an unseen object, it is difficult for him to recall such feelings. In this case, if someone tells him that this unseen object shares the same sense of

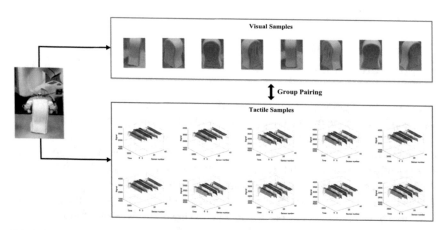

Fig. 9.1 A typical visual–tactile data collection procedure, which is adopted from the PHAC-2 datasets [2]. Generally speaking, the visual and tactile measurements are obtained independently and therefore there does not exist sample-to-sample fully paired information. On the other hand, since all of the visual and tactile measurements are collected from one single object, there exists a coarse group-pairing relation between them, where the group is determined by the object instance

touch with the apple, he can quickly establish the feeling of touch about this object. Such strategies have been preliminarily utilized as the virtual sense of touch in the advertisement. For online shopping, the tactile measurements of the merchandise can be collected before selling. However, showing such tactile data to the user is of no sense. When the user hopes to obtain the sense of touch about some object, the Web site could use the corresponding tactile data to retrieve some images of other objects and provide the images to help the user to establish the sensor of touch for the new object.

The most demanding requirement for the visual–tactile cross-modal matching is to develop a suitable machining model that can support the similarity search for visual and tactile data. In this sense, this work is a special cross-modal retrieval task. It takes one type of data as the query to retrieve relevant data of another type. For example, a user can use a text to retrieve relevant pictures or videos. In recent years, cross-modal retrieval has drawn much attention due to the rapid growth of multimodal and multimedia data. Various methods have been proposed to measure the content similarity between different modalities. For a comprehensive survey on the recent progress of cross-modal retrieval, refer to [16]. The representative methods include canonical correlation analysis, partial least square, topic model, deep learning, and so on.

Therefore, the idea of cross-modal correspondence is used to partially solve this problem. When users search information by submitting a query sample, they can obtain search results across various modalities, which is more comprehensive given that different modalities of data can provide complementary information to each other. Visual–tactile cross-modal matching aims to take one type of tactile data as the query to retrieve relevant visual data. In Fig. 9.2, a scheme of the proposed visual–tactile cross-modal matching framework is presented, which contains training and retrieving stages and will be detailed in the subsequent sections. Under this framework, how to effectively perform cross-modal matching between tactile and visual measurements is still a challenging problem. The main difficulty lies in how to measure the content similarity between different modalities of data, which is referred as the heterogeneity gap.

The problem investigated in this chapter is highly relevant to the humans' synesthesia, a perceptual condition in which the stimulation of one sense triggers an automatic, involuntary experience in another sense. Figure 9.3 shows a live example which shows that visual–tactile synesthesia is very common in our life. Unfortunately, little is known about how synesthesia develops and only a few types of synesthesia have been scientifically evaluated.

On the other hand, the sparse dictionary learning method has found great success in many measurement domains, such as [18]. The main idea of the original coupled dictionary learning method [5] is to learn two dictionaries for the two modalities in a coupled manner such that the sparse coefficients are equal in the original or some transformed space. Reference [19] brought coupled dictionary learning into supervised sparse coding for cross-modal retrieval, which is called supervised coupled dictionary learning with group structures for multimodal retrieval. It can utilize the class information to jointly learn discriminative multimodal dictionaries as well as

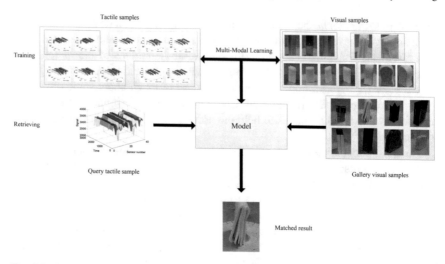

Fig. 9.2 A scheme of the visual–tactile cross-matching framework. The part above the dashed line shows the training stage, where two sets of visual samples and tactile samples are provided. The colored boxes are used to surround the samples belonging the same class. It should be noted that the sample-to-sample correspondence information is unavailable, but the group-to-group correspondence information is available. For each group, the visual modality and the tactile modality may exhibit different numbers of samples. Using such weakly paired training set, the multimodal learning can be performed to obtain a model. The part below the dashed line shows that retrieving stage. In this stage, a gallery visual set and a query tactile sample are given. Both of them are fed into the model and the retrieved image is used as the matched result

Fig. 9.3 A Chinese proverb: Once bitten by a snake, one shies at coiled rope for ten years. This image is adopted from the Web site https:// www.suibi8.com/essay/ 76a3e3-7775203.html

mapping functions between different modalities. Very recently, Ref. [12] presented a generalized coupled dictionary learning technique for the task of cross-modal matching. The approach can seamlessly handle both paired as well as unpaired data in the two modalities in the same framework. Reference [15] presented a technique which jointly learns projections of data in two domains, and a latent dictionary which can succinctly represent both the domains in the projected low-dimensional space was developed for transfer learning. However, none of those work addresses the visual–tactile cross-modal matching problem. To this end, a novel dictionary learning model to tackle the visual–tactile cross-modal matching problem is presented. It can simultaneously learn the projection subspace and the latent common dictionary for the weakly paired visual and tactile modalities. An optimization algorithm is developed to effectively solve the common dictionary learning problem and a visual–tactile cross-modal matching problem. Experimental validations on the PHAC-2 datasets are performed to show the effectiveness of the proposed visual–tactile cross-modal matching framework and methods.

The rest of this chapter is organized as follows: In Sect. 9.2, the investigated visual–tactile matching problem is formulated. Section 9.3 is used to introduce the proposed learning and matching algorithms, respectively. The experimental evaluations are shown in Sect. 9.4.

9.2 Problem Formulation

This section formulates the problem of visual–tactile matching which is illustrated in Fig. 9.2. This framework contains two stages. In the training stage, the available visual and tactile samples are used to learn a model. In the retrieving stage, the learned model and the gallery visual sample set are used to search the matched results for a query tactile sample.

Given N tactile samples

$$T = [t_1 \ t_2 \cdots t_N] \in R^{d_T \times N},$$

and M visual samples

$$V = [v_1 \ v_2 \cdots v_M] \in R^{d_V \times M},$$

where d_T and d_V represent the dimensions of the tactile feature and visual feature vectors, respectively, the visual–tactile matching can be formulated as retrieving the relevant sample in unlabeled gallery visual dataset

$$\mathcal{F} = \{f_1 \ f_2 \cdots f_{N_G}\} \subset R^{d_V},$$

where N_G is the number of the visual samples in gallery set, in response to the tactile query of $t \in R^{d_T}$.

In this work, it is assumed that all of the training samples originated from G classes. Even though, learning an effective model for visual–tactile matching is still difficult, due to the following reasons:

1. $d_T \neq d_V$: Since visual modality and tactile modality exhibit very different characteristics, their feature vectors may show different dimensions. This prevents them from being compared directly. In some extreme cases, even though $d_T = d_V$ may hold, it is still difficult, if not possible, to compare visual and tactile samples by using the conventional Euclidean distance.

2. $N \neq M$: Since visual data and the tactile data may be collected independently by different operators, their numbers may be different. This makes the
pairing between the modalities very difficult. In some extreme cases, even though
$N = M$ may hold, it is still difficult, if not possible, to establish the sample-to-
sample correspondence between the visual and tactile modalities.

The goal of this work is to develop a visual–tactile matching method using the
multimodal training datasets T and V. Based on this method, the most similar visual
data in the gallery set $\mathcal{F}$ can be searched for the tactile query sample t.

Before closing this section, it is noted that a dual matching problem can be formulated as searching the most similar tactile data in a gallery tactile set for a visual query
sample. From the perspective of methodology, this does not incur extra difficulties.
However, such a problem is currently poorly motivated because the retrieved tactile
samples do not provide vivid information to the user.

9.3   Common Dictionary Learning Method

9.3.1   Proposed Model

The dictionary learning method provides effective strategy to unify multimodal data
since the original feature vectors can formulate some comparable coding vectors.
A conventional multimodal dictionary learning method tries to solve the following
optimization problem

$$\min_{D_T, D_V, X, Y} \mathcal{L}_O = \|T - D_T X\|_F^2 + \|V - D_V Y\|_F^2 \\ + \mathcal{C}(X, Y), \tag{9.1}$$

where $D_T \in R^{d_T \times K}$ is the tactile dictionary and $D_V \in R^{d_V \times K}$ is the visual dictionary;
$X \in R^{K \times N}$ is the tactile coding matrix and $Y \in R^{K \times M}$ is the visual coding matrix.
The number of K is the size of the dictionary which should be prescribed by the
designer. The coupled term $\mathcal{C}(X, Y)$ can be used to impose some constraints on
the intermodality relation and the intramodality relation. This term has different
realization forms in existing work. Since the dictionaries D_T and D_V are implicitly
coupled, their relation is not obvious, and this prevents the coding matrices X and
Y from being connected using some sophisticating tool such as joint sparsity. In
fact, since D_T and D_V reflect the characteristics of the unpaired tactile and visual
modalities, their relation is complicated. A natural remedy is to explicitly impose
constraints on the relation between D_T and D_V. However, this is not straightforward
since the dimensions d_T and d_V may not equal.

In this work, a common dictionary across different modalities is learned. This can be realized only when the tactile samples and the visual samples are transformed into a common subspace. To this end, the following linear projections are resorted.

$$T \rightarrow W_T^T T, \quad V \rightarrow W_V^T V,$$

where $W_T \in R^{d_T \times d}$ and $W_V \in R^{d_V \times d}$ are the projection matrices, and d is the dimension of the learned subspace. The basic idea is illustrated in Fig. 9.4. After performing such a transformation, the samples in projected tactile space and projected visual space can be comparable and a common dictionary can be designed to give a unified description of them. The optimization problem which focuses on the reconstruction error in the projected subspace can be reformulated as

$$\min_{\substack{W_T, W_V, \\ D, X, Y}} \mathscr{L}_R = \left\| W_T^T T - DX \right\|_F^2 + \left\| W_V^T V - DY \right\|_F^2, \tag{9.2}$$

where $D \in R^{d \times K}$ is the common dictionary, which provides a basis for establishing more complicated relationships between the coding matrices X and Y.

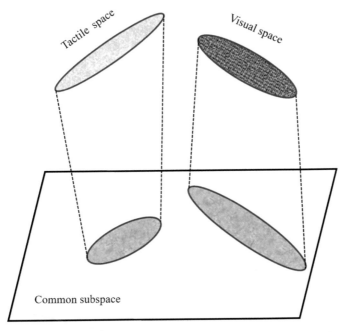

Fig. 9.4 An illustration for the projection. Though tactile samples and visual samples lie in different space, they can project some common subspace, which can be used to develop the common dictionary

Nevertheless, the optimization problem in the above formulation obviously leads to trivial solutions $W_T = W_V = D = 0$. To avoid this point, the orthogonality $W_T^T W_T = I$, $W_V^T W_V = I$ are imposed, and the transformations W_T and W_V must be required to preserve the useful information presented in original samples. This leads to the following additional objective function

$$\mathscr{L}_P = ||T - W_T W_T^T T||_F^2 + ||V - W_V W_V^T V||_F^2. \tag{9.3}$$

Then the following naive multimodal common dictionary learning model can be established as

$$\begin{aligned} \min_{\substack{W_T, W_V, \\ D, X, Y}} \quad & \mathscr{L}_R + \lambda \mathscr{L}_P, \\ \text{s.t.} \quad & ||d_k||_2 = 1 \text{ for } k = 1, 2, \ldots, K, \\ & W_T^T W_T = I, \quad W_V^T W_V = I \end{aligned} \tag{9.4}$$

where λ is the penalty parameter. Note that d_k is used to denote the kth column of D and the constraint on d_k is imposed to avoid the large solution.

Though a common dictionary D can be learned from (9.4), it does not incorporate the class label information and may result in poor performance. An intuitive method to tackle this problem is to impose the sparsity on the coding vectors and require the samples belonging to the same class share the same sparsity pattern [19]. This can be realized by imposing the constraints on the row-sparsity of X_g and Y_g, which denote the coefficient matrix associated to those data belonging to the gth class. However, since the common dictionary is developed for both visual and tactile samples, their coding vectors may share the same patterns. Therefore, the row-sparsity can be imposed on the combined coding matrix $[X_g \ Y_g]$. The resulting loss function can be constructed as

$$\mathscr{L}_G = \sum_{g=1}^{G} ||[X_g \ Y_g]||_{2,1}, \tag{9.5}$$

where $|| \cdot ||_{2,1}$ is the sum of the 2-norm of each row in the matrix and therefore encourages the row-sparsity. Figure 9.5 shows an illustration about this coding strategy. Note that without the common dictionary D, it is impossible to establish the joint group sparsity between X_g and Y_g.

The multimodal common dictionary learning problem can then be formulated as

$$\begin{aligned} \min_{\substack{W_T, W_V, \\ D, X, Y}} \quad & \mathscr{L}_R + \lambda \mathscr{L}_P + \gamma \mathscr{L}_G, \\ \text{s.t.} \quad & ||d_k||_2 = 1 \text{ for } k = 1, 2, \ldots, K, \\ & W_T^T W_T = I, \quad W_V^T W_V = I \end{aligned} \tag{9.6}$$

In the above optimization problem, the reconstruction term $\mathscr{L}_R$ is used to control the data fidelity, the regularization term $\mathscr{L}_P$ is used to avoid the trivial solution, and the group sparsity term $\mathscr{L}_G$ is used to model class-wise intermodality relationship,

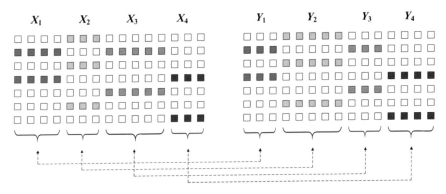

X_1 X_2 X_3 X_4 Y_1 Y_2 Y_3 Y_4

Fig. 9.5 An illustration for the coding strategy. The number of groups is set as $G = 4$. The empty square represents zero element and the solid square represents nonzero element. Different colors are used to represent different classes. For each class $g = 1, 2, 3, 4$, it is required that all of the column vectors in X_g and Y_g to share the same sparsity pattern, but the values of columns in matrices X_g and Y_g are not required to be equal. The dashed lines shown in the bottom, which connect two groups of X_g and Y_g, are the only available group-pairing information

Fig. 9.6 Illustration of the basic idea of the common dictionary method. Using the common dictionary, both samples of visual and tactile modality can be transformed into visual coding vectors and tactile coding vectors. Then joint sparsity can be used to exploit the intrinsic relation between the coding vectors

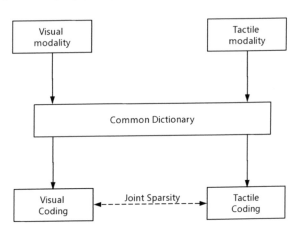

whose role is penalized using the parameter γ. In Fig. 9.6, how the common dictionary unifies the visual and tactile modalities is illustrated.

9.3.2 Optimization Algorithm

Although there are many variables in (9.6), they can be alternatively optimized as follows.

9.3.2.1   Updating the Coding Vectors

In this step, X and Y are updated. By fixing other variables, (9.6) is reduced to the following problems:

$$\min_{X,Y} \quad \mathscr{L}_R + \gamma \mathscr{L}_G. \tag{9.7}$$

It can be transformed as:

$$\min_{X,Y} \left\| W_T^T T - DX \right\|_F^2 + \| W_V^T V - DY \|_F^2$$
$$+ \sum_{g=1}^{G} (\|[X_g \ Y_g]\|_{2,1}). \tag{9.8}$$

This is a convex optimization and many off-the-shelf algorithms can be utilized to solve it. In this work, the solutions are obtained using SPARSE modeling software [11].

9.3.2.2   Updating the Dictionary Coefficients

In this step, the common dictionary D is updated. By fixing other variables, (9.6) can be reduced as

$$\min_{D} \quad \left\| [W_T^T T \ W_V^T V] - D[X \ Y] \right\|_F^2$$
$$\text{s.t.} \quad \|d_k\|_2 = 1 \ \text{for} \ k = 1, 2, \ldots, K. \tag{9.9}$$

This is a classical dictionary learning problems that can be easily solved using the block-coordinate descent method [19].

9.3.2.3   Updating the Projection Matrices

In this step, the projection matrices W_T and W_V are updated. By fixing other variables, (9.6) is reduced to the following independent subproblems:

$$\begin{cases} \min_{W_T} \quad \left\| W_T^T T - DX \right\|_F^2 + \lambda \| T - W_T W_T^T T \|_F^2 \\ \text{s.t.} \quad W_T^T W_T = I \\ \\ \min_{W_V} \quad \left\| W_V^T V - DY \right\|_F^2 + \lambda \| V - W_V W_V^T V \|_F^2 \\ \text{s.t.} \quad W_V^T W_V = I \end{cases} \tag{9.10}$$

Due to the orthogonalization constraints, those problems involve optimization on the Stiefel manifold. The Crank–Nicolson-like update scheme developed in [17] is employed to solve it.

9.3.2.4 Algorithm Summarization

The above procedures are repeated until convergence. The whole algorithm is summarized in Algorithm 5.

Algorithm 5 Common Dictionary Learning

Input: Tactile dataset T and visual dataset V.
Output: Solutions W_T, W_V and D.
1: Initialize W_T, W_V and D.
2: **while** Not convergent **do**
3:     Fix W_T, W_V and D, update X and Y by Eq.(9.8).
4:     Fix W_T, W_V, X and Y, update D by Eqs.(9.9).
5:     Fix X, Y and D, update W_T and W_V by Eqs.(9.10).
6: **end while**

In practice, W_T, W_V, and D are initialized to be random matrices with appropriate dimensions. The algorithm is empirically shown good convergent property because the objective function is minimized in each step. The termination is declared when the difference between subsequence objective function values is smaller than 10^{-3}.

9.3.3 Cross-Modality Matching

The above learning procedure provides solutions which are denoted as W_T^*, W_V^*, and D^*. The obtained solutions can be used to develop the visual–tactile matching algorithm. Given the gallery visual sample set $\mathscr{F} = \{f_i\}_{i=1}^N$ and the query tactile sample t, the following optimization problem should be solved:

$$\min_{x,y,f} \left\| W_T^{*T} t - D^* x \right\|_2^2 + \left\| f - D^* y \right\|_F^2$$
$$+ \gamma \|x\ y\|_{2,1}.$$

(9.11)

This problem is also nonconvex, and therefore, the alternative optimization method is resorted. The iterations are divided into the following stages. For convenience, the superscript t is used to indicate the iteration number.

1. Initialize

$$x^{(0)} = \underset{x}{\operatorname{argmin}} \left\| W_T^{*T} t - D^* x \right\|_2^2 + \gamma \|x\|_1$$

and $y^{(0)} = x^{(0)}$.

2. Update f as

$$f^{(t)} = D^* y^{(t-1)}.$$

3. Update x and y as

$$\{x^{(t)}, y^{(t)}\} = \underset{x,y}{\operatorname{argmin}} \left\| W_T^{*T} t - D^* x \right\|_2^2 + \left\| f^{(t)} - D^* y \right\|_2^2$$
$$+ \gamma \|x \ \ y\|_{2,1}. \tag{9.12}$$

After the iteration procedure is converged, the best-matched result can be searched as

$$f^* = \underset{f_i \in \mathcal{F}}{\operatorname{argmin}} \|D^* y^* - W_V^{*T} f_i\|_2,$$

where the term $D^* y^*$ represents the mapped visual sample in the latent space, and y^* is used to denote the obtained optimum solution of y. In practice, all of data in the gallery visual set can be ranked according to the distance to $D^* y^*$ as the retrieved results of the query tactile data.

9.3.4 Discussions

The differences between some relevant work and our previous work are briefly discussed here.

One of the most popular cross-modal matching algorithms is SliM[2] which was originally developed by [19]. In that work, the authors separately learned the dictionaries for each modality and the sparsity penalty term was developed as

$$\hat{\mathcal{L}}_G = \sum_{g=1}^{G} (\|X_g\|_{2,1} + \|Y_g\|_{2,1}). \tag{9.13}$$

Compared with (9.5), the term in (9.13) did not establish the relation between modalities using the joint sparsity. Equation (9.5) encourages the coding vectors in different modality to share the same sparsity pattern if they belong to the same class. This exploits more intrinsic connections between visual and tactile modalities. In addition, the work in [19] requires the exact sample-to-sample correspondence information which is unavailable in our visual–tactile cross-modal matching problem.

Currently there are only very few works relaxing the full pairing in multimodal data. Refs. [8, 14] extended the traditional maximum covariance analysis and canonical correlation analysis methods to deal with weakly paired data fusion problem. However, their work focused on the dimension reduction and no dictionary learning technology was involved. In this work, the tasks of dimension reduction and dictionary learning are simultaneously performed for the weakly paired visual–tactile multimodal data.

The most relevant work is [12], which developed a generalized coupled dictionary learning approach for cross-modal retrieval. This work combined the cluster canonical correlation analysis technology [14] and the coupled dictionary learning technology. Since the former is a maximization problem and the latter is a minimization problem, the authors had to introduce extra parameters which complicated the optimization objective function. In addition, two separated dictionaries are learned and therefore the joint sparsity between modalities could not be exploited.

The joint sparsity has been utilized in some of previous work. Reference [9] used the joint sparse coding method to solve the multifingered tactile object recognition problem, and Ref. [10] used the relaxed joint sparse coding method to solve the visual–tactile fusion recognition problem. It should be noted that the weak-pairing problem has been touched in [10] using the sparse coding method. However, both [9, 10] regarded all of the training samples as the dictionary atoms, while in this work the common dictionary learning is addressed. In addition, both [9, 10] concern the object recognition, while this work addresses the cross-modal matching for retrieval, which is a relative new application. Therefore, this work is a nontrivial extension of our previous work in [9, 10].

9.4 Experimental Results

9.4.1 Dataset

The cross-modal matching methods are demonstrated on the Penn Haptic Adjective Corpus 2 (PHAC-2) dataset [2, 4]. PHAC-2 contains 60 household objects (Fig. 9.7), among them 53 household objects exhibit 8 visual images and 10 tactile samples, while the rest 7 objects admit 8 visual images only. Table 9.1 lists the data description according to the material category, where the item $\sharp$Obj represents the number of the objects belonging to this category, $\sharp$Obj* represents the number of the objects which exhibit both visual and tactile samples. $\sharp$TrainObj* objects are randomly selected for training and remaining $\sharp$TestObj* objects for evaluating the recognition performance. The split is randomly performed for 10 times, and the averaged performance is reported. By this protocol, it is ensured that one single object does not appear in both training and testing sets. For each row in Table 9.1, there is

$$\sharp\text{Obj}^* = \sharp\text{TrainObj}^* + \sharp\text{TestObj}^*.$$

Table 9.1 Dataset description

Material	♯Obj	♯Obj*	♯TrainObj*	♯TestObj*
Foam	16	14	7	7
Organic	5	4	2	2
Fabric	7	7	4	3
Plastic	13	13	7	6
Paper	12	10	5	5
Stone	2	2	1	1
Glass	2	1	0	1
Metal	3	2	1	1
Total	60	53	27	26

Fig. 9.7 Sample images of PHAC datasets. The original images are adopted from [2], with slight modification. The red boxes are used to surround the objects which only admit tactile sequences but no images. Such objects can only be used for testing, but not training. See more details in Table I and the text

Since each training object exhibits 8 visual images and 10 tactile sequences, there are $M = 27 \times 8 = 216$ and $N = 27 \times 10 = 270$. For these ♯TestObj* objects for evaluation, all tactile samples belonging to them are used for probe and all visual samples belong to them are used for gallery set. Therefore, there is $N = 26 \times 10 = 260$. The number of the query tactile samples is $26 \times 8 = 208$.

Similar to [12], the Rank-1 recognition accuracy is used for performance evaluation, which is defined as the percentage of correctly classified Rank-1 results overall query tactile samples.

9.4.2 Compared Methods

Since there does not exist explicit-pairing relation between the visual sample and the tactile sample, many existing cross-modal matching and recognition methods such as SliM^2 cannot be used. Therefore, the following popular method which does not require the fully-pairing information for performance comparison is adopted.

1. WMCA: This method was proposed in [8]. It tries to optimize

$$\max_{W, W', \Pi} Tr[W^T V \Pi T^T W']$$

to determine projection matrices $W \in R^{d_V \times d}$, $W' \in R^{d_T \times d}$, and pairing matrix $\Pi \in \{0, 1\}^{M \times N}$. Some extra constraint conditions should be imposed on the pairing matrix Π to incorporate the group-pairing information. WMCA method uses an iterative maximization procedure to automatically determine suitable pairings within the groups. The final pairings lead to a dimensionality-reduction mapping that is guaranteed to locally maximize the covariance between the modalities.

2. C-CCA: This method was proposed in [14] to learn discriminant low-dimensional representations that maximize the correlation between the two sets while segregating the different classes on the learned space. C-CCA problem is formulated as,

$$\max_{w, v} \frac{w^T \Sigma_{VT} v}{\sqrt{w^T \Sigma_{VV} w} \sqrt{v^T \Sigma_{TT} v}}$$

where the covariance matrices Σ_{VT}, Σ_{VT}, and Σ_{VT} are defined as

$$\Sigma_{VT} = \frac{1}{\sum_{g=1}^{G} |V_g||T_g|} \sum_{g=1}^{G} \sum_{i=1}^{|V_g|} \sum_{j=1}^{|T_g|} v_i t_j^T$$

$$\Sigma_{VV} = \frac{1}{\sum_{g=1}^{G} |V_g||T_g|} \sum_{g=1}^{G} \sum_{i=1}^{|V_g|} |T_g| v_i v_i^T$$

$$\Sigma_{TT} = \frac{1}{\sum_{g=1}^{G} |V_g||T_g|} \sum_{g=1}^{G} \sum_{j=1}^{|T_g|} |X_g| t_j t_j^T$$

where $T_g (V_g)$ is the sub-matrix of $T(V)$ and is associated to those tactile(visual) data belonging to the gth class. $|T_g|$ and $|V_g|$ denote the numbers of columns in T_g and V_g, respectively.

3. GCDL: The Generalized Coupled Dictionary Learning Method was recently proposed in [12]. This approach can seamlessly handle both paired as well as unpaired data in the two modalities in a unified framework. It can be formulated as

$$\min_{D_T, D_V, W_V, W_T, X, Y} \|T - D_T X\|_F^2 + \|V - D_V Y\|_F^2$$
$$+ \alpha_T \|X\|_1 + \alpha_V \|Y\|_1 \qquad (9.14)$$
$$+ \rho \sum_{i=1}^{N} \sum_{j=1}^{M} (k_{ij} - \frac{\langle W_V x_i, W_T y_j \rangle}{\|W_V x_i\|_2 \|W_T y_j\|_2})^2,$$

where α_T, α_V, ρ, and k_{ij} are parameters. In addition, Ref. [12] developed two extensions of GCDL, named GCDL-1 and GCDL-2, which will also be used for comparison.

The difference among the above methods are significant: Both WMCA and C-CCA perform the joint dimension reduction. However, WMCA tries to recover the latent-pairing relation between samples, while C-CCA imposes virtual-pairing relation among all samples belonging to the same class in different modalities. GCDL is a combination of dictionary learning method and C-CCA method and therefore is highly relevant to our work. However, GCDL learned separate dictionary for each modality, and the dimension reduction is performed on the sparse coding vectors, while our work learns common dictionary for all modalities and develop the joint sparsity to connect different modalities. Therefore, the comparison with those methods can effectively disclose the performance of the proposed method. For the dictionary learning method GCDL and the proposed one, the size of dictionary is fixed as $K = 150$, unless otherwise stated. The regulation parameters in the all of the algorithms (such as λ and γ in the proposed method, and α_x, α_y and ρ in GCDL) are carefully tuned to obtain the best results.

9.4.3   Performance Comparison

To analyze the role of the learned latent subspace, the number of dimension d is progressively increased and all of the methods are run to observe their performances. In Fig. 9.8, the averaged accuracy versus the dimension d is illustrated. From those results, the following observations are obtained (Fig. 9.9):

Fig. 9.8 Recognition accuracy versus the dimension d

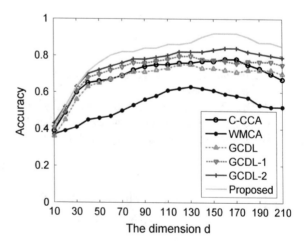

Fig. 9.9 Recognition accuracy versus the size K

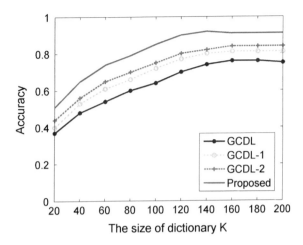

1. The dimension reduction and the latent subspace learning are indeed effective, since all of the methods archive their best performance in the interval $d \in [130, 170]$.
2. The performance of the proposed method is almost consistently better than the other ones. Especially, the difference between red and megane lines shows that the common dictionary and joint sparsity are more suitable for connecting the visual and tactile modalities.
3. When d is small (about $10 \sim 30$), the performances of all methods are close. However, with the increasing of d, the merit of the proposed method becomes significant. This is due to the joint learning of the latent subspace and the common dictionary.
4. The performance of GCDL is not so sensitive to the dimension number d. The possible reason is that the dimension reduction is performed on the obtained coding vectors but not the original samples.
5. WMCA performs rather poor. The reason is that it imposes pairing relation during the learning stage. However, for PHAC-2 dataset, the sample-to-sample relation may not exist. Therefore, the group correspondence strategy adopted by C-CCA, GCDL, and the proposed one is more reasonable.

In Figs. 9.10 and 9.11, two matching examples are given by submitting two query tactile samples. For further analysis, the top-3 ranked visual image results for each method are listed.

Figure 9.10 shows the result corresponding to a tactile sample of object *Charcoal Foam*. In this case, WMCA gets rather poor results. Because the returned results are related to the object *Black Eraser*, which is of different material with *Charcoal Foam*. C-CCA, GCDL, and GCDL-1, though get some wrong results, still correctly recognize the material *Foam*. For this example, both GCDL-2 and proposed method obtain perfect results.

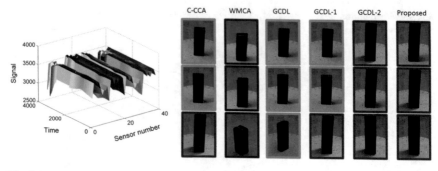

Fig. 9.10 Matched results for the query tactile sample *Charcoal Foam* shown in the left panel. From top to bottom: Rank-1, Rank-2, and Rank-3 results. The results surrounded with red, blue, and green boxes correspond to the objects *Charcoal Foam, Black Eraser, Black Foam*, respectively

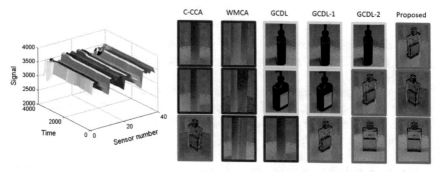

Fig. 9.11 Matched results for the query tactile sample *Glass Container* shown in the left panel. From top to bottom: Rank-1, Rank-2, and Rank-3 results. The results surrounded with red, blue, and green boxes correspond to the objects *Glass Container, Aluminum Channel, Soap Dispenser*, respectively

In Fig. 9.11, a more difficult example is demonstrated. Here the user may submit the tactile query of the object *Glass Container*, which belongs to the category *Glass*. It can be seen from Table I that there are no training samples about this category. That is to say, all of the training samples are not related to *Glass*, but the user needs to retrieve a tactile sample belonging to *Glass* from the visual gallery set. In this case, WMCA and GCDL find completely wrong results. C-CCA and GCDL-1 find the correct one until Rank-3 is returned. GCDL-2 gets the correct Rank-2 and Rank-3 results. The proposed method, however, archives perfect results. This shows the power of the joint sparsity which is based on the common dictionary, which can be used to transfer the knowledge between different materials.

9.4.4 Parameter Selection

There are several important parameters in the developed method, such as d, K, λ and γ. From the above results, it can be seen that all of the methods achieve stable results when the dimension number d is in the interval $[110, 150]$. The roles of the other parameters are investigated. To attenuate the influences of the selection of d, the value of d is enumerated from the set $\{110, 120, 130, 140, 150\}$ in the following comparison and the best results are reported.

The parameter K is the size of the dictionary, and it is a common parameter for all of the dictionary learning methods including GCDL. Therefore, the methods GCDL, GCDL-1, GCDL-2, and the proposed method are compared. Figure 9.9 demonstrates the results, from which the following observations are obtained:

1. All of the methods achieve the best results around $K = 130 \sim 150$. This also shows the roles of dictionary learning.
2. When the size of dictionary is small (such as $10 \sim 50$), the performance of all of the methods are poor. However, with the increasing of K, the performance of the proposed method shows obvious advantages.
3. When $K \geq 150$, all of method achieve saturation or worse performances and the proposed method performs consistently better than other dictionary learning methods.

9.5 Summary

In this work, the visual–tactile cross-modal matching problem is investigated. It is formulated as retrieving the relevant sample in unlabeled gallery visual dataset in response to the tactile query sample. A dictionary learning model which can simultaneously learn the projection subspace and the latent common dictionary for the visual and tactile measurements is developed. The experimental results show that using appropriate training dataset composed of weakly paired visual and tactile samples, an effective visual–tactile cross-modal matching method can be established. This work presents a solution to the matching problem using the tactile GA kernel and visual covariance descriptors. Nevertheless, the procedure described herein is easily extendable to other modalities and features.

Retrieving images from touch information is a relative new field and more efforts should be performed. Before closing this paper, we recall an old story *Blind Men and an Elephant*[1] which provides negative evidence for this work. The main problem originates from the fact that the tactile measurements usually represent the local surface of an object, while visual image may capture the global information. The relation between visual and tactile measurements is very complicated and is far from solved.

---

[1] https://en.wikipedia.org/wiki/Blind_men_and_an_elephant.

References

1. https://www.syntouchinc.com/texture-gallery/
2. Chu, V., McMahon, I., Riano, L., McDonald, C.G., He, Q., Perez-Tejada, J.M., Arrigo, M., Darrell, T., Kuchenbecker, K.J.: Robotic learning of haptic adjectives through physical interaction. Robot Auton. Syst. **63**, 279–292 (2015)
3. Internet shopping and buying behavior of college students: Dh, L., Am, F., D, L. Serv. Mark. Q. **627**, 123–138 (2006)
4. Gao, Y., Hendricks, L.A., Kuchenbecker, K.J., Darrell, T.: Deep learning for tactile understanding from visual and haptic data. IEEE International Conference on Robotics and Automation (ICRA) **2016**, 536–543 (2016)
5. Huang, D.A., Wang, Y.C.F.: Coupled dictionary and feature space learning with applications to cross-domain image synthesis and recognition. In: Proceedings IEEE International Conference on Computer Vision, pp. 2496–2503 (2013)
6. Kim, J., Forsythe, S.: Adoption of sensory enabling technology for online apparel shopping. Eur. J. Mark. **43**, 1101–1120 (2009)
7. Klatzky, R.L., Lederman, S.J., Matula, D.E.: Haptic exploration in the presence of vision. J. Exp. Psychol. Hum. Percept. Perform. 726–743 (1993)
8. Lampert, C., Krömer, O.: Weakly-paired maximum covariance analysis for multimodal dimensionality reduction and transfer learning. Comput. Vis.-ECCV **2010**, 566–579 (2010)
9. Liu, H., Guo, D., Sun, F.: Object recognition using tactile measurements: kernel sparse coding methods. IEEE Trans. Instrum. Meas. **65**(3), 656–665 (2016)
10. Liu, H., Yu, Y., Sun, F., Gu, J.: Visual-tactile fusion for object recognition. IEEE Trans. Autom. Sci. Eng. **14**(2), 996–1008 (2017)
11. Mairal, J., Bach, F., Ponce, J., Sapiro, G.: Online learning for matrix factorization and sparse coding. J. Mach. Learn. Res. **11**(Jan), 19–60 (2010)
12. Mandal, D., Biswas, S.: Generalized coupled dictionary learning approach with applications to cross-modal matching. IEEE Trans. Image Process. **25**(8), 3826–3837 (2016)
13. Peck, J., Childers, T.L.: Individual differences in haptic information processing: the need for touch scale. J. Consum. Res. 430–442 (2003)
14. Rasiwasia, N., Mahajan, D., Mahadevan, V., Aggarwal, G.: Cluster canonical correlation analysis. In: Proceedings International Conference on Artificial Intelligence Statistics, pp. 823–831 (2014)
15. Shekhar, S., Patel, V.M., Nguyen, H.V., Chellappa, R.: Coupled projections for adaptation of dictionaries. TIP (2016)
16. Wang, K., Yin, Q., Wang, W., Wu, S., Wang, L.: A comprehensive survey on cross-modal retrieval. arXiv preprint arXiv:1607.06215 (2016)
17. Wen, Z., Yin, W.: A feasible method for optimization with orthogonality constraints. Math. Program. 1–38 (2013)
18. Zhang, L., Zhang, D.: Evolutionary cost-sensitive discriminative learning with application to vision and olfaction. IEEE Trans. Instrum. Meas. **66**(2), 198–211 (2017)
19. Zhuang, Y., Wang, Y., Wu, F., Zhang, Y., Lu, W.: Supervised coupled dictionary learning with group structures for multi-modal retrieval. In: AAAI, pp. 1070–1076 (2013)

Part IV
Conclusions

This part of this book comprises one chapter, which summarizes the main work of this book and presents some important future directions.

Chapter 10
Conclusions

10.1 The Roles of Sparse Coding in Robotic Tactile Perception

This book comprehensively introduces sparse coding and dictionary learning and shows their applications in robotic tactile perception. Merits of sparse coding methods are validated using extensive experiments, which include but not limited to *robustness, flexibility to incorporate structured information*, and *capability to deal with multi-modal fusion*. Under the developed unified sparse coding framework, the following robotic tactile perception and understanding problems are systematically addressed.

1. *Multi-Fingered Fusion*. The relation among different fingers is very complicated because the fingers usually contact different regions of objects. In addition, the grasp pose also strongly influences the recognition performance. In Chaps. 3 and 4, the joint sparse coding method is utilized to tackle this problem. The developed model is elegant, flexible, and effective to address the *between-finger* problem, while previous work usually considers the *fingertip* problem only.
2. *Multi-Task Recognition*. It is found that tactile attribute is comprehensive and many tactile adjectives could be used to describe the properties about the objects. This naturally forms the multi-task learning task. In Chaps. 5 and 6, the multi-adjective attribute information is incorporated in the multi-task dictionary learning method. It shows that the sparse coding framework is very flexible to incorporate such structured information to increase performance.
3. *Multi-Modal Fusion*. A very important merit of the sparse coding is its capability to deal with multi-modal fusion. In Chap. 7, the great challenges of visual-tactile fusion problem are shown, which is difficult to deal with using conventional machine learning methods. However, this problem can be easily solved using the sparse coding and dictionary learning methods which are developed in Chaps. 7 and 8, respectively. Furthermore, such methods are used for cross-modal matching and retrieval in Chap. 9.

© Springer Nature Singapore Pte Ltd. 2018
H. Liu and F. Sun, *Robotic Tactile Perception and Understanding*,
https://doi.org/10.1007/978-981-10-6171-4_10

Using the developed sparse coding and dictionary learning methods, a series of robotic perception problems including tactile perception and visual perception can be solved. In addition, some extensions of tactile perception in material recognition and retrieval are also demonstrated. This work shows potential applications in some specific domains including fabric industry and and Internet shopping.

10.2   Prospects

This book divides all tasks of tactile perception and visual–tactile fusion perception into two stages: *Representation* and *Coding*. The representation stage, which is illustrated in Chap. 2, is not the focus of this book, and therefore, some hand-crafted feature descriptors are adopted to characterize the tactile and visual signals. The subsequent coding stage, which is rather general, can therefore be used for different feature descriptors. In this sense, the proposed methods can be extended to more applications which have been shown in Chap. 8.

Nevertheless, dividing the perception task into two independent stages brings some limitations. Recently, deep learning technology shows extremely powerful capability to realize the so-called *End-to-End* learning which seamlessly integrates all learning components including feature learning and classifier learning. Motivated by this point, we may combine the deep learning and sparse coding to develop a more comprehensive architecture as shown in Fig. 10.1. It clearly shows that the deep structure can be used to automatically extract the feature vectors for visual and tactile modalities, and the sparse coding module can be used for multi-modal fusion with various structured constraints.

We believe such an architecture will play important roles in future robotic perception.

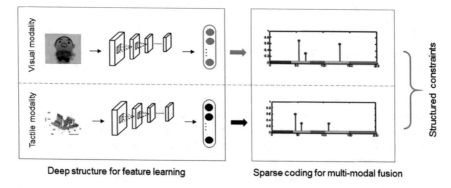

Deep structure for feature learning   Sparse coding for multi-modal fusion

Fig. 10.1 A more comprehensive architecture for multi-modal fusion learning. This architecture takes the advantage of deep structure for feature learning, and sparse coding for multi-modal fusion

On the other hand, the conventional deep learning architecture totally neglects the information provided by the hand-crafted feature descriptors and strongly depends on large amounts of training samples to automatically extract the feature vectors, which may be un-interpretable. In addition, it is very difficult to collect large amounts of training samples for tactile modalities. This provides great challenges for tactile deep learning. A possible solution to solve this problem is to develop some hybrid models which seamlessly incorporate the merits of data-driven mechanism and the prior knowledge which is provided by the hand-crafted feature descriptors.

Printed in the United States
By Bookmasters